■ *Transgressions of Reading*

■ *Post-Contemporary*

Interventions

Series Editors:

Stanley Fish and

Fredric Jameson

TRANSGRESSIONS *of Reading*

Narrative Engagement as Exile and Return

Robert D. Newman

DUKE UNIVERSITY PRESS *Durham and London 1993*

© 1993 Duke University Press

All rights reserved

Printed in the United States

of America on

acid-free paper ∞

Library of Congress

Cataloging-in-Publication

Data appear on the last

printed page of this book.

to my father, an exile

Contents

Preface

Memory believes before knowing remembers.
—*Faulkner,* LIGHT IN AUGUST

I offer Faulkner's arresting aphorism as an introduction to this book because it embodies many of its premises. I vividly recall Faulkner's sentence striking my mind with a ringing sense of truth when I first encountered it as an adolescent. Its power still moves me each time I read it aloud to another American literature survey class, hoping to instill the lyrical awe in my students that I seek to recover in myself. After I envision Faulkner's magical words drifting out of my mouth like vapor trails, I shatter whatever spell I may have created by asking what the words mean. The ensuing struggle to find an answer never fails to remind me of my own groping toward a response, a groping which this book continues and extends.

Faulkner offers memory as a repository of raw experiences and distinguishes it from knowing as a remembering, a translation of these experiences. The world imprints itself in our memories and we interpret these memories with the structures and frameworks of knowledge. In this way, we derive meaning from our memories, remembering through our articulation of them and articulating in order to remember. One important way we structure our experiences is by composing stories, shaped according to the demands culture places on us and we place on ourselves. The emotional and intellectual excitement we garner from reading or viewing stories, I argue, stems from repeating this process of memory and knowing; in effect, narrating these narratives. Rather than operating through a Coleridgean suspension of disbelief, narratives command our attention and belief because they recapitulate the manner in which we creatively shape and remember our lives.

Through narratives we engage our world and ourselves. We do so by drawing on patterns that evoke what is most personal and necessary to sustain and broaden our fragile sense of continuity between who we were, are, and wish to be. As a creative act, the process of narrative engagement is both dynamic and subtle. It involves a psychodrama during which we shape the texts we encounter while revealing and remaking ourselves in the course of that shaping. The rise and fall of gauzy curtains on our inner complex of stages do not simply coincide with the opening and closing of a text. Instead, they rise and fall continuously and to varying degrees during and after the encounter, while we simultaneously usher memories of other texts onto our mental panorama of intersecting performances. The nature of this identity quest that is the conditional interaction between readers and texts and what motivates it are the subjects of this book.

Attempts precisely and conclusively to map such broad and shifting terrain are, like endeavors to grasp a handful of sand, doomed to inadequacy. *Transgressions of Reading* instead recognizes and investigates knowing as narration, as a relational process rather than a totalizing product. As such my project aims to describe rather than to circumscribe by articulating inclusive and flexible ways of approaching the experience of narrative engagement. Rather than eschewing social or historical approaches, for example, the psychological emphasis I accord my paradigm intends links with these approaches. The portrayal of our investment in the transgressive embraces cultural as well as specific literary and psychoanalytic issues. By expanding notions of narrative and loosening definitions of genre, the book proposes inextricable connections between reading texts and reading our own selves.

I am pleased to acknowledge my indebtedness to the individuals and institutions that assisted me in the preparation of this book. Earlier versions of Chapters one, four, and six appeared in *New Historical Literary Study: Essays on Reproducing Texts, Representing History* edited by Jeffrey Cox and Larry Reynolds, *James Joyce Quarterly*, and *Modern Fiction Studies*, respectively. All works by Max Ernst copyright 1992 ARS, N.Y./SPADEM/ ADAGP. I am grateful for permission to use these materials here.

Most of the book was written during a Fall 1990 Faculty Development leave granted by Texas A&M University. Prior research grants from the National Endowment for the Humanities, Texas A&M's College of Liberal Arts, and the Interdisciplinary Group for Historical Literary Study afforded me the time to study the issues I address. The Interdisciplinary Group also provided a much needed intellectual forum in which I developed and tested many of my ideas. I also wish to thank my Dean, Daniel Fallon, and my present and former Department Heads, J. Lawrence Mitchell and Hamlin Hill, for their support.

Several people generously critiqued my ideas and in other ways provided invaluable help. Laurence Buell, Richard Costa, Elliott Gose, S. K. Heninger, Phillip Herring, Margot Norris, Mary Ann O'Farrell, Hortense Spillers, Robert Spoo, and Weldon Thornton kindly commented on parts of the manuscript. Jeff Cox carefully read the manuscript and offered many thoughtful suggestions. Reynolds Smith provided good counsel and sound editorial advice. I am most grateful to Larry Reynolds for his encouragement and for his enthusiastic and combative engagement with my work. And to Vicky, who reminds me of what is most important.

Introduction

I have been a sojourner in a foreign land.—EXODUS 2:22

This book is an attempt to explore the dynamics of narrative engagement by considering the interplay of erotic and tragic elements implicit in that engagement. I am interested in what goes on in the private hermitage of our minds as we illuminate the grids of black marks on white pages—what in the "Proteus" episode of *Ulysses* Stephen Dedalus terms signs on a white field—and in how our perspective adjusts and is adjusted by transactions with narrative. I contend that this illumination is an ongoing process of vision and revision that approximates the authorial experience, thereby narrating the narrative with which it is engaged. Furthermore, this engagement empowers and reveals the narrative as a complex mind in itself, like the mind of the reader, governed by the revelations and displacements of memory. I therefore assume memory to be the shaping power of narrative and will establish analogies between the interpretive processes of reading and psychoanalysis. The psychoanalytic case history is no less a history or a story than the narrative of historical events or the interpretation of a work of fiction, art, or film. I consider both reader and narrative as texts in that they are both composites of messages and codes to be unravelled. I also maintain that the loss engendered by the invasion of the Imaginary by the Symbolic Order in the individual's psychic life motivates the reading process in an attempt to recover the ideal Imaginary state while narrative memory inevitably recapitulates this loss.[1]

The narrative recreation of the exile reveals the fluidity of genre between biography and history as symptomatic of a more profound unsettling of fixed binaryism. Exiles continually define themselves in relation to what is absent, their homeland, which they simultaneously embrace and deny. Their recreation of that homeland, necessarily infused with irony, demonstrates memory as a revisionary act and history as an exercise in narrative memory. Exiles' memories of homeland are not constants, but are constantly changing due to their experience as exiles. Their mental returns are guided by the necessity of making that home, which was once an extension of Self, Other, in part so as to preserve the home that now is. This necessitates alienation from oneself, the Self that was and that still is present as an influence upon and aspect of the present Self. Hence, irony is a natural vehicle for the writer as exile. The authorial Self is extended into the character functioning within a setting that recalls a previous Self of the author through a present interpretation, and thus must be ironically distanced as Other.

Readers engaged by a text function much like exiles, viewing the narrative as a type of homeland in which they can no longer live. They are shifted between narrative and metanarrative constructions while each construction adjusts continually the reader's perspective on the other. However, because metanarratives (both those explicit in the text and those implicitly erected by the readers' engagement with the text) depend to a large degree upon narratives for their subject matter, readers need to visit this homeland often. Metanarratives remind readers of their actual distance from the narrative which is seducing them. They are conflicted by opposing urges to yield and to resist while metanarratives, as polemics, also seduce through the illusions they create.

At the level of metanarrative, readers adopt the comfortable pose of omniscience, joining the narrator in the interpretive act through the discourse of rational analysis. Playing critic, readers exile themselves from vicarious participation in the narrative to observe and judge it. However, this omniscient pose is another spell conjured by their desire for autonomous order and a means by which the self-conscious authors may tweak their deluded confidantes. The rational construct created by the seemingly objective stance may be exposed as ephemeral, the metanarrative as necessarily contaminated by the narrative, thereby revealing the metanarrative itself as no more than a story. Irony similarly highlights the perspectivity of the exile's mnemonic visions, and reveals ideas of home and return as fictional constructs. The exile, who chooses the ironic mode or is chosen by it, creates a mirror for the reader's experience while infiltrating and modifying that experience.

In posing readers as exiles whose desire for return shapes their journey through the narrative memory of the text and whose desire is in turn shaped by that narrative memory, I offer a paradigm which describes the fragmented experience of narrative engagement. The dynamics of this paradigm, yearning and loss, appropriately are shifting contingencies. The reading of literature, history, art, film, or personal narrative is by no means limited to a singular text or event. Instead the engagement occurs primarily in the margins. We do not read or observe without the flood of memory continually relating present to past experience. Events and the images they conjure bleed from the immediate focus of the text into other events and images both from within and outside the text. The desires which motivate memory arrange these links, but the recognition that similarity is infused with difference and repetition with change constitutes a trauma, an awareness by the exile that origin is recoverable only through mnemonic traces that blend into phantasm.[2]

We might view memory as a narrative of homecoming just as we see narrative as an act of memory. In either case, readers function as wanderers, perpetually exiled by their desire for the order of metanarration which both obstructs and enters into their engagement with the narrative. Just as they wander the text in search of the illusion of unity, smoothing its folds to meet the contours of their present desires, the margins of the text invade and alter the path they wander. Their return home can never be completed because their image of home changes.

In a letter to Jacob Burckhardt, Nietzsche wrote "every name in history is I . . ."[3] Much contemporary literary theory has encouraged us to view reading and writing as based in the inevitable self-referentiality of language or in its blocking of its own significations. Historical interpretation has often become trans-historical. The binary conventions used by traditional historiography are attacked and linear history is replaced by concepts of systematic rupture. Subjectivity is seen as a culturally constituted category, an extension of an ideology which the interpreter must expose. However, one problem we risk in adapting literary theory to history is an interpretive hegemony where unravelling the master code of language is performed through an equally exclusive model. Edward Said has attempted a way out of this impasse by promoting a broader cultural criticism that transcends disciplinary boundaries. His opposition of "filiation" and "affiliation" reveals how political power molds the perceptions of individual writers while pragmatically situating structure so as to avoid overly general models.[4]

In choosing the re-creation of the exile as my paradigm for narrative engagement and the interpretive experience, I am proposing a model of *disaffiliation*. In this model, structure is situated as a perpetually sliding signifier, generated by the revisionary mix of desires and repressions at work in the interaction between the narrative memories of text and reader (or events and interpreter).[5] Disaffiliation, however, assumes prior affiliation and the exile as model offers the memories of that affiliation, its loss, and the conflict between the liberation of wandering and the desire to return as primary constituents in the dynamics of narrative engagement.

In collapsing the distinction between the fictional and the factual, I am drawing on Roland Barthes's merging of *mimesis* and *diegesis* and on Paul Ricoeur's assumptions concerning the allegorical equivalence of structure in historical and narrative events.[6] I do so to set up an equivalence between the reader of a novel, the historian composing a narrative about the past, the viewer of a film or visual narrative, and the psychoanalyst constructing a case history (all of whom I have labeled above as readers both for the purpose of simplicity and to indicate the commonality of their endeavor). Like Hayden White, particularly in his analysis of the tropological basis of historiography, I contend that all narratives of interpretation are involved with extended figures that generate representation. I focus on the reader or viewer rather than the author, filmmaker, or artist both to demonstrate the effects of that mediation and to show that such mediation is an ongoing dynamic whereby the reader assumes the role of creator.[7]

In *One Hundred Years of Solitude*, Gabriel García Márquez describes an insomnia plague that has seized the village of Macondo and José Arcadio Buendía's attempts to protect the town against the resultant loss of memory by labeling everything with its name and function. However, Buendía's well-intentioned system cannot anticipate the vagrant desires of many of his fellow townspeople:

In all the houses keys to memorizing objects and feelings had been written. But the system demanded so much vigilance and moral strength that many succumbed to the spell of an imaginary reality, one invented by themselves, which was less practical for them but more comforting. Pilar Ternera was the one who contributed most to popularize that mystification when she conceived the trick of reading the past in cards as she had read the future before. By means of that recourse the insomniacs began to live in a world built on the uncertain alternatives of the cards, where a father was remembered faintly as the dark man who had arrived at the beginning of April and a mother was remembered only as the dark woman who wore a gold ring on her left hand, and where a birth date was reduced to the last Tuesday on which a lark sang in the laurel tree. Defeated by those practices of consolation, José Arcadio Buendía then decided to build the memory machine that he had desired once in order to remember the marvelous inventions of the gypsies. The artifact was based on the possibility of reviewing every morning, from beginning to end, the totality of knowledge acquired during one's life. He conceived of it as a spinning dictionary that a person placed on the axis could operate by means of a lever, so that in a very few hours there would pass before his eyes the notions most necessary for life.[8]

García Márquez presents a situation where the past becomes as fictionalized as the future. Furthermore, Buendía's spinning dictionary, like the mystical consolation he rejects, is based upon personal selection, upon infinite permutations, albeit from a finite source. Attempts to reconstruct the past require the reconstruction of memory, a selective and partial remembering necessarily accompanied by massive forgetting. The reconstruction can never be comprehensive because it is ordered by desires that are situational and personal as well as by ones that are universal. Desire itself can never be fully satiated, although the quest to do so motivates our yearning for the illusory comforts of narrative closure and theoretical totalization.

Like Buendía's memory machine, readers' desires to render objective, complete judgments regarding their object of study rest upon a faith in the provisional suspension of the subjectivity implicit in the inevitable dialogic relationship between interpreter and object of interpretation. Interpretive discourses consist of a dynamic dialogue, an ongoing interchange between Self (interpreter) and Other (object of interpretation), whereby Otherness is consistently internalized by the Self as well as projected with codes of desire and repression inherited from the Self back onto the Other. The psychoanalytic analogy is relevant here. Lacan links Freud's processes of displacement and condensation in dream interpretation to the literary tropes of metonymy and metaphor, respectively. For Lacan, desire is manifested by our attempts to integrate metaphorically the metonymy of disconnected serial events, attempts that cannot fully be satisfied. This metaphoric urge can be related to Freud's view of transference whereby the patient transfers unconscious wishes onto his analyst:

> The content of the wish had appeared first of all in the patient's consciousness without any memories of the surrounding circumstances which would have assigned it to a past time. The wish which was present was then, owing to the compulsion to associate which was dominant in her consciousness, linked to my person, with which the patient was legitimately concerned; and as the result of this *mesalliance*—which I describe as a "false connection"—the same affect

was provoked which had forced the patient long before to repudiate this forbidden wish.[9]

The shift in the analogy where the patient (text) is imposing a sense of order upon the analyst (interpreter), however, not only suggests the dialogic nature of the psychoanalytic relationship but also the oscillations involved in the interactions between interpreter and text.[10] The illusions of objectivity and totality neglect these oscillations and the transference that catalyzes them.

Lacanian psychoanalysis holds that the unconscious always speaks in response to the desire of the Other and that its Symbolic Order lies in a "transindividual" space between Self and Other.[11] Freud's definition of hysteria makes pantomime the symptomatic locus of the Imaginary.[12] In the hysterical, discourse achieves its etymological intent ("dis" plus "currere" = "to run in different directions"). Furthermore, it continually internalizes and projects the presence of Otherness and therefore is most effectively presented in forms of the grotesque. In the grotesque, the illusion of an integrated autonomy of Self is transgressed and repressions and fetishes are projected in exaggerated forms. Bodies are expressed as being synecdochic or being multiple, their lower parts emphasized over their heads with more attention to openings and orifices than to images of closure or completion.[13] When the grotesque dominates in a narrative, traditional hierarchies are upset. An ending seldom occurs without the dissipation of hysteria or the hysteric unless it is an ending that does not resolve the tensions it has aroused, but causes them to extend beyond the physical confines of the narrative. These tensions are presented within apocalyptic events where the horrific dominates and order has collapsed. Readers come face to face with the presentation of their repressions and an uneasy conflict of identity occurs. The pleasure of narrative engagement, the participation in the acting out of repressions through identification with the Other, is accompanied by a quest for the restoration of order through the eradication of the Other. The desire for an end joins the resistance to ending. In Freudian terms, Eros battles Thanatos as the need for narration encounters the necessity to remedy it.

Peter Brooks argues that the master trope in making sense of narrative is an anticipation of retrospection where the past is read as present and the present past in relation to a future we know to be already in place waiting for us to reach it. In other words, narrative constitutes an effort to reach origins through endings. Structural and imagistic repetitions, recognized by memory, inform the narrative and metanarrative structures and rehearse this desire for closure and return. However, these repetitions also interrupt the movement forward that will lead to the satisfaction of that desire. Repetition therefore can be seen as an expression of the conflicting desires of narrative memory—the exile's wish to return home and his need to wander. The journey toward the Imaginary ideal state as an end to the alienation from unity and order and the pleasure of deviance realized in the journeying both persist through repetition.

In hysterical discourse, transgressions of order intensify readers' experiences of deviance. The Other appears exaggerated because it is no longer safely contained. Rather than being dictated by the direction of events, it dictates them and does so by destabilizing. While a yearning for a return to containment is consequently aroused in readers, so too is their recognition of identity and a dynamic between their internalization and their projection of the Other occurs. Again, repetition offers an indication and an expression of this dynamic, but repetition with a difference. In the hysterical, repetition becomes compulsive, demonic.[14] And the need for alleviation on the part of hysterics, a need with which readers also identify, is indicated by the prevalence of the apocalyptic in their discourse and the discourse concerning them. Thus, the annihilation of order which hysterics and their discourse effect becomes also a revelation of the desire for self-annihilation, for a final transgression that will end all transgressions.

The texts I have chosen for studying the paradigm of exile and return are heterogeneous in themselves and in combination with one another. They deliberately induce psychic dislocation in their readers and frame attempts at order as quests for power and possession, thereby underscoring the poetics of transgression with which this book is concerned. By arousing both the transgressor and the protector of order within us, these texts call attention to the borders of identity while simultaneously disrupting them.

By structuring the book around such a nontraditional combination of texts, I wish to emphasize the attraction to anomaly with which the discussions of all of the texts are involved. Each chapter explores readers' paradoxical cognitive and emotional impulses toward the anomalous in narrative as a dialogue of conflicting and oscillating desires. The desire to subsume the transgressive so that Symbolic integrity is maintained motivates the narrative quest. This motivation, however, intersects with and is continually adjusted by an equally powerful and originary motivation to rupture the Symbolic Order in order that readers might end their exilic status.

The paradigm of exile and return indeed could be applied to a variety of transgressive texts from a number of different narrative "types," a possibility that attests to the richness and flexibility of the paradigm. While I do not mean my particular choices of texts to be in any way exclusive, I do consider them ultimately to present an effective range of narratives. That many of the narratives chosen are authored by people who were/are themselves political or, in the case of Joyce, philosophical exiles provides further intersections between historical events and narratives about those events. The book then presents a kind of sampling that easily could be extended. Thus, the theoretical possibilities expressed here do not end with it.

I attempt not to set up simple binary categories but to demonstrate that exile and return enter into a variety of exchanges and permutations in which the reader seeks both fragmentation and reconsolidation. Exposing this pattern of reader engagement with narrative demonstrates all paradigms to be contingent just as it shows contingencies to be paradigms. Although I use exile and return to describe both a reading of *Psycho* and of *The White Hotel*, for example, the specific dynamics by which this paradigm expresses a reader's engagement with each text are markedly different. Exile and return becomes an elastic descriptive pattern by which to articulate a dynamic process, not an inflexible, categorical formula.

Chapter one examines the generic patterns of narrative engagement by discussing three texts, one a reconstruction of historical events, the second a work of fiction, and the third a fiction disguising itself as a psychoanalytic history. The story of Jim Jones, exiled patriarch of the People's Temple, who, in a grotesque parody of Moses, brought his people to the Promised Land of Guyana, is examined through the narrative constructed by James Reston, Jr. in *Our Father Who Art in Hell* after the mass suicide of 911 of Jones's followers. Reston's portrait becomes a contemporary *Heart of Darkness*, dominated by the motif of the double, in which he plays Marlow to Jones's Kurtz. The obsession with loss involves historian and subject in a fetishization of memory that becomes a narrative of the death drive.

Chilean exile Ariel Dorfman's first novel written in English, *Mascara*, in which the protagonist and narrator is literally faceless, presents both a political allegory as well as an allegory of the reading process. The narrative focuses on the secretive and the obscene while considering the betrayals of memory to show identity to be predicated on disaffiliation. As faceless voyeur, the narrator of *Mascara* mirrors the plight of readers, their desire to incorporate the Other in order to project the Self as imaginative ideal and to become amnesiacs regarding their exilic condition. Like *Our Father Who Art in Hell*, *Mascara* spills into the compulsive repetition of hysterical discourse, fixating the narrative memory produced by the engagement of reader and text in trauma.

The chapter concludes with a reading of Freud's *Moses and Monotheism* as an expression of Freud's own fear of imminent exile. In doing so, it posits all narratives as allegories of temporality wherein readers see themselves reflected as absences which they must in turn resist.

Although these three narratives are vastly dissimilar from the perspective of genre, the engagement between reader and text in all of them has fascinating correspondences. All convey the transgressive and the hysterical discourse which informs their respective histories. Furthermore, this discourse derives from and impels the conflicting desires and mnemonic revisions of the exile, thereby creating a mirror for the interpreter as well.

The second and third chapters investigate the visual dimensions of narrative engagement from the perspectives of the art narrative and the moving picture. Chapter two uses Max Ernst's collage novel, *Une Semaine de bonté*, as its case study of the transgressions of art narrative and of the nature of looking as possession. After asserting the figural genesis of narrative and the temporality of perception, this chapter discusses narrative engagement as paradoxical in turning a structural impulse into a deconstructive effect. The inscription of time in space by viewers, the narrative engagement between them and the images they view, is performed within a personal dialogue of yearning and loss that operates through mental forgeries. Ernst's novelistic pastiche employs hybridization as a narrative and rhetorical technique to expose this process. By positioning its readers doubly as voyeur and object, victimizer and victim, *Une Semaine de bonté* intentionally warps the Symbolic language that permits them to aesthetically separate images from themselves. Ernst confronts readers with the revelation that they are objects of their own look, exiles trying to deceive themselves that they have returned home.

The third chapter discusses the postmodern horror film, specifically *Psycho*, *Night of the Living Dead*, and *Blue Velvet*, to explore further the implications of hysterical discourse in narrative engagement. In addition to investigating an aesthetics of disgust, it considers the attraction of the transgressive and anomalous exhibited in engagements with the self-consuming (both figuratively and literally) narratives of these films. Postmodern horror films deliberately fetishize while advertising and exaggerating this fetishization to induce fragmentation in their viewers. By compelling obsessive responses of attraction and denial, these films manipulate their viewers to internalize and to project the presence of Otherness while upsetting the illusion of an integrated autonomy of Self. Such viewing embraces the threat posed by postmodern horror films, their exposure of our concept of Self as a performance for Others. In this manner, they rehearse an impulse to negate the identity imposed by our exile into the Symbolic realm of language and social order and to return to the undifferentiated state of the Imaginary.

The structurally central chapter of this book marks its turn to a focus on literary narratives. Like the preceding chapters on visual narrative, the chapters on literary narrative move from a modern text to postmodern ones while pointing out stylistic and hermeneutic resonances that breach historical boundaries. I am aware of the distinctions between modernism's aestheticism, political self-marginalization, and transhistorical perspective and postmodernism's parodic fragmentation, plural and provisional politicizing, and concentration on the uncertainty of historical knowledge through its undermining of totalizing systems.[15] My emphasis, however, is on the reader's dual role as reader and meta-reader, one who yields and one who resists yielding, exile and returnee. This paradigm for narrative engagement bridges both periods, converging the structuralist stress on *langue* with the poststructuralist insistence on *parole*. The interplay between the quest for a code and the independent significance of each individual message reenacts a hermeneutic circle as a protean and ceaseless dialogue between reader and text that involves selection and change. Reading, like the exile's quest for home, approximates rather than attains.

Joyce's *Ulysses* marks the culmination of modernism by the period's most famous exile. Joyce's use of the coincidence of contraries as a structural and thematic model deliberately espouses multiplicity and paradox, producing counter-narratives that also signal the novel as a precursor of postmodernism. In applying its parallax view to the concepts of messenger and message by using them as tropes, *Ulysses* forces meaning to shift perspective and radiate in alternative directions. In the interplay of exile and return, reading moves from part to whole, from fetish to allotropy, as paradigms become contingencies and contingencies paradigms. Chapter four discusses how messenger figures layer the novel's messages. In this manner, they function as signposts in the narrative to call attention to the reader's double motivation to create and to suspect order. By oscillating between allusions to Aristotelian and Hermetic philosophy, Joyce uses messenger figures to transgress and to restore narrative memory. By involving its readers in the urge to return while estranging them from what they are returning to, *Ulysses* highlights their exilic status.

Chapters five and six examine the revisions of narrative memory in the reader's experience as exile in two postmodern novels—*The Unbearable Lightness of Being* and *The White Hotel*. Czechoslovakian exile Milan

Kundera's novel functions in terms of betrayals on the levels of plot and narrative structure. These betrayals operate by negating or shifting authority, by refusing to endorse or to sustain the endorsement of philosophical petitions in both literary and metaliterary contexts. They constitute a revisionist aesthetic, attacking the teleological assumptions of novels by telling the story of the reader's misreadings. Each perspectival swing disrupts its predecessor, dislodging hegemonic imperatives and refusing the comfort of totality, so that the reader's engagement becomes a series of renegotiations. Kundera hybridizes his novel to foreground this process as a textual erotics enhanced by and enhancing anxiety. Learning to read Kundera means learning to read with what Kierkegaard terms "sympathetic antipathy," a condition that fosters return and re-creation.

The interplay of the erotic and the tragic that animates narrative engagement is poignantly dramatized in D. M. Thomas's *The White Hotel*. Thomas's novel combines history, fiction, and psychoanalysis as subjects in a narrative that propels the reader simultaneously backward and forward in a quest for meaning. As the narrative writes over itself like a palimpsest, the reader alternates wearing the masks of psychoanalytic detective, historian, hysteric, fetishizer of the fantastic, victim of trauma, plagiarist, and aesthete while engaging the psychic duplicity generated by the text. Drawing on the notion of metaphor as repression in its investigation of the sublime, Chapter six characterizes the paradoxical dynamics of *The White Hotel* as proleptic repression. It further argues that the novel's structure is both decentering and regenerative in its dependence on mirrors to create a chiasmus of terror and pleasure that leads readers to question and to revise their own desire for and resistance to closure.

The concluding chapter brings Julia Kristeva's concept of abjection to bear on pornographic narratives to inquire into the feminine as exile. Contrary to the rational distinctions formed by phallogocentric language and naming, abjection focuses attention on thresholds which function as scenes of generation and negation, attraction and repulsion, Eros and Thanatos. It also follows the psychoanalytic design by tying identity formation to experiences of and through the body and to repressions of those experiences. Pornographic narratives deliberately fetishize the corporeal sites wherein Kristeva locates abjection and also fetishize the reader's or viewer's engagement by devaluing or eliminating context. By representing the feminine only as a hole to be filled by monolithic phallic meaning, pornographic narratives seek to incorporate the feminine as object while exiling it as subject. Chapter seven explores how pornographic narratives both serve and react against the Symbolic. It discusses how the reader or viewer as voyeur revolves between sadistic and masochistic positions in a dialogue of exile and return which engages abjection while attempting to eliminate it.

Transgressions of Reading considers narratives as living forms that are given shape by, and in turn give shape to, their narrators. The arrangement of words, images, or events for the purpose of presenting an explanation also tells the story of the presenter, or re-presenter. Furthermore, narratives of words, images, or events, which are also narratives of Self, are by no means exclusive. While each has an integrity that metamorphoses with the integrity of the reader who encounters it, a reader whose own integrity is also adjusted by that encounter, all tell the story of exile and return, which is the ongoing account of narrative engagement.

Exiling History: Hysterical Transgression in Historical Narrative

I became my own obituary.—Sartre, LES MOTS

The news reports of the assassination of Congressman Leo Ryan and of mass suicide at Jonestown on November 18, 1978 were both chilling and fascinating. Each day boldfaced headlines declared the new body count, and each day the number increased. Our attention fixed on that number as if its magnitude could somehow offer us a means of measuring, of quantifying this macabre event, of putting it on some scale by which we could assess the weight of tragedies. An exiled cult seeking a Promised Land in Guyana, proclaiming its principles with the fervor of a tent meeting, and finally protecting its purity against unknown and unseen persecutors by a self-induced Armageddon; here was our Biblical consciousness hyperbolically dramatized. Here was Moses and Masada, the Garden of Eden and the Fall, the mesmerizing preacher and Satan subsumed into one story. And, most traumatizing, here were our cultural myths, our universal narratives, confronting us as gruesome revelations.

The protagonist of this story, Jim Jones, was savior, God, and angel of death to his followers. Addicted to quaaludes, cognac, antidepressants, valium, and nembutal, having eliminated his body's natural defenses through massive doses of antibiotics, Jones would have died from natural causes within ten days after the apocalypse at Jonestown according to his doctor. His monstrous power and twisted passion are most fully revealed in the 900 hours of tapes he made at Jonestown—his attempt to preserve the holy word, his words. Jones's contradictions underscore our paradoxical reactions to the Jonestown calamity. Like Hazel Motes preaching the Church of Christ without Christ, Jones used his ministerial zeal to convert his followers to atheism. A crusading socialist who practiced capitalism, his sermons in the swamps of Guyana mixed the rhetoric of faith healing, political revolution, and paranoia.

To strengthen his followers' bonds to him, Jones worked to eradicate their blood ties with relatives in the States. Sometimes White Nights (a name chosen by Jones to counteract the racism he felt inherent in the term "black night"), all-night mass meetings during which Jones whipped his followers into hysterical frenzies, became testimonials in which Jonestown residents would take turns spinning stories about how they would like to maim and torture their fallen relatives. Jones exhorted them, applauding the most inventive with his high-pitched squeals of laughter. The tapes give us one little girl explaining to a delighted Jones how she would cut up her father's body and then invite her other relatives over to eat it.

Jones promised death, murder, and suicide to his followers. He heaped doses of profanity on his religious phrases while vocalizing imagined apocalyptic scenes. Inventing snipers and warning against an imminent invasion by Fascist troops who would torture the Jonestown babies and elderly first, Jones rehearsed his self-proclaimed "Greatest Decision in History." And indeed it was the children, followed by the elderly, who lined up first to receive the toxic sacrament. Their savior, unable to steel himself sufficiently with a fistful of barbiturates to take the poison, asked a nurse to shoot him in the temple.

Yet Jones's voice cannot be summarily dismissed as lunatic. His professed cause was just, the elimination of racism and the elevation of the oppressed. His followers numbered in the thousands. He was appointed by Mayor Moscone to the San Francisco Housing Authority Commission in 1976 and was frequently feted and lauded by local politicians. Walter Mondale courted him to deliver the votes of his followers to the Carter campaign. Even during the last months of Jonestown, when the rantings of the White Nights would pierce the jungle, representatives of the Soviet government negotiated with Jones to bring his settlement to the Soviet Union. Jones calculated his appeal and his deviousness well beyond the capacities of the irrational madman. And because of this, our need as interpreters to distance him as merely crazy is frustrated. On some level we recognize that, in different circumstances, we might have been among Jim Jones's followers and therefore our involvement in the tragedy of Jonestown is enhanced.

Attempts to interpret the story of Jim Jones are attempts to exorcise complicity in his story—attempts to play patient and analyst, priest and confessor, simultaneously. Yet we unconsciously recognize this complicity in our initial attraction to the story. With Jim Jones we reenact and transgress cultural myths, achieve vicarious pleasure in his power to command and manipulate them, and can punish ourselves for this delight by participating in his demise.

Making Sense of the Jonestown Suicides by Judith Weightman and Jesus and Jim Jones by Steve Rose present sociological and religious perspectives, respectively, on the People's Temple.[1] Rebecca Moore, whose sisters, Carolyn and Annie, and nephew, Kimo, died at Jonestown, proposes to offer a history of "the believers, rather than of the non-believers, or the ex-believers" in A Sympathetic History of Jonestown, but her history understandably tends to focus on the betrayal and manipulation by Jones of these believers.[2] I find James Reston's account, Our Father Who Art in Hell, the most intelligent and compelling in its effort to attach allegorical significance to the events at Jonestown. Also, Reston is both a novelist and a historian and is therefore sensitive to the links between these two genres.

Reston views the deaths at Jonestown as a consequence of the "spiritual floundering of post-Vietnam America":[3]

> Before I left for Guyana the first time, I saw Jones and his demise as a novel in real life, one of those rare public events which possess the essential elements of compelling fiction: mystery and horror, a primeval setting, a theme close to the raw, primordial instincts of man, a plot stretching belief and imagination, and a villain of satanic power who had used arguments I cared about on race and Vietnam and social progress to produce this ghoulish spectacle. The story tapped my morbid fascination, but it also questioned my political rootedness. Was the Jonestown calamity simply the reductio ad absurdum of 1960s thinking and practice? (150).

This "novel in real life" was a contemporary Heart of Darkness, and Reston plays Marlow to Jones's Kurtz. Jones was the brilliant leader whose mission warped in the primal jungle, a cultural hero who unleashed his culture's dark, repressed urges when he freed it of its constraints. He would "exterminate the brutes," and his uncanny legacy, "the horror, the horror," would echo in his chronicler's mind as he recognized a cultural, and by extension a personal, doppelgänger.

Reston tells us the Jonestown community was founded upon the three qualities for which Dostoevski's Grand Inquisitor said humankind thirsted: miracle, mystery, and authority (58). Jones's followers called him "Father" or "Dad," titles whose implications convey these three qualities. He demanded their idolatry, fostering allegiance through public humiliation, and he stoked this idolatry by staging dramatic proof of his healing powers, even faking an assassination attempt from which he miraculously healed himself. He promulgated a doctrine of Christian atheism that placed himself as the realization of God in man:

> In *me*, the twain have been married. In this dispensation, I have taken on the body, the same body that walked in the plains of Palmyra, of whom Solomon said his hair is black as a raven, and, who, as Isaiah said, 7:20, would shave with a razor. I *do* shave with a razor. My hair *is* black as a raven's. I came as the God to eliminate all your false Gods. Men have dastardly distorted the spirit that I have, but it was necessary for me to come upon the scene and I have. From time to time, I shall show you proofs, so that you will have no further need of religion. I have repeatedly resurrected the dead before your eyes. You have never seen anyone shot down before your eyes and heal themselves, yet I, the socialist leader, have done it. I am the only God you've ever seen, with blood gushing out of his chest, who, after the nurses put their fingers in the bullet holes, just wiped his hand across his chest, and closed them. Your God is one of the people. He is the instrument of all you've ever desired, all that freedom embraces, all that justice embodies, all that sensitivity involves. That is what your God is.
>
> I must say that it is a great effort to be God. I would lean upon another, but no other in the consciousness we are evolving in has the faculties that I possess. When they do, I will be glad to hold his coat. In the meantime, I shall be God, and beside me, there shall be no other. If you don't need a God, then fine, I'm no problem to you. But if you need a God, I'm going to nose out that other God, because it's a false God, so you can get the right concept in your mind. If you're holding onto that Sky God, I'll nose him out ten lengths every time.
>
> And when all this has been done, I shall go into the obscurity of the conscious collective principle of socialism, and I shall have no further intrusion into the affairs of man.

"With that," Reston reports, "he would take the Bible and fling it before him, spit on it, and stamp on it with his feet. He would raise his bare arm to the roof of his Temple and shout, 'If there is a God in the sky, I say, FUCK YOU,' and when he was not struck dead on the spot, this was his proof of the silliness of the Sky God and proof of their superstition" (56–57). As

Father, Jones became the God that his followers lacked and created meaning for their disenchanted lives. He offered a panacea for disillusionment
and, in a culture full of disillusioned people, his appeal was magnetic, not
least of all to the narrator of his story.

Reston's account begins much like Marlow's, waiting for his ship to
depart for a journey down a jungle river. He also quickly establishes the
motif of the double that dominates *Heart of Darkness* and infiltrates his
narrative. Since Caucasian travelers are scarce, one of the deckhands jok-
ingly calls Reston "Jim Jones":

> It was a joke that time, but two days later, as I boarded the *Pomeroon*
> again for the return, the same thing happened, but with an edge to it.
> "You Jim Jones?" a muscular, unsmiling Oriental shouted over to me,
> and before I could answer he said, "If you Jim Jones, you a skunk.
> Jump overboard, I say," and he turned away angrily. The report had
> just been published in the *Guyana Chronicle*, the government news-
> paper, that seventeen of the children at Jonestown had been adopted
> Guyanese. Many still believed that Jim Jones had a double in Jones-
> town, that he was still alive (4).

Just as Marlow discovers the repressed disease of his culture and of himself in Kurtz, we witness Reston's discovery of the same in his narration of
Jones's story:

> Jim Jones was the singular product of the last thirty years of Ameri-
> can history, and his following was the blend of disaffected blacks and
> whites for whom modern America provided no answer in religion,
> political action, or education. His overwhelming success in Califor-
> nia, where he built the single largest Protestant membership of any
> church in that state in little more than four years, dramatizes the void
> he filled. His success was deeply rooted in the general failure of the
> 1970's. Without Richard Nixon, without the Vietnam War, without
> the demise of the civil rights movement or the departure of the tra-
> ditional church from social action, without the current trend toward
> self-concern and hedonism, there would have been no Jim Jones (228).

Reston's personal and political investment had been subverted by 1970s
America's abandonment of the social mission of the sixties and by its immersion in narcissism and cynical forgetfulness. "It could have been different," he laments, "the 1970s could have been the Second Reconstruction
in American history, an active, inspiring attempt to bind up the nation's
wounds, to care for those who had borne the pain and the defeat of Viet-

nam and for those who had resisted it as immoral, to ensure that those for whom the civil rights struggle had been waged were not left in a void after the gains of the sixties" (229). Reston's resultant alienation explains his and the cultists' attraction to Jones, whom Reston characterizes as "the true Alienated Man in an age when alienation had ceased to be fashionable" (230). It also explains the disconnected images—quotes from the Bible tacked to rafters, Santayana's famous epigram "those who do not remember the past are condemned to repeat it" emblazoned above Jones's chair, a SMILE sign—he recalls from his trip to Jonestown on November 27, 1978, deeply tinged with irony in the aftermath of a holocaust. Reston's narrative reveals the dynamic interplay of attraction and repulsion at work in his memory. It is an attraction to a restoration of purpose, a historical telos, an Imaginary ideal which he found so profoundly absent in contemporary cultural life. And it is a repulsion from the perversion of that ideal, the recognition of the Other intruding into that most precious domain—the illusory unity of Self—in this instance projected onto an integrated social mission. In other words, Reston recognizes the cultist in himself, and through this recognition he achieves the status of both analyst and analysand. Rather than becoming dominated by the mystique of Jones so that the repetitions of his narrative memory become the compulsive repetitions of the cultist, continually acting out his enthrallment in the power of that mystique, he can respond critically to that power. In this sense his narrative becomes a dialogue, a reciprocal relationship between the analyst and analysand whose collaboration determines its shape.

The story of Jim Jones and the People's Temple, Reston's "novel in real life," bears comparison to stories as diverse as those of Manson, Hitler, Kurtz, or Sutpen. All of these, whether "historical" or "fictional," contain a generic plot structure—that of the exile or outcast who forges a Promised Land out of an obsession with loss, thereby dooming the dream to destruction. The exile as wanderer can only realize the object of his search through self-annihilation, so that the wish to return to an origin becomes the desire for an ending. And this plot of identity suicide usually includes a Manichean quest to eradicate the Other as unconscious projection of the Self. The return to the ideal Imaginary is premised on the death of the Real, the object of history becomes the end of history.

Jameson's theory of expressive causality presents one model for approaching the exile as protagonist and meta-code. Jameson draws on Althusser's concept of history as an absent cause in which the causes of present social effects can be approached only through perceptions of functions that we experience as "Necessity."[4] Expressive causality places a sequence of historical events into an underlying interpretive allegory. This exercise of narratological will views the present as a satisfaction of gene- alogical desire, a realization of the past rather than simply an effect. In *The Content of the Form*, Hayden White interprets Jameson's narratological causality in the following manner:

> The seizure by consciousness of a past in such a way as to define the present as a fulfillment rather than as an effect is precisely what is represented in a narrativization of a sequence of historical events so as to reveal every thing early in it as a prefiguration of a project to be realized in some future. Considered as a basis for a specific kind of human agency, narrativization sublimates necessity into a symbol of possible freedom.
>
> The narrativization of history, for example, transforms every pres- ent into a "past future," on the one side, and a "future past," on the other. Considered as a transition between a past and a future, every present is at once a realization of projects performed by past human agents and a determination of a field of possible projects to be realized by living human agents in their future.[5]

In this sense, interpreters of history function like characters in a novel in that their mission is to realize the inherent potentialities of the plot in which they are engaged. In doing so, they tie events together so that they lead to conclusions which, retrospectively, subsume beginnings as part of their process.

Expressive causality helps to define the shape of narrative memory, but its view of genealogical desire fails to consider sufficiently the degree to which simultaneous attraction to and repulsion from loss informs narra- tive memory's dynamics. Readers as exiles from an ideal Imaginary state seek to recover that state by wandering the text, only to continually wander into recognitions of their exiled condition. Although genealogical desire empowers them to assign direction and purpose to their wandering, the return to homeland is still not accomplished. While the search for an end- ing motivates their journey, the fear of ending that journey, of finding the Imaginary unrestored, impels them to resist conclusion. Once again, the transgressive, particularly in hysterical extremes where the discourse of repetition.becomes compulsive, offers us insight into the flirtation with the death drive. The master text to apply to this understanding is Freud's *Beyond the Pleasure Principle*.

Beyond the Pleasure Principle views repetition as the essence of drives, but paradoxically views the individual's basic need to reproduce his earliest states as indicative of the desire to abolish all drives, a death instinct (Thanatos). Like the pleasure principle (Eros), Thanatos is an internal force. Indeed, Freud considers it the supreme form of the pleasure principle in its complete reduction of tension, and at times terms it the "Nirvana Principle," thereby linking pleasure with annihilation.[6] According to Freud, all living beings possess this internal tendency toward the end of life as the end of life's drives and the restoration of an original, tension-free state. Life's diversities, instigated by traumas and subsequent repressions, represent detours, wanderings from this path. Ironically, Freud's own discourse in *Beyond the Pleasure Principle* lacks his usual clarity and logic. As if resisting his proclamation of the primacy of the death drive, Freud fills the text with contradictions and blurred references. At times he seems to grope toward conclusions, and we might take this groping not as indicative of Freud's lack of a comprehensive understanding of his subject but rather as an unconscious resistance to that understanding.

Narrative engagement with a fictional text or with events in history, characterized as it is by yearning and resistance, recapitulates the narrative of life. Our engagement with literary and historical texts becomes the arena in which the contest between Eros and Thanatos is performed. We are exiles from our origin, yearning for return and possessed by our sense of loss of that origin while simultaneously resisting that yearning because of the pleasures of wandering and our fear of the loss of those pleasures. Interpretation, as an act of memory, is controlled by these opposed urges. We travel a text in quest of an ending that will retrospectively impose order by relieving the tensions generated by the plot, thereby returning us to a beginning. In doing so, we seek the beginning of history in its end.

The discourse of repetition, signalling the death drive, catalyzes and is catalyzed by narrative memory. It functions as an indication of ending while, ironically, it tentatively halts progress toward the end. Freud termed repetition a "demon," and we witness the demonic aspect in the cadences of Jim Jones's orations. Repetition in the transgressive discourse of the hysteric becomes compulsive, transgressing the normal function of repetition within discourse. Rather than relaxing tension, it contributes to it. Rather than coalescing to augment order, it disperses order and destabilizes through its constancy. Hysterical transgression combines Eros and Thanatos, bringing erotic excitement to loss. It fetishizes memory, inducing sexual frenzy in infinite repetition, and undermines narrative by collapsing beginnings and endings while eliminating middles. Exiles have nowhere to wander, but must spin endlessly in the same place. They have found a home, an Imaginary ideal, but it is no resting place. And Father has castrated their memories.

II

The new historian, the genealogist, will know what to make of this masquerade. He will not be too serious to enjoy it; on the contrary, he will push the masquerade to its limits and prepare the great carnival of time where masks are constantly reappearing. Genealogy is history in the form of a concerted carnival.—Foucault, "Nietzsche, Genealogy, History"

Ariel Dorfman adopts the language of the land to which he is exiled to give voice to memories of the land from which he is exiled.[7] In doing so, he offers an example of the movement from filiation to affiliation although his focus remains on disaffiliation, on the fact that his identity will always be predicated on his exilic status. Indeed, this act underscores the gap between experience and representation of experience, and demonstrates language to be but part of the makeup that constitutes the mask. *Mascara* deals with acquiring and losing identities, with self-possession through the possession of others, with the deceptions of memory. The text becomes a mirror in which the narrator's facelessness reveals the reader's face.

Dorfman presents the story of an unnamed character who is born without a recognizable face. No one, not even his parents, remembers who he is, and therefore he is able to become the perfect voyeur. To enhance this vocation, he destroys all records of his identity, including his fingerprints. Unable to forget a face, he perceives the hidden faces of others and captures them in photographs, thereby acquiring power over them by possessing evidence of their secrets. Photography as an act of erotic possession is more satisfying to him than sex: "A photograph: now, you can fuck a photograph forever"; "to own another human being, the only thing necessary is to kidnap her intimacy, to deflower with my camera what my eyes had already explored."[8] His employment as assistant to the archivist of photography files at the Department of Traffic Accidents enables him to acquire a collection of photographs that depicts its subjects in their most private and grotesque moments. For this featureless narrator, all faces are false. By putting on their socially authorized masks, they respond to a historical rather than a genetic imperative:

> The first face a little one sees is not something far away, outside, like a mirror in the sky. Not so. The first thing any child sees is the inside

of his father's face, he sees the maneuvers that his own features must start rehearsing and that are constantly being sewn onto him like an umbrella of skin against the rain. In order to keep out other, possibly worse, invaders, he adopts his father's shell. Human beings are trapped inside the dead faces of their remote ancestors, repeated from generation to generation (32).

Mascara's narrator finds his perfect love, his twin, in Oriana, an amnesiac whose memory past the age of four is nonexistent. This child-woman with no past mirrors his lack of a face and permits him the opportunity to dictate the parameters of her identity and thereby substitute his authority for society's:

> For her, every day shall be as a first birth, with all the fresh air that came at the beginning of Creation. And the person who accompanies her, the person who can show her the perpetually recent contours of the universe, will be as a god. . . . I can rewrite and recapture the whole of human history. We can be each of the past's lovers, each character in each novel: and it will always be my narrating her, a thousand and one times if that is necessary (80–81).

However, the narrator fears the disruption of his Edenic situation by the reemergence of Oriana's past, an adult Oriana, "normal: someone with a past, with a mask" (77), hiding within the child Oriana and waiting to reclaim her face. In order to prevent this, he seeks the skills of the plastic surgeon, Dr. Mavirelli, whom he addresses in the sections of the novel which he narrates. While he attempts to blackmail this remaker of faces to unmake Oriana's past, he intentionally and ironically misremembers Mavirelli's name, offering instead a panoply of variations.

Mavirelli responds to him in the third section of the novel and reveals himself as a double of the narrator. He has achieved professional prominence by reconstructing the faces of important public figures to match public desires as expressed in opinion polls, even re-creating the face of one popular victim of sudden death on the face of his successor. Like the narrator's photography, Mavirelli's surgery functions as a means of erotic possession; penetration constitutes control:

> All right, I admit it, I start to think that I am possessing that face: that small apparatus is like a metallic clitoris, which I am inserting into the precise intersecting line of the brain. . . . Tell me, of what use is it to change somebody's twisted nose if his memory persists in remem-

bering the old one and, therefore, continues to twist the new one until it resembles the nose that will not vanish from that memory? That is why my operations have such an incredible degree of success: because along with the old skin, they eliminate the old habits, the past (140).

In the epilogue, we discover that Mavirelli has given his face to the narrator and can die smiling, having conferred his identity rather than having had identity conferred on him.

From the narrator's Kafkaesque job to the Gestapo-like repossessors of the hands of the dead to the two unidentified investigators who become rude interrogators in the epilogue, Dorfman's references to the political oppression in his native Chile are clear. Totalitarian authority renders memory a fraud. Like the plastic surgeon, its "efforts are made in order to suppress a revelation" (35), to enforce the repetition of sameness, and to erase the personal. Social identity is predicated on the loss of the Self, and resistance to that loss ironically is fostered through anonymity. But aside from a political allegory, *Mascara* also presents an allegory of the reading process.

As faceless voyeur, the narrator functions like a generic reader. His vicarious pleasure derives from subsuming the Other and using its sameness or difference to affirm his ideal projection of the Self. In the wish to attain that imaginative ideal, to revise memory so as to eliminate the recognition of his exilic condition, the reader, like the narrator, desires privation rather than plenitude, return rather than journeying, and manipulates whomever and whatever he encounters in order to conserve the fixed center of his desire. By focusing on origins and elevating them to myth, he represses the knowledge of loss and willfully attains the status of amnesiac. In effect, the reader ends history in order to recreate it.

Dorfman uses first-person narration to better convey the obsessive quest, the death drive toward the Imaginary. Even though the section narrated by Mavirelli revises those of the faceless narrator, the tone and perspective of the narrative voice remain consistent until the epilogue. The faceless narrator and the plastic surgeon, like the social Gestapo they resist, are thieves of memory. However, their figurative and tonal parallels, the propensity of their discourse toward the grotesque and the cynical, inject repetition into the text and activate its readers' narrative memories while suggesting metanarrative constructions to them. Their similarities are reified as the novel concludes with the initial narrator putting on Mavirelli's face, thereby compelling its readers, like Narcissus, to stare into their own reflections. Whether or not they drown depends on the extent to which they have established a reciprocal dialogue with the narrative or have been possessed by it.

Hysterical transgression again fetishizes memory and eroticizes loss. Just as the faceless narrator loses his voyeuristic distance in his obsession with Oriana, allowing himself to become possessed by her in his wish to possess her, Mavirelli gives up his life to impress his identity without first having to erase a prior image. Both wish to invade the insides of another and father a new individual who is a replication of themselves. In *Mascara*, they combine to succeed, and this merging catalyzes their readers' identifications. The narrative reaches into their private recesses and affirms their fetishes, fusing Eros and Thanatos, while they participate in its conclusion. Chameleon-like, they permit the novel to stamp its face upon their own. This yielding constitutes a transgressive act, one which the narrative endorses and which its readers compulsively repeat, deriving pleasure from their loss of Self.

Yet readers wish to play Dr. Mavirelli to the text as much as they desire to be molded by it, and therefore are impelled to resist the compulsion to be subsumed which hypnotically promises to lessen the tension produced by their journey through the novel. Instead, they make their own incisions into the face of the text and stitch it back together in the image of their own narrative memories. Furthermore, they must refashion their handiwork to accord with the mutable demands of that memory. By oscillating between yielding and resisting, readers again perform the role of exile.[9] Their conflicting impulses to journey and to return are regulated by the desires of memory which assert themselves only to fade and to be replaced by another assertion, like so many applications of makeup.

We have seen the discourse of the hysteric, the pantomimic language of the Imaginary, at work in both a historical narrative and a work of fiction. Both types of narrative are conditioned by the judgments inherent in description, and the descriptions in both cases contain a complex of symbols that relate to universal patterns. The engagement of the historian or reader with the narrative of events is continually mediated by a dialogic process akin to psychoanalytic transference where Otherness is internalized and projected. Repetition offers the means and the evidence for this process and, as the foundation of memory, refers backward in the narrative to propel it forward. This paradox mirrors and is dictated by the readers' conflicting desires for excitement and stasis. However, hysterical discourse transgresses this dialogic process by rendering repetition compulsive, thereby destroying the movement forward and freezing the narrative memory in trauma.

Lacan contends that Freud made distinctions between repeating (*wieder-holen*) and reproduction (*reproduzieren*). While reproduction consists of the actual reexperiencing of the original traumatic event, repetition confronts this past event in symbolic form.[10] Hysterical discourse reproduces the tragic vision inherent in the end product of narrative—its temporality. The aspiration to be liberated from history inherent in the quest for the Imaginary is undercut by the historical underpinnings of the Imaginary. Interpreters or readers, who are subsumed by the thanatotic urge of hysterical discourse, become fixated on trauma. They lose the critical distance necessary for a dialogue with the text so that their narrative memories endlessly replicate the trauma reproduced in the narrative memory of the text.

III

By searching out origins, one becomes a crab. The historian looks backward, eventually he believes backward.—Nietzsche, TWILIGHT OF THE IDOLS

To conclude this discussion, I wish briefly to examine what amounts to a work of fiction that masquerades as a history. Originally titled *The Man Moses: A Historical Novel*, Freud's *Moses and Monotheism* attempts to extend the principle of primal forfeiture that he presented in *Totem and Taboo* to Jewish monotheism. Its discussion of the archetypal exile, Moses, however, succeeds more as a narrative of its author's psyche. Freud argues that Moses was actually an aristocratic Egyptian who descended from his position to side with the children of Israel and imposed the monotheistic religion that revolved around the Egyptian sun god, Aten, on the Semitic tribes. Freud contends that Moses was subsequently killed by his people and that the worship of the god of Moses melded with the worship of a volcano god, Yahweh, through whom the Jewish people repressed their guilt for murdering their leader. However, this repressed trauma returned as the Jewish prophets advanced a religion based on ethics by focusing on the Mosaic god and enhancing the guilt of the people.[11]

Although Freud's assertions have not been given much credence by historians and Biblical scholars, *Moses and Monotheism* does offer much material by which to analyze its author's engagement with the events he narrates.[12] As James Strachey's editorial note informs us, its construction is extremely unorthodox for Freud. It consists of three essays of greatly varying lengths and contains two prefaces, one located at the beginning of the third essay and another halfway through that essay. What is perhaps most striking is the sputtering quality of the argument, again uncharacteristic of Freud. The work is full of parenthetical remarks, repetitions, and recapitulations, and contains several apologies by Freud for these distractions. These features begin to make sense when we place Freud's history of Moses in the context of Freud's own desires.

Moses and Monotheism was four years in composition (1934–38), well above Freud's standard for a work of this length. During these four years, Freud witnessed increasingly ominous signs in Austrian politics that were to climax in the Nazi occupation of Vienna and force his departure to London with the manuscript of *Moses and Monotheism* among his possessions. Freud's attention to the prototypical exile therefore is symptomatic of his anxiety over his own imminent exile. His argument that Moses was an aristocratic Egyptian who left his country because of its oppressive tactics toward the Jews dramatizes his own dilemma as a member of Austria's intellectual elite who could no longer tolerate his country's slide into anti-Semitic hooliganism. Freud viewed the rejection of psychoanalysis by the political establishment as the symbolic murder of himself as the lawgiver of psychoanalysis just as he argued that Moses, the lawgiver of his people, was slain by them. His contention that the Jewish prophets brought about the return of the Mosaic god indicates his desire that his disciples, the Jewish prophets of psychoanalysis, reinstate his teachings. The consequent guilt suffered by the children of Israel from the return of repressed trauma constitutes Freud's secret wish for retribution.

The fits and starts that characterize the narrative are symptomatic of Freud's ambivalence concerning the entire notion of exile. His attachment to Vienna was as extreme as the attachment to Egypt he manufactures for Moses. Unconsciously he recognized that the departure from his homeland would preserve that homeland only in the postures of his memory, and would be manifested only through condensation and displacement. His reconstructions therefore would be informed by the very methodology of the law he had preached—the law of psychoanalysis. The stone tablets into which Freud had engraved that law had suffered numerous cracks and crumblings during the 1930s, a period during which some of his disciples, in his eyes, became infidels. Perhaps their proposed revisions to his law secretly tested his own faith. Perhaps his narrative of Moses represented his working out his anxiety concerning both exile and living by the very law he dictated.

Freud writes of his interpretation of the story of Moses:

Its evidential value seems to me strong enough for me to venture on a further step and to posit the assertion that the archaic heritage of human beings comprises not only dispositions but also subject-matter—memory-traces of the experience of earlier generations. In this way the compass as well as the importance of the archaic heritage would be significantly extended.[13]

What he is arguing is a universal history based on a universal memory of trauma. Ricoeur draws on this argument to posit all narrative, whether historical or fictional, as an allegory of temporality.[14] I have attempted to demonstrate that the fear of loss generated by awareness of the corrosive power of time embodies the tragic underpinnings of all narratives. Although methods of historiography, like techniques of fiction, vary, the dynamics of narrative engagement always involve conflicting desires to yield to and to resist this traumatic recognition. While repetitions within narrative reproduce and enhance the function of memory by offering signs of origin, hysterical repetition, like hysterical memory, arouses trauma by excising the marginalia that typically accompany the encounter with origin. The tragic experience in this instance is not diminished by the mediative intrusion of signs, symbols, or other projections. Instead, the reflection of the Self encountered is an absent Self, and the subsequent reverberations of this perception constrict any future encounters.

As interpreters, we function as exiles. Our desires and our denials, our masks and our absences, our alienation and our yearning for omniscience all come into play as we seek and resist our origins in our narrations of narrative. Our visions of home altered by the revisions of memory, we are condemned to wander our texts eternally, recreating history in our quest to conclude it.

2 Disrupting the Look: Ernst and the Kindness of Transgression

I

We are beyond the stage of reverence for works of art as divine and objects deserving our worship. The impression they produce is one of a more reflective kind, and the emotions they arouse require a higher test.
—Hegel, THE PHILOSOPHY OF FINE ARTS

E H. Gombrich begins his monumental *Art and Illusion* by exposing the illusion within a mundane act of representation in which most of us engage daily. He asks that we take advantage of the steamy bathroom mirror after a shower to trace the outline of our heads' reflection on its surface and then to clear the area enclosed by the outline. By doing so, we will find the image in the mirror to be precisely half the size of our actual head rather than the exact face-to-face representation we assume.[1] I cite Gombrich's tale of the shrunken head as a prelude to taking the measure of another source of self-knowledge. Instead of the bathroom mirror, I wish to consider the work of art at which viewers gaze and in which they find themselves gazing back deeply altered. I wish to examine how the narrative of the artwork engages and is engaged by the narrative of the Self and to consider where this dynamic is paradoxical in turning a structural impulse into a deconstructive effect.

To consider art as narrative is to begin with a departure from traditional aesthetics. In his *Laocoön* of 1766, G. E. Lessing considers painting to be incapable of narration because its imitation is static rather than progressive. According to Lessing, attempts to express stories in pictorial imagery rather than language lead painting into "abandoning its proper sphere and degenerating" into allegorical forms.[2] Lessing extends the difference between painting and poetry to the opposition of space and time, a link which has been fortified in the aesthetics of Romanticism and Russian formalism, as well as in the observations of a contemporary narrative theorist like Seymour Chatman, who deems the term "pictorial narrative" oxymoronic.[3]

Motivated in large part by Roland Barthes's claim for the polysemy of images, however, several recent critics have questioned Lessing's categorical distinction.[4] In his study of the interplay between imagery and textuality, Nelson Goodman uses a linguistic model for his conception of the icon. His summary of his essay "The Way the World Is" describes this model:

> I began by dropping the picture theory of language and ended by adopting the language theory of pictures. I rejected the picture theory of language on the ground that the structure of a depiction does not conform to the structure of the world. But I then concluded that there is no such thing as the structure of the world for anything to conform or fail to conform to. You might say that the picture theory of language is as false and as true as the picture theory of pictures; or, in other words, that what is false is not the picture theory of language but a certain absolutistic notion concerning both pictures and language.[5]

In *Languages of Art*, Goodman locates the text-image boundary in the differences between sign-types, which he argues are the result of practical applications rather than *a priori* metaphysical distinctions. He states, "Realism is relative, determined by the system of representation standard for a given culture or person at a given time."[6]

In *Iconology*, W. J. T. Mitchell analyzes Goodman, Gombrich, Lessing, Burke, and Marx to confirm the linguistic model for the workings of the pictorial image. Since ideas are understood as images, Mitchell contends that "ideology, the science of ideas, is really an iconology, a theory of imagery."[7] Perhaps drawing from Fredric Jameson's notion of the political unconscious, he proposes that space and time in the arts be considered in a dialectical struggle in which the ideological roles and relationships of the two concepts shift with historical contingencies. By emphasizing the ideological and dialectical nature of the image and stressing its polyvalent functions, then, Mitchell helps to break the mold into which Lessing had cast notions of artistic production and response.

Wendy Steiner examines the empowering of the perceiver in departures from the Albertian model of the Renaissance, which posited perception as atemporal. "To equate reality and its representation, realism, with atemporality," Steiner argues, "is to destroy the logical basis of realism—the concept of identity as a repetition traversing time."[8] She goes on to analyze the undercutting in modern painting of Alberti's single point perspective through such narrative factors as multiplicity and repetition.

With the aid of Steiner, Mitchell, and Goodman, we can attribute Lessing's exclusion of picture from narrative, and his consequent disparagement of allegory which finds further expression in Coleridge's elevation of symbol over allegory,[9] to an ignorance of the figural genesis of narrative. Indeed, time is knowable always in terms of space, constituted in images, which are figures fixed in space, that refer to it. As Paul de Man argues in "The Rhetoric of Temporality," although it is "the originary constitutive category" in allegory, time is ultimately defined through allegory's spatial design.[10] The referent always precedes the image as an anterior sign with which the image as present sign can never coincide. Perception is therefore apperception; what is perceived is always invested with and colored by previous perceptions. In allegory, the anterior referent becomes ideal and is projected within and by the narrative structure.[11] Although it is excluded from the present, the present seeks to recapture it, to reinstitute it in the here and now. However, these attempts can result only in approximations, so that the idealizations of memory lead inevitably to a reconfirmation of one's exilic status from those ideals, to an awareness of the fictional condition of perception.

The nature of engaging images is allegorical in that viewers invest images with life and tend to consecrate that animation in some fashion as an ideal representation. Like the narrative action of all allegory, the narrative action of this engagement is autotelic. The inscription of time in space by viewers, as well as artists, is filtered through a perceptual field tinged by the personal dialectic of yearning and loss. Viewing is framed by what is projected into a picture, a frame which may be unable to contain lingering transgressions that may signal both the inaccessibility of the projections and the constraining effects of the assumptions on which those projections are premised.[12] Multiplicity, fragmentation, and repetition become self-commentaries that occlude the sheen of the ideal, producing an awareness of time as something other than a fixed moment. It is this awareness, the detachment of the metaphoric from the metonymic, that generates contradiction and struggle within viewers. In these disruptive junctures, the frame of the Symbolic Order is also cracked and the sense of ideal return and stasis is revealed as a period of entrapment. To use Walter Benjamin's term, the image as allegorical agent has been emptied of its "aura" and is displayed as a convenience that is endlessly reproducible, a token with which exiles temporarily may deceive themselves that they have returned home.[13]

The narrative that ensues between viewers and images, like our morning rituals with our images in the mirror, operates through mental forgeries. Chief among these is the wedge we drive between our intellectual and emotional responses so we may elevate the former and suppress the latter. Our cognitive defenses permit us to believe a disjunction exists between art objects and reality, and allow us to keep our powerful emotional responses to the images before us at bay. Both Goodman and David Freedberg have written persuasively in an effort to heal this breach.

Goodman's critique of the prevailing dichotomy between the cognitive and the emotive charges "this pretty effectively keeps us from seeing that in aesthetic experience the *emotions function cognitively*."[14] Freedberg attributes the separation of cognition and emotion to a fear of the strength of images. In a discussion that considers a wide variety of images and rituals, he argues that this fear is based on a fear of the body and on the need to distinguish between the divine and the mundane. Intellectual distance from the emotions, endorsed by the humanistic tradition, provides a refuge from the animal drives of the body and permits the illusion of severing this link to our instinctive selves. By abstracting our responses to images, particularly images of the body, we maintain this illusion. Furthermore, the enlivening of an image emulates divine action and threatens a hierarchical array that informs our inherited worldview. Freedberg questions these distinctions as well as those differences which traditionally have been invoked to categorize artworks as canonical or noncanonical.[15]

Art which deliberately indulges in heterogeneous discourses unsettles cognitive boundaries so that its viewers' emotions may no longer be suppressed within their response. Since understanding is akin to ownership, the subversion of reason thwarts the oppression of others through the look of the Other. Furthermore, this subversion undermines the dictates of the Symbolic through which hierarchies are disseminated and perpetuated. By overtly and ironically eroticizing the body as fetish, art may politicize the act of looking, exposing its potential as a mechanism of power that controls the bodies of others. This parody of voyeurism may show it as an omnipresent exercise in possession which must always bare the image to understand, and therefore master it. Freedburg asserts that, bound up as it is in desire and in the drive for possession, all looking in the West is essentially masculine.[16] While endorsing Freedburg's assertion, this study will endeavor to offer transgressive examples that, in contesting the prevailing power, feminize the observer. Although looking is masculine and possessive, transgressive art can subvert the Law of masculine possession by deliberately advertising or parodying it. In this process, viewers may glimpse the lost homeland of the Imaginary and, integrating cognition and emotion, experience where and from what they have been exiled.

The transgressive example on which I wish to focus as my case study for the above discussion is Max Ernst's collage novel, *Une Semaine de bonté*. As an explicitly narrative sequence based on the pastiche of collage, *Une Semaine de bonté* constitutes a heterogeneous discourse which both uses hybridization as a narrative technique and presents images which are themselves hybrids. In *Problems of Art*, Susanne Langer rejects hybrid works as aesthetic deviants, stating "there can be no happy marriages in art— only successful rapes."[17] Ernst's anomalies take aim at the purveyors of aesthetic truths and at the system of mastery they serve. In doing so, they exult in raping the rapist.

II

Art, like the God of the Jews, feasts on holocausts.
—Flaubert, Letter to Louise Colet, August 1853

In 1933 Max Ernst traveled to northern Italy for a holiday visit with François Hugo and Maria de Gramont, his suitcase stuffed with the raw materials for his fifth collage novel. In three weeks, the illustrations he had clipped from French pulp novels, popular books on astronomy and natural science, scientific journals, and natural history magazines would become the 182 collages of *Une Semaine de bonté* (*A Week of Kindness*), which would be published in Paris in five paperbound booklets issued individually during 1934. Hitler's rise to power figures prominently in the irony of Ernst's title and in the images of catastrophe and entrapment that dominate the book. The Nazis would later denounce Ernst as a degenerate artist and display his work in the *Entartete Kunst* exhibition that traveled through Germany in 1937. Indeed, the disparate elements of Ernst's collages respond to the pernicious imposition of identity occurring in his homeland.

Une Semaine de bonté differs from Ernst's previous collage novels, *Répétitions* and *Les Malheurs des Immortels* (*The Misfortunes of the Immortals*) in collaboration with Paul Eluard in 1922, *La Femme 100 Têtes* (*The Hundred Headed Woman*) in 1929, and *Rêve d'Une Petite Fille qui voulut entrer au Carmel* (*A Little Girl Dreams of Taking the Veil*) in 1930, most significantly by the absence of captions.[18] In bypassing its primary vehicle, language, Ernst undermined the Symbolic. To enhance pictorial relationships, Ernst also revised the format of his previous efforts where the collage appeared on the right-hand page and the facing page was left blank. In addition to increasing the size of his figures in *Une Semaine de bonté*, Ernst placed collages on both right- and left-hand pages. These changes intensify the emphasis on commentary through and among images rather than words and help to free the reader's play of responses from the dictates of the Symbolic. However, Ernst's neglect of linguistic tags and emphasis on the pictorial paradoxically encourage the imposition of the Symbolic at the same time they frustrate it, thus dramatizing its dominance. Although the absence of captions initially limits readers from constructing meaning through language so that we depend more on the development and interplay of visual themes, this absence also motivates us to supply our own captions, to project our own Symbolic terms into the frame.

Ernst attended the University of Bonn as a philosophy student during a time when Kokoschka, Kandinsky, Jawlensky, Picasso, Braque, and Rouault erupted onto the increasingly internationalist art scene to which Ernst was drawn. As a student, Ernst's interests gravitated to iconoclasts like Freud and Nietzsche. He studied abnormal psychology and planned a book on art made by the inmates of a nearby asylum. In Nietzsche, Ernst found a life-long influence in his revolt against culturally authorized categories of knowledge and identity. In his biography of Ernst, John Russell quotes the artist remarking of *The Gay Science*, a copy of which he had heavily annotated since his student days, "there, if ever, is a book which speaks to the future. The whole of surrealism is in it, if you know how to read."[19] Russell directs his readers to passages in *The Gay Science*, particularly Book two, paragraphs 57 and 58, that Ernst had marked as a student, passages which were to guide his own work:

> This has given me the greatest trouble and still does: to realize that what things *are called* is incomparably more important than what they are. . . . What at first was appearance becomes in the end, almost invariably, the essence and is effective as such. How foolish it would be to suppose that one only needs to point out this origin and this misty shroud of delusion in order to *destroy* the world that counts for real, so-called *"reality."* We can destroy only as creators.—But let us not forget this either: it is enough to create new names and estimations and probabilities in order to create in the long run new "things."[20]

Nietzsche's hyperbolic hammering at the boundaries of Aristotelian order empowered Ernst to seek new ways of naming. He dallied with the Dadaists, whose name mocks the paternalistic state, in a creative effort to destroy. In deliberately abandoning the rules of reason, Ernst embraced Breton's *Surrealist Manifesto* and its call for the arbitrary, the derisive, and the hallucinatory. Rather than reject the world, however, his work reacts to it. He termed his collages "phallustrades" because he sought a new way of fathering but was aware that the contradictory elements he yoked together constituted political and social commentaries. In his verbal collage as essay, "Beyond Painting," Ernst defines the phallustrade as a register of the current state of human tragedy:

> A phallustrade is a typical product of black humor. A sagging relief, taken from the lung of a 47-year old smoker, is another. . . . It seems to me one can say that collage is a hypersensitive and rigorously true instrument, like a seismograph, capable of registering the exact quantity of possibilities for human happiness in each epoch. The quantity of black humor contained in each authentic collage is found there in the inverse proportion of the possibilities of happiness (objective and subjective).[21]

Ernst's phallustrades, then, are also parricides, designed to destroy authority and convention by restoring the Dionysiac and libidinous from their repressed status.[22]

Nietzsche's offensive against Aristotle's law of non-contradiction and the metaphysics that is its legacy found another front in Ernst's collages. As a Nietzschean artist of upheaval, Ernst devoted his work to the demolition of culturally inscribed perspectives and used collage as his technique of destruction. Calling for "the pairing of two realities which apparently cannot be paired on a plane apparently not suited to them,"[23] Ernst promoted paradox to instill estrangement in his viewers. His collages disturb because they display the familiar in contexts contradictory to those which sustain its familiarity. Their principle of substitution transforms coherence into a dialogue between parts and reveals continuity as a mutable patchwork. Indeed, Ernst concluded "Beyond Painting" with the capitalized proclamation "IDENTITY WILL BE CONVULSIVE OR WILL NOT EXIST."

Ernst's use of the collage novel as an assault on the confines of identity is evident in the title of his earlier *La Femme 100 Têtes*. Here he plays on the similarity between the pronunciations of the French words for "one hundred," *cent*, and "without," *sans*. The title character simultaneously has one hundred heads and is without a head. Her identity is not uniform, but multiple or absent. However, her variability and inconsistency are not limited to the pages on which she appears. By undermining narrative logic and the control of reason, the collage novels also dislodge their readers' sense of identity.

In her rejection of the linkage of Romantic and Neoplatonic heritages to Surrealism, Margot Norris places Ernst within a biocentric rather than anthropocentric context.[24] She reads his work as an attempt to reclaim art from the domain of reason and from the humanistic tradition which had placed it there. Ernst recognized that with the fall into the Symbolic the Imaginary must present itself through the language of the Symbolic. He therefore devoted his efforts to warping that language so that the images he produced were recognizably perverse. Norris terms the effect of his expressions "semiotic derangement," the function of which "is not only to demonstrate the inadequacy of reason when confronted with the irrational, but also to frustrate and dislodge the 'other,' the reader, the viewer, as subject."[25] Ernst's basic materials are scraps of popular culture, representations of everyday aspirations. These conventions, coupled with allusions to classical and ideal forms, constitute deceptive lures for his readers in that the presentation of bodies as accumulations of disparate parts subverts any ideal harmony. Using oxymoron as their primary rhetorical technique, then, Ernst's collages destabilize any sense of cohesive reader identity.

Une Semaine de bonté, as the title indicates, is divided into seven parts corresponding to the days of the week. Each chapter heading contains an element associated with the day, a characteristic example, and a quotation to establish the tone of the action. The imagery includes typical Surrealist interests like alchemy and Freudian dream symbolism, but unlike the intended results of the processes behind these interests, the narrative fails to coalesce into a unified whole. Its narration is strikingly antinarrative. Although M. E. Warlick has compiled an impressive discussion of the relationships between *Une Semaine de bonté* and alchemical symbolism and process, he has failed to grasp this point.[26] The novel does not move toward any state of spiritual purity. No philosopher's stone is attained nor is Jungian individuation achieved. Similarly, the encounter with horrors that may be deemed cultural repressions produces no alleviation of these horrors as the Freudian process would dictate. *Une Semaine de bonté* offers no clear conclusion, no reconciliation of opposites, no restoration of psychic wholeness.

The first book, "Sunday," has the Lion of Belfort as its role-shifting protagonist. Military officer, seducer, murderer, sadist, enforcer, and transgressor, the Lion of Belfort fills the sabbath day with violence and perversity. Like the classical and mythic allusions in many of Ernst's paintings and collages, the Lion of Belfort has its historical referent fractured and parodied. As Evan M. Maurer explains, the Lion of Belfort refers to an immense stone statue by Frédéric-Auguste Bartholdi, sculptor of the Statue of Liberty, carved into the rock cliff on the eastern side of Belfort near the German border. The wounded yet heroic lion depicted represents the French defenders of Belfort and their leader, Colonel Denfert-Rochereau, who stood their ground against a much larger Prussian army.[27] Considering the Nazi menace, the contemporary significance for Ernst is obvious. However, Sunday's lion-headed protagonist ranges far from being an honorable protector of home and instead appears complicitous with that which threatens it.

The first collage establishes the frame-within-the-frame motif that recurs throughout *Une Semaine de bonté.* The lion-headed man, adorned in an officer's uniform decorated with numerous medals of valor, gazes over his shoulder at a gauzy portrait of Napoleon while being attacked or embraced (it is not clear which) by a young lion (figure 1). In addition to establishing the historical associations with the Lion of Belfort, this collage reveals the threat of conquest that lurks in the background of the entire novel. The filmy, dream-like representation of Napoleon suggests the possibility of imminent transformation into another conqueror, perhaps the Nazi Führer. The cub's attack on the lion-headed man looks forward to Wednesday, the Oedipus section of the novel. If we read its posture as an embrace, we might see the pair as suggesting a lineage of continuing tragedy when posi-

Figure 1

Figure 2

tioned under the vanquisher portrayed above them.[28] In either sense, the gaze of both lion figures is directed toward the Napoleon portrait and their expressions of horror are reactions to it. Napoleon is the creator-father of the Lion of Belfort, who is the creator-father of the lion cub, who both desires (embraces) and hates (attacks) the father. The line is one of descent, from man to beast, and the nakedness of the latter reveals the brute within the first father. As viewers, we are implicated in the line of descent for we look at the picture of them looking.

Conquest and entrapment as extensions of male desire are reflected in the images of pain, dismemberment, and enslavement that make up "Le Lion de Belfort." The second collage depicts a scene in an art gallery (figure 2). A nobly dressed lion-headed man strolls gallantly through the corridor, while a well-dressed young woman clings to his arm. The couple's rich and multi-layered clothing contrasts with the art displayed in the gallery: a picture featuring a female breast in an oval frame and a statue of a woman who is nude except for a chastity belt, one stocking, and some constraining bands. Behind the lion-headed man, another man bends his face closely to the oval-framed picture and stares intently.

The collage exposes the masculine gaze behind culturally sanctioned ways of looking as fetishistic and exploitative. The posturing lion-headed man's authoritative explanations are meekly accepted by his consort, whose sex is manifested by the accoutrements of fashion. On either side of her, representations of the female body appear. However, they are, like her, fashion statements. The three female figures form a kind of triptych in which the female observer is no less objectified than are the two nude images. Bound by devices designed to frustrate movement and sexuality, the statue's appeal is pornographic. It implies that the control of natural impulses has been subjugated by the observer, so that the body is converted to property. The faceless image in the oval frame has been synecdochized as a breast, to the obsessed delight of one gallery patron who comments on the male viewer of the collage. The oval frame suggests a mirror, which reflects the relationship between the well-dressed young lady and her lion-headed paramour. Like the picture in the oval frame for the obsessed patron, the young woman is on display for the lion-headed man. Whether or not she sees a reflection of herself is not clear, but her status as an observer in the gallery certainly comments on the reader's. By positioning the young woman to watch how others see her, Ernst feminizes his readers and turns their gaze back on them. He reveals that gaze as the look of male desire which must impinge upon, fragment, or embellish the female body in order to possess it. The bodiless head, mounted like an animal's in the background of the collage, no longer looks or lusts, and thus appears angelic, decorated with wings.[29]

Scenes of orgy, torture, murder, and punishment with the lion-headed man in various incarnations as seducer, torturer, murderer, and executioner follow. In one set of facing pages, a lion-headed man nonchalantly tickles the foot of an inert woman bound to a bed on the left-hand page, while on the right-hand page a lion-faced man beats an obviously pained and bloodied woman with a cane (figures 3 and 4). Both women are eviscerated, a recurrent image in the Sunday book. Having removed his victims' internal organs, the lion-headed man perversely seeks signs of life from the dead woman and obliterates the remaining ones from the dying woman. In both cases, he is the oppressor of the exposed female flesh, the depraved agent of extinction. In both collages, however, the torturers do not seem to enjoy the torture; it is as if they act only to titillate the viewer.

The bourgeoning loss of reason finds full realization in the guillotining collage (figure 5). The lion-headed man, his coat emblazoned with a military medal, triumphantly thrusts toward the reader the human head which the guillotine in the background has just severed from its torso. The fact that the guillotine has been lifted back up and is ready for another victim

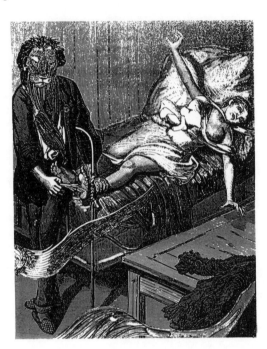

Figures 3, 4, 5 (left to right)

unveils a frightening narrative for readers projecting themselves into the scene. By forcing us to take the low angle point of view of victims, on their knees looking up, Ernst evokes a sense of subject as child gazing up at the face of the lion-father. In that face is seen the castrator, the Other.

The sundering of the head and body marks the demise of rationality, a demise which is enhanced by shredding the elements of the Symbolic from their established referents. The detached and dripping head which occupies the center of the collage mirrors the mind viewing it, its reliance on social and intellectual conventions battered by Ernst's assault.

Although some art critics, especially Maurer, have noted the influence of Freud's case history of Dora on the second book of *Une Semaine de bonté*, "L'Eau," none have considered the extent to which Ernst directly draws on Freud for his imagery. In fact, "L'Eau" can be read paradoxically as a partial dramatization of the Dora case which also dismisses Freud's authority by ridiculing his interpretation. In this manner, it takes the point of view of Dora, who quit her analysis before it was completed. "L'Eau" dwells on the water imagery that figures prominently in Dora's traumas and dreams, and in Freud's extensive and defensive interpretation of them, to assert female dominance and disregard. In order to clarify these associations, I

wish to devote some space to a summary of the Dora case history.

"Fragment of an Analysis of a Case of Hysteria" (1905) is Freud's land-mark case for asserting the sexual-organic basis of hysterical symptoms. However, the title word "fragment" signals its lack of conclusion as well as its curious method of narration. Dora broke off the analysis before its completion, and Freud narrates the case history in a disjointed, looping manner that can be seen as an attempt to defend himself against her action as much as to analyze her symptoms. Steven Marcus likens the narrative form of this case history to a modern experimental novel and elucidates the numerous double plots, inversions, and betrayals that characterize the case.[30] Indeed, Freud's boast to Wilhelm Fliess that "the case has opened smoothly to my collection of picklocks" seems to have been wishful think-ing from the start.[31]

As both Marcus's and Peter Gay's reconceptualizations of Victorian cul-ture have demonstrated, the case of the eighteen-year-old girl is a remark-able, but by no means isolated, example of Victorian domestic intrigue.[32] A contributing factor to Dora's hysterical symptoms is her awareness of her father's sexual liaison with the wife of a couple, noted in Freud's history as the K.'s, with whom her parents had become close friends. Both Frau and

Herr K. had befriended Dora and, on two occasions, Herr K. had made sexual advances toward her. When she was fourteen, Herr K. arranged to be alone with her and "suddenly clasped the girl to him and pressed a kiss upon her lips." Dora responded with "a violent feeling of disgust," but continued their relationship. Just after she had seen Freud for the first time, when she was sixteen, Herr K. and she were walking by a lake when he "had the audacity to make her a proposal." This time Dora slapped Herr K., hurried away, and reported the incident to her father. Herr K. denied the incident and told Dora's father that he had heard from Frau K. that Dora "used to read Mantegazza's *Physiology of Love* and books of that sort in their house by the lake. It was most likely, he had added, that she had been over-excited by such reading and had merely 'fancied' the whole scene she had described." Dora's father accepted Herr K.'s explanation and the dramatic change in Dora's personality dates from the time of this acceptance. He turned her over to Freud for treatment with the request, "please try to bring her to reason." [33]

Freud's analysis of Dora centers on two of her dreams, the first of which occurred three nights in succession at the place on the lake where the scene with Herr K. had taken place. It is this dream which figures prominently in "L'Eau":

> A house was on fire. My father was standing beside my bed and woke me up. I dressed quickly. Mother wanted to stop and save her jewel-case; but Father said "I refuse to let myself and my two children be burnt for the sake of your jewel-case." We hurried downstairs, and as soon as I was outside I woke up. (64)

Dora relates that she once woke from an afternoon nap to discover Herr K. standing beside her and that he had also given her an expensive jewel-case as a present.

Freud makes the obvious links between jewel-case and female genitalia, and expands this link to a reticule with which Dora fidgets during one of their sessions and, more broadly, to the shell of Venus. He approaches the fire in the dream through its antithesis, water, connecting the accident at night to childhood bed-wetting. Just as Herr K. had stood beside her, Freud concludes, so had her father during her childhood to prevent her from wetting her bed. Her shock at Herr K.'s indiscretions is inseparable from the pain her father has caused her by abandoning her for Frau K.

Freud also launches into a discussion of the aetiology of hysteria in childhood masturbation and considers bed-wetting as a symptom of this activity. Wetness, he contends, has primal erotic associations:

In consequence of certain connections which can easily be made from it, the word "wet" served in the dream-thoughts as a nodal point between several groups of ideas. "Wet" was connected not only with the bed-wetting, but also with the group of ideas relating to sexual temptation which lay suppressed behind the content of the dream. Dora knew that there was a kind of getting wet involved in sexual intercourse, and that during the act of copulation the man presented the woman with something liquid *in the form of drops*. She also knew the precise danger lay precisely in that, and that it was her business to protect her genitals from being moistened. (90)

Freud clearly sees that the "reason" to which Dora's father urges him to bring his daughter means convincing Dora to ignore his infidelity. However, he also presses his own reason on his readers to an extent that, playing analysts themselves, their suspicions ought to be aroused. Marcus points out that while Freud's narrative behaves like a modern novel, he takes elaborate pains to distance himself from such potential accusations and to proclaim himself, above all, a scientist. Distancing himself from anything but empirical intentions, Freud writes,

I must now turn to consider a further complication to which I should certainly give no space if I were a man of letters engaged upon the creation of a mental state like this for a short story, instead of a medical man engaged upon its dissection. The element to which I must now allude can only serve to obscure and efface the outlines of the fine poetic conflict which we have been able to ascribe to Dora. This element would rightly fall a sacrifice to the censorship of a writer, for he, after all, simplifies and abstracts when he appears in the character of a psychologist. But in the world of reality, which I am trying to depict here, a complication of motives, an accumulation and conjunction of mental activities—in a word, overdetermination—is the rule. (59–60)

But Freud is as duplicitous in his explanation of Dora's case as her father was in seeking treatment for her. Freud, however, disguises his duplicity with the voice of scientific reason. Dora terminates their sessions after Freud contends Herr K.'s rebuttal of her charges were at the root of her current disorder. Freud argues that Dora desired Herr K.'s advances to be serious ones, proposals that would lead to marriage, rather than behavior that would be denied and halted. He concludes "that the slap Dora gave him [Herr K.] by no means signified a final 'No' on her part" (109).

Rather than the promoter of objective truth, Freud is here clearly the projector of his own wishes. The slap that Dora gives him by abruptly ending her analysis continues to sting him through the five years it took to publish the case: "Her breaking off so unexpectedly, just when my hopes of a successful termination of the treatment were at their highest, and her thus bringing those hopes to nothing—this was an unmistakable act of vengeance on her part" (109). In his postscript to the case, Freud blames himself for not mastering the transference at the proper time. "I ought to have said to her," he writes, "it is from Herr K. that you have made a transference on to me" (118). It is a transference only Freud has made.

Ever the enemy of the posturings of scientific reason, Ernst adapts the salient features of the Dora case to poke fun at Freud's authority. The Monday book begins with three collages depicting scenes of catastrophe. In each a disproportionately gigantic woman appears. In the initial collage, she plunges with a train from a collapsed bridge into the water beneath. However, the woman, unlike the train, is intact, and her tremendous size renders the situation largely nonthreatening for her. In the second collage (figure 6), a sleeping woman is foregrounded while behind her a collapsed bridge has pressed hundreds of figures into a teeming mass of havoc. The

Figure 6

Figure 7

third collage presents another gargantuan figure, who stands unconcerned before a spire as rising water envelopes the roofs of the town.

Whether or not we accept Renée Hubert's contention that these catastrophes "serve to purify a stifling world," the Sleeping Beauty motif for which she also argues is clearly established in figure 6.[34] However, no Prince Charming seems imminent for this Sleeping Beauty, nor does she appear to need one. The victims in this collage, and for the most part throughout "L'Eau," are male. Females generally remain asleep, unaffected by the disasters of consciousness and culture, empowered by their passivity. Rescue of the damsel in distress by the heroic male (or the hysterical female by the insightful psychoanalyst) is unnecessary and unwanted.

The next collage in "L'Eau" (figure 7) extends Ernst's expression of the Dora case to specific aspects of Freud's analysis. Freud's comments on the sexual connotations of water and the aetiology of hysteria in masturbation are depicted by placing a woman dressed in a low-cut bodice in the middle of a raging stream. Her face is covered by a scallop shell, the shell of Venus Freud mentions along with the jewel box as symbols of female genitalia. Between her legs she holds a long rod. The effect of this collage is certainly disconcerting, primarily because its sexual significations conflict. By obscuring the woman's face with the scallop shell, Ernst takes his cue from Freud and subsumes her identity completely within her sex organ. The rod which she holds between her legs, however, conveys androgyny or, if employed for masturbation or mock intercourse, sexual satisfaction achieved through a phallic instrument.[35] The parody behind Ernst's expression of Freud's analysis is clear only in the context of the other collages of "L'Eau," which feature women asleep in bed as massive volumes of water inundate all around them. Ernst takes Freud's conclusions regarding bed-wetting to an absurd extreme.

Two collages portray a woman asleep in bed amid a flood while being watched by a man (figures 8 and 9). These collages obviously allude to Dora's experience of waking to the watchful eye of Herr K. and to Freud's presumptive link of this experience with Dora's father standing beside her bed to stop her childhood bedwetting. The voyeur in figure 8 stands behind bars to observe the recumbent bare-breasted woman, his pornographic fascination imprisoning him. In figure 9, an aristocratically dressed man also studies a sleeping woman. This time the woman is clothed, but her face betrays her rapturous dreams. The man stands among the bedroom furniture unaffected by the flood waters which are drowning two others.

In addition to assuming a transference on the part of Dora from Herr K. to himself, Freud contends that earlier he was replacing her father in her imagination (118). Ernst's reading of Freud plays with this contention, for the paternal authority which places itself above the flood waters in figure 9 receives no attention from the female. She conjures her own visions, which may include the destruction of the two men (selected from the triad of Herr K., her father, and Freud, the members of which Freud has claimed may substitute for one another) in the foreground who cling desperately to their phallic spars. However, the spars, like Freud's phallocentric conjectures, have no mooring in Ernst's collage. Dora refuses to participate any longer.

The title page of the Tuesday book, "La Cour du dragon," contains an epigraph from a work of occult erotica by the "Comte de Permission" entitled *Visions*. By describing the attempts by two men to collar and sexually possess a female whose form fluctuates between that of a dog and a woman, the quotation reintroduces the horrific zoomorphic images that dominate "Le Lion de Belfort" and that also pervade this third book. The settings are primarily bourgeois domestic scenes, oppressively crowded with garish furnishings. However, it is the actions and interactions of the characters that amplify this oppression. As Norris adeptly diagnoses, "the violence of the earlier works is replaced in this book with a different kind of power

Figures 8 and 9

play—the tendering of homage, obeisance, reverence—as figures bow to the 'other'."³⁶ Indeed, the well-appointed interiors presented in "La Cour du dragon" feature acts of petty pleading and dependency.

Again the pictures on the walls function as revelatory mirrors, reflecting people or objects in the room transformed into poses that comment on the scenes beneath. They also reflect our judgmental status back at us, casting us as Others for which the characters in the collages obsequiously perform. The pernicious aspects of this status are further enhanced by the recurring motif of eavesdropping. Characters frequently peer from behind doors and look furtively over their shoulders.

A winged woman, an aristocratic woman, and a servant garbed in eastern attire (Maurer refers to him as a Turk, Norris as an Algerian) are the principal characters of this book.³⁷ In figure 10, the bat-winged woman's vampiric associations are rendered explicit.³⁸ She kneels with her mouth to the throat of a child whose arms are held by the servant and another man. The bowl beneath them suggests the child is to be bled. In the background, a matronly woman who might be a governess stands impassively. An elaborately coiffured dog draped by a snake is perched on a chair in

Figure 10

the foreground. The picture on the wall depicts a woman adjusting her funereal veil.

The collage portrays the death force of cultural vampirism, initiating its children by sucking the freeplay of the Imaginary from them. Their entrance into the manners of citizenry practiced within the well-bred apartments of the dragon's court is presided over by the portrait of the figure dressed in mourning. Like her veiled identity, the manner in which she mirrors the reader is ambiguous. Does she clothe herself in mourning out of sorrow or convention?

Figure 11 presents another scene of collusion and desperation. The woman, now adorned in bird's wings, kneels with her head in her hands next to a dragon while the eastern servant peers at them from behind a door. Rather than colluding with men to victimize a child, she herself appears as victim. The viewings of her private moment by servant and reader are violations of sorts. In a painting above the sofa on which she kneels, the servant is shown kissing the hand of the aristocratic woman. Whether the action in the painting reveals a past event that causes the winged woman's present despair or foretells a future occurrence, the servant's connivance is

Figure 11

unmistakable. He is both sycophant and conspirator, an actor who mimes for the approval of others. The paintings in this and other collages in the Tuesday book transform his participation in the melodramatic scenes enacted beneath them in a manner which deepens his involvement. As mirrorings, they also implicate the reader. Our complicity as voyeurs is therefore doubled, our controlling eyes converted to those of spies, servants of the eye of the Other. With every bow of the head, with every kiss of a lady's hand, with every report of a secret, we augment our bondage to a life of parlor games.

The Wednesday book, "Oedipe," hybridizes its figures by placing bird heads on human forms. The crisis of identity thereby expressed underscores the myth invoked in the title, a tale involving a search for self-knowledge, and also relates to a psychological crisis Ernst experienced during his youth. Ernst had become a withdrawn child as a result of his horror over the death of his older sister in 1897. When he was fourteen in 1906, the birth of his younger sister coincided with his discovery of the death of his precious pink cockatoo. Ernst was never capable of separating the two events, even as an adult. In "Some Data on the Youth of M.E. as told by himself," Ernst describes his reactions in the third person:

> The *perturbation* of the youth was so enormous that he fainted. In his imagination he connected both events and charged the baby with extinction of the bird's life. A series of mystical crises, fits of hysteria, exaltations and depressions followed. A dangerous confusion between birds and humans became encrusted in his mind and asserted itself in his drawings and paintings. The obsession haunted him until he erected the *Birds' Memorial Monument* in 1927, and even later Max identified himself voluntarily with *Loplop, the Superior of the Birds*.[39]

Instead of the totemic and benign Loplop, however, Ernst forges shocking images of violence, entrapment, and pursuit through his bird-headed characters in "Oedipe." Birds and humans exchange roles, so that the bird-headed figures persecute and confine the humans (figure 12). Bird tames man, training him to perform unnatural pet tricks (figure 13). One of the quotes on the title page attributes the eradication of monsters from the earth to "the efforts of the authorities." The quote is obviously ironic in the context of the book which follows it, for the monsters have become the authorities.

The ruptures of identity with which "Oedipe" confronts the reader climax in figure 14. A train has halted before the head of a sphinx which is visible through the window and open door of one of its berths. A bird-headed man occupies one seat in the compartment and on the floor before him the collage presents only the lower half of a human body which seems dead or unconscious. The sphinx is itself assaulted by weasel-like animals which are climbing over its left shoulder and up the side of its head. The eyes of the sphinx seem to gaze intently at the bird-headed man who has turned his face away from the gaze. In an inversion of the Oedipus myth, it is the sphinx who appears to ponder the riddle before him. One hybridized form contemplates another and both face the reader. The head of the prostrate figure is absent so there is no confirmation of its being human. Even if such confirmation existed, the figure appears lifeless, so the reader's engagement is directed toward the two monsters. They constitute the mirror in this collage. The riddle they present cannot be solved, at least not rationally. Ernst has stopped the train at the end of the line for reason.

Book five contains the last three days of the week of kindness. Thursday is presented through two examples, "Le Rire du coq" ("The Rooster's Laughter") and "Ile de Paques" ("Easter Island"). The irony of the col-

Figures 12, 13, 14 (left to right)

Figures 15, 16, 17 (left to right)

lage novel's title is replicated in the title of the first example, a title which is immediately contradicted by one of its epigraphs—"Laughter is probably doomed to disappear." Instead of humor, Ernst offers sixteen scenes of frenetic aggression. The victims are women, and they are pursued, kidnapped, tortured, disemboweled, and murdered by crowing rooster-headed men. Sadistic punishment is meted out in Gothic chambers (figure 15) by these depraved cocks, and Ernst fashions their heads to anatomically locate gender at the site of thought.

In the next example, Ernst indulges his fascination with the uncanny rock engravings of Easter Island by adorning the male figures with Easter Island heads. As a result, the hybridized characters in this section differ from the previous animal-headed men in having a human-forged icon as their source of identity. Nonetheless the themes of seduction, violence, and punishment continue as well as the commentary on the reader. Figure 16 depicts an Easter-Island-headed man examining himself in a hand mirror while a bare-breasted woman watches him through a window. The woman's role is consequently doubled, and she functions to launch the reader into the play of paradoxical signifiers. Although her nudity makes her an object for the reader's erotic gaze, the fact that she too watches and that she faces us while doing so implicates us in her voyeurism. Ernst par-

tially feminizes the voyeuristic stare and cracks the solidly male purview of the Symbolic gaze. However, the vanity of looking, as indicated by the Easter-Island-headed man, still occupies the center of the collage.

Friday is named "L'Interieur de la vue" ("The Interior of Sight") and is composed of what Ernst terms "Trois poèmes visibles" ("Three visible poems"), sequences of collages in units of six, four, and two, respectively. Ernst puns on the Romantic concept of sight as interior vision by using interiors—human bones, skinless bodies—to constitute his forms. He also deconstructs Romantic unity by combining these elements with plants, stones, and other unrelated objects to create a discontinuous mass. In figure 17, an image combining *La femme 100 têtes* and classical sculpture is merged with cacti, squid, and rocks. The stamen of a flower extends from her vagina. The doubling and proliferation within this collage attack abstract constancy, transgress aesthetic categories, and instead induce the semantic derangement Norris notes.

Friday concludes with a pair of collages that Russell has called "a last love-letter to pure surrealism."[40] The last of these (figure 18) shows two facing rows of eyes, seven on the right and an implied seven on the left, on either side of a stark and limitless road. Only a spherical adornment on the eyebrow of the closest figure on the left breaks the suggestion of

Figure 18

mirrored duplication. A stacked triad of balls sits on the road between the rows of eyes and is duplicated on the horizon at what would appear to be a vastly increased magnitude. Otherwise only an arrangement of eggs in the foreground is included in this stylistic departure from the complicated and elaborate contents of the majority of *Une Semaine de bonté*'s collages.

Again the mirroring doubles back on the reader. The seven eyes indicate the seven days of the week of kindness, each day marked by the hegemony of the Other, a hegemony of vision enforced by subjugating the object of the gaze. The collage speaks to the composition of "I" as a performance for the eye of the Other, a situation which deprives one access to the multiplicity of self. Ernst positions his readers doubly as victimizer and victim. By looking we impose our vision, yet the self-referentiality of the collage ultimately renders us the object of our look. Ernst thereby loosens the grip of the Symbolic so that vision is momentarily free to bounce ambiguously back and forth down the infinite Imaginary road.

Une Semaine de bonté closes with the Saturday section, "La Clé des chants" ("The Key to Songs"), ten collages in which women become the central figures. Although images of fear, seduction, and entrapment persist, no masculine authority is overtly pictured. The final three collages feature floating women as if the horrors of the week of kindness have finally abated,

Figure 19

freeing them to luxuriate in the sensual drift of dreams. Or perhaps they suggest the only reprieve is to be found in the dream world.

In the novel's last collage (figure 19), the motif of role reversal recurs. A woman floats above a staircase at the top of which a small bird stands while a broken piece of masonry tumbles down the steps. The staircase imagery might send us again to Freud, who associated the climbing of stairs in dreams as a symbol of copulation. In *The Interpretation of Dreams*, Freud reports what he labels "A Staircase Dream," the imagery of which Maurer suggests might well have been a stimulus for Ernst's collage:[41]

> I was running down the staircase in pursuit of a little girl who had done something to me, in order to punish her. . . . I caught hold of her; but I don't know whether I hit her, for I suddenly found myself in the middle of the staircase copulating with the child (as it were in the air). It was not a real copulation; I was only rubbing my genitals against her external genitals, and while I did so I saw them extremely distinctly, as well as her head, which was turned upwards and sideways.[42]

Ernst situates the girl in the air above the staircase with her head turned upwards and sideways, but removes the dreamer of Freud's record. In doing so, he eliminates the punisher, the agent of phallic will, and portrays the girl acting rather than being acted upon, dreaming rather than being dreamt. The tumbling piece of masonry might be from the rational pillars of Freud's interpretive system. Ernst declares those pillars collapsed, liberating the girl to float beyond a rapacious world where kindness means pain.

III

Every work of art is an uncommitted crime.—Adorno, MINIMA MORALIA

In his discussion of consecration rites involved in the final stages of completing an image and thereby bringing it to life, Freedberg quotes Richard Gombrich's description of the *netra pinkama* (eye-ceremony) of the Theravada Buddhists of Ceylon. The painting in of the eyes is the last act in the creation of the statue of Buddha:

> The craftsman paints in the eyes at an auspicious moment and is left alone in the closed temple with only his colleagues, while everyone else stands clear even of the outer door. Moreover, the craftsman does not dare to look the statue in the face, but keeps his back to it and paints sideways or over his shoulder while looking into a mirror, which catches the gaze of the image he is bringing to life. As soon as the painting is done the craftsman himself has a dangerous gaze. He is led out blindfolded and the covering is only removed from his eyes when they will first fall upon something which he then symbolically destroys with a sword stroke.[43]

By giving sight to his image, the image maker grants it life. Inherent in the power of looking is the means to arrange the order of things as well as to impose one's vision on those whom the looker has reduced to the condition of things. The Buddhist artist creates a representation of his creator and inherits the power of its gaze, a power he knows he must disperse to maintain the dichotomy of divine and human. In the same manner that the maker of idols acquires the power of idols, worshippers of images (idolaters) may project the images they worship. However, to sustain both their function as idolaters and the ideal status of the image they worship, they, like the Buddhist artist with his symbolic sword stroke, must disavow their act of projection. This process of disavowal can be explained by a psychoanalytic principle Lacan has labeled "foreclosure."[44]

Lacan was no stranger to aesthetic debate. He was a contributor to the Surrealist publication, *Minotaure*, and Dali in particular acknowledges Lacan's influence on his critical method. Drawing on Freud's analysis of the Wolf Man, Lacan focuses on Freud's use of the word "*Verwerfung*" (repudiation) and its distinction from *"Verdrängung"* (repression). Freud writes,

> We are already acquainted with the attitude which our patient first adopted to the problem of castration. He rejected [*er verwarf*] castration, and held to his theory of intercourse by the anus. When I speak of his having rejected it, the first meaning of the phrase is that he would have nothing to do with it, in the sense of a repression [i.e., the rejection (*Verwerfung*) was unlike a repression (*Verdrängung*)]. This really involved no judgment upon the question of its existence, but it was the same as if it did not exist.[45]

Lacan reads *Verwerfung*, for which he proposes *"forclusion"* (foreclosure) as the French equivalent, as distinct from repression in that it rejects something as if it never existed. In the case of the Wolf Man, foreclosure is manifested in his disavowal of the absence of the penis in a woman and his insistence on the anus as the site of intercourse. Appropriating Freud's essay, "Negation" (1925), and his own theory of the Symbolic, Lacan defines foreclosure in terms of its relation to the primary process of integration into the Symbolic Order. Laplanche and Pontalis summarize this process as involving two complementary operations:

> "the *Einbeziehung ins Ich*, introduction into the subject, and the *Ausstossung aus dem Ich*, expulsion from the subject." The first of these operations is what Lacan calls "symbolisation" or "primary" *Bejahung* (postulation, affirmation); the second "constitutes the Real inasmuch as this is the domain which subsists outside symbolisation." So foreclosure consists in not symbolising what ought to be symbolised (castration): it is a "symbolic abolition." Whence Lacan's formula for the hallucination . . . "what has been foreclosed from the Symbolic appears in the Real."[46]

Foreclosure excludes what should be symbolized, thereby creating a gap in the signifier (a "symbolic abolition"). The signifier is then forced to find expression in the Real, the realm outside the subject, often as a hallucination.

Not only does foreclosure describe the Wolf Man's rejection of the absence of the phallus, it also applies to the process by which idolaters exclude the presence of the phallic. They repudiate as aspects of their act of perception their voyeuristic position and its quest for mastery of the objects of their gaze. Rather than acknowledging their perceptions of the image as a product of their desires, observers approach the image as an aesthetic ideal and thereby sustain the sense of discrepancy between themselves and it. Their foreclosure masks their service to the Symbolic and enables them to function as inscribers of its hierarchies.

Art like Ernst's, which intentionally parodies attempts to idealize or idolize it and which calls attention to its viewers' relation to it, confronts us with what we have foreclosed. In essence, the return of the foreclosed in Lacan's Real is expressed through Ernst's surreal, hallucinatory images. By disrupting the steadiness of their viewers' gaze and of the Gaze which works through them, they unleash a protean play of signification that fractures any frames imposed on them. In this way, Ernst holds his viewers accountable for looking by revealing to them the nature of their look.

3 Cannibals and Clock-Teasers: Narrating the Postmodern Horror Film

I

Those arts which sustain anguish and the recovery from anguish within us are the heirs of religion.—Bataille, LITERATURE AND EVIL

According to Paul Ricoeur, "we understand ourselves only by the long detour of the signs of humanity deposited in cultural works."[1] In this chapter, I hope to shorten the detour between these signs and what they signify. The cultural works I wish to consider—postmodern horror films—intentionally do violence to the signs of humanity, and to the humans, which are deposited within them. Our attempts to understand ourselves as something other than random victims of malicious fate are thereby stymied by this genre, which has proliferated to become a reigning popular form in current entertainment. I am interested in the pattern of psychological response this form describes; how as viewers we become attracted to what typically would repulse us. Our desire to be entertained by what we fear and what disgusts us, the proliferation of *humour noir,* comments on our sense of powerlessness and confusion as well as the means by which we seek power and order. Not only do postmodern horror films consciously violate cultural taboos, but their manner of narration cannibalizes their own structure, rendering interpretive constructs ephemeral. By obsessively bringing to light what typically is obscured and by doing so in a way that self-consciously undercuts both themselves and their audience, postmodern horror films reflect our need to reconsider both what we know and how we know it.

In a sense, the viewing of a film replicates a dream state, a darkened environment where the outside world, including in most cases the rest of the audience, is temporarily excluded while a parade of images flickers before us. This alone explains the attraction, a desire to dream while awake, and to engage and be engaged by the images on the screen which indulge our narcissism. However, our narcissistic engagement is not entirely passive. Although, unlike dreams, the images are generated independent of us, the screen on which they are projected functions like a gigantic mirror in which we see ourselves reflected. The images that elicit the most profound identifications are those that awaken our own screen memories,[2] so that the images projected at us from the screen interact with those pulled from our memories and projected from us onto those on the film screen. In an inversion of the principle of persistence of vision, a principle on which the illusion of moving pictures is based, the illusion of a distinction between film and personal mnemonic images masks the ongoing exchange between viewer and film text.

In the horror film, these exchanges are disturbing because the identifications made are representations of the forbidden, what we have excluded or masked in ourselves to satisfy cultural dictates. The screen memories awakened pertain to the formation of self as a process of repression, and this recognition stirs both a yearning for those aspects we have lost as well as a repulsion from the forbidden to protect the illusion of integrity of Self. The primary threat embodied in and posed by the postmodern horror film is therefore its exposure of our concept of Self as a performance for Others.

The personal screen memory itself is a displacement resulting from a compromise between repressed elements and unconscious defenses, and the engagement between narrative and viewer is also characterized by displacement. The Latin root of "emotion"—*emovere* meaning "to move away from or out of"—offers an indication of the dynamics of this engagement. Identification with the film image occurs through an awakening of unconscious wishes via a memory trace; in effect, through a transference whereby the past is experienced with a strong sense of immediacy. As Freud explains, transference as a manner of remembering is enhanced by unconscious repetition and, as we shall see, the emphasis on repetition that characterizes postmodern horror films dramatizes this process.[3] The triggering of emotion which accompanies the transference also signals a reaction to ("a movement out of") the memory performed by an unconscious transmutation of the identification taking place between repressed memory and image—a countertransference.[4] This displacement is an exilic movement, a moving out from the memory, a renewal of repression necessary to escape fixation. The exilic release reestablishes narrative movement within viewers so that they may in turn continue to engage that movement with the film narrative until another threat occurs. These displacements are not isolated nor are they infrequent. Instead, the pattern of exile and return is an ongoing dynamic that characterizes the manner in which viewers engage and are engaged by the films they watch.

Similarly, viewers' interventions in the film text and its interventions in their lives demonstrate a desire both to master narrative and be mastered by it. Narrative progression is continually interrupted by the repetition indicative of fetishizing, so that meaning is selectively attributed within an ongoing process. Indeed, narrative progression is spurred by the quest for such a stasis, for control over the flow of words and images achieved through the imposition of a design. The resultant fixation temporarily postpones the inevitable advance of the narrative, performing a clock-tease that promotes the illusion of mastery. Within the erotic drive to insert purpose and to regulate reaction, the thrill of suspense derives from such clock-teases. They promise both the satisfaction of the erotic drive and its termination, and therefore conflict the viewer with impulses to yearn and to resist. By continually undercutting suggested solutions, suspense narratives play to these impulses and both sustain and frustrate desire.

The potential for conclusion insinuated by a tease is as intimidating as it is exciting. The death drive as well as Eros catalyze the urge to inflict meaning, for the outcome is cessation. In order to sustain narrative, the mastery of it compels the need to be mastered by it. In the same manner, obsessions through which screen memories expose themselves are as disruptive as they are revelatory. Attraction to narrative is an attraction to a sense of coherent identity that is in reality a product of mastery by Others. Since identity, the narrative of Self, is structured both by projections onto the eyes of Others and by repressions, the countering of repression by the exposed screen memory threatens that identity with extinction and therefore requires displacement. That our engagement with narrative is characterized by such advances and retreats, by impulses toward exile and return, indicates our paradoxical and tenuous sense of Self.

I choose to focus my discussion on the horror film, particularly the postmodern horror film, because it self-consciously reproduces and explodes the dynamics of narrative engagement. In invoking the term "postmodern," I am not referring solely to a chronological distinction. Instead, I use the term primarily for its stylistic and hermeneutical implications, for its emphasis on the ludic and the undermining of totalizing structures through self-conscious declarations of fictionality and transience. I use the term "horror" with James Twitchell's distinction between terror and horror in mind: "terror is external and short-lived; horror is more internal and long-lasting."[5] Although Twitchell's definition of terror dismisses its contemporary political ramifications, his delineation of horror through sustained psychological effects serves my purposes. By "postmodern horror films," I am referring to works which deliberately fetishize to induce fragmentation in the viewer. They proclaim interruptions of narrative flow and dramatize efforts at displacement, compelling obsessive responses of attraction and denial. Viewers are manipulated into a recognition of the gaze emanating from the movie screen as a mirror image and their attempts to escape this recognition are deliberately frustrated.[6] Destroying aesthetic distance through the absence of comforting closure produces a sense of horror not suddenly dispelled by turning on the house lights. The internal chord that continues to resonate is an awareness of having witnessed a reenactment of the drama of self-formation, an awareness that thwarts the capacity for disengagement by haunting us with the desire for what we are not.

I place films like Alfred Hitchcock's *Psycho* and *The Birds*, Brian De-Palma's *Dressed to Kill* and *Body Double*, George Romero's *Night of the Living Dead*, John Landis's *An American Werewolf in London*, and David Lynch's *Blue Velvet* in the category of postmodern horror. Unlike other well-directed contemporary horror films such as Nicolas Roeg's *Don't Look Now*, William Friedkin's *The Exorcist*, Roman Polanski's *Rosemary's Baby*, and Michael Wadleigh's *Wolfen*, these films employ the self-consciousness of a black, intellectual humor to accompany lurid shock. In doing so, they force a radical fluctuation in their viewers between horrifying immediacy and abstract self-consciousness that rends them into two conflicting halves. While they may duplicate the formulas of other horror films, postmodern horror films use formulas as an invitation for parody and as an appeal for thought. For example, the formula of titillation preceding brutality which is a staple of slasher films like *Nightmare on Elm Street* is foregrounded in a postmodern horror film like *Dressed to Kill* to force the viewer into an awareness of this psychodynamic. Implicit and explicit commentaries are fused to depictions of frightening brutality; intellectual irony pushes against extreme emotion.

If we can see repression as exile from memory, the horror film functions as the return of the repressed, a return beset with displacements and obsessions. If we consider the need to eliminate sources of discomfort from the conscious mind, we can understand why pleasure is sought in exile, in wandering away from difficult memories. Why then do we subject ourselves, under the guise of entertainment, to frightening encounters with gigantic grotesques? An archetypal perspective might suggest our attraction to a darkened theatre as partaking in a collective memory of a cave-dwelling past where petroglyphs painted to record culture have become the moving images projected before us. Indeed, horror films depart from usual film etiquette in generating group (tribal) interaction as witnessed by the shrieks and screams that are elicited from the audience. *The Rocky Horror Picture Show*, for example, which parodies the traditional elements of the horror film, has achieved cult status through the elaborate rituals practiced by its audience. Our propensity for horror films might be viewed as a need to practice controlling one of our primary impulses, the impulse to flee, and thus as a kind of counterphobia or confidence derived from overcoming fearful objects. Indeed, in his essay "Repression" (1915) Freud defines the title word as "a preliminary stage of condemnation, something between flight and condemnation."[7]

Taking a clue from Marx, who labeled capitalists vampires and werewolves, we also might see horror iconography as an ideologically unifying reaction to political oppression. Or we might extend the analyses of fairy tales undertaken by Bruno Bettelheim and others to horror myths as James Twitchell has done.[8] Just as fairy tales prepare children for the anxieties of separation, Twitchell sees horror myths as fables of sexual identity, preparing teenagers for the anxieties of reproduction.

Although I see validity in each of the above arguments, I consider our attraction to horror films primarily as an attraction to transgression. As the aforementioned dialectical process of exile and return indicates, however, I also regard this attraction as complicated by opposite and dependent reactions. Tzvetan Todorov asserts that nineteenth-century fantasy "is nothing but the bad conscience of this positivist era."[9] I contend our viewing of postmodern horror films rehearses an impulse to negate the identity imposed by our exile into the Symbolic realm of language and social order and to return to the undifferentiated state of the Imaginary. During the process of viewing these films, we approximate this return and, as a result, alter our status as exiles, an alteration we are then obliged to revamp. These continuing adjustments comprise our narrative engagement.

The postmodern expression of the horror genre, through its self-consuming and open-ended narration and its assaults on stable identity and uniform time, differs from earlier incarnations of this genre. Although presenting disruptive alternatives, classic horror films, and the Gothic tradition from which they derive, tend ultimately to reinforce traditional cultural frameworks through closure and audience identification with a hero who eradicates the threat from the outside.[10] Postmodern horror denies its viewers the solace of stable form and works to undermine the disavowal that insulates them and permits them to take pleasure in the viewing experience. This disavowal is usually accomplished through the belief in linearity and closure so that identification contains little ultimate risk. The thrill of vicarious adventure is attained because we believe the threat to the protagonist will be vanquished. Indeed, the attraction of cinematic identification arises from the joy of participating in the disruption of the order of things while feeling assured of its eventual restoration. We can enter the cave of the theatre, and by extension the cave of the Self, to battle demons and face annihilation and know we will emerge unscathed.

The postmodern horror film, however, alters these expectations. The narrative is often as dismembered as the victims within it. In its fascination with anomaly, its embracing of contradictions and the transgressive, the horror film represents a cognitive threat.[11] The viewer's identification with a stable hero or heroine is undercut by a parade of interchangeable victims so that unity of character is violated.[12] Furthermore, the film is often presented through the point of view of the victimizer rather than the victim, thereby double-binding the audience which finds its distance as spectators via identity with the perpetrator of what it wishes to disavow. Deprived of the reassurance of identification, let alone redemption, the security of closure, and the comfort of disavowal, postmodern audiences are rendered as defenseless as the victims they view. Like these victims, they are cast in a submissive role and, since the victims are more often than not female, we may say that the audience too is simultaneously feminized and violated.[13]

By denying their audiences access to pleasure and victimizing them for seeking it, postmodern horror films reenact the misogynistic underpinnings of our culture. However, the psychodynamics of these reenactments are again paradoxical because of the attraction of transgression. By inviting identification with the breaker of the Law, the destroyer of the Symbolic Order, postmodern horror films also give their audiences access to the pleasure of a pre-Oedipal condition, before the intrusion of the Father, Law, and language. Thus, they celebrate a world, the desire for which we have been taught to repress, but confound our participation in this celebration by foregrounding the misogynistic trappings of the transgressive. These films self-consciously reveal an aspect of the look they invite to be possessive, the look of the pornographer who imprisons nature within the Symbolic.

The psychoanalytic analogue to the paradigm of exile and return for narrative engagement in postmodern horror films is hysteria, where the viewer plays both analyst and analysand. The displacements generated in us by the narrative are akin to the repressions of a hysteric in which the emotional source of the repression is represented through a physical malady, usually a fetishized part of the body. In the engagement with a film narrative, however, the transference to the body is performed for us by the film since the focus of horror is typically an anomalous physical transformation. The bearer of the anomaly threatens the "normal" humans within the film and, by extension, our culturally inscribed sense of self which is attached to normality. The depiction of horror on the screen which magnifies us in its mirror also hysterically repeats our repressions of memory, converting them to physical grotesques which demand obsessive attention and which in turn generate acts of displacement and denial in us.

Similarly, our attempts to explain the narrative to ourselves are haunted by the very prohibitions we are attempting to explain away. Our attempts at aesthetic distance are undermined by our desire for the unknown and by the thrill of transgression. At the same time, the postmodern horror film comments on our quest for aesthetic distance as voyeurism by making us watch ourselves watching, thereby shattering the aesthetic. In this way, the viewer's desire to remain a viewer, an analyst, a master of narrative, is sustained by never being brought to satisfactory closure. What inhibits this closure and sustains our role as analysand is our simultaneous attraction to that which masters us, the revelation of ourselves to ourselves through a representation. Narrative engagement, characterized by repetition and turning away, therefore proceeds regressively.

According to Freud, hysteria is based upon a disgust with the body which produces its desexualization so that erotic sensations deemed improper are repressed and their libidinal energy displaced. In an 1897 letter to Wilhelm Fliess, Freud uses a corporeal trope to postulate repression as a rejection of memory: "To put it crudely, the memory actually stinks just as in the present the object stinks; and in the same manner as we turn away our sense organ (the head and nose) in disgust, the preconscious and the sense of consciousness turn away from memory. This is *repression*." [14] Freud goes on to explain that because libidinal energy is displaced, "obliged to proceed in a *regressive* direction (as happens in dreams)," hysteria psychically sustains its desire unsatisfied:

> Libido and disgust would seem to be associatively linked. We owe it to the former that the memory cannot lead to general unpleasure and the like, but that it finds a psychic use; and we owe it to the latter that this use furnishes nothing but symptoms instead of aim-directed ideas. [15]

In its attack on the body, indeed its frequent depiction of slashing and dismembering bodies, the horror film proceeds hysterically through regressive narration to excite digust. In doing so, it presents a negative aesthetic, an alternative to Kant's concept of the sublime. In section 48 of the "Analytic of the Sublime" from *The Critique of Judgment,* Kant writes,

> There is only one kind of ugliness which cannot be represented in accordance with nature without destroying all aesthetic satisfaction, and consequently artificial beauty, viz., that which excites disgust. For in this singular sensation which rests on mere imagination, the object is represented as if it were obtruding itself for our enjoyment, while we strive against it with all our might.[16]

Disgust as passionate denial of a representation offered for our enjoyment, a sensation arising from "mere imagination," is also the sensation elicited by horror films. Indeed, their aesthetic effect depends upon the fascination for prohibition to produce satisfaction. That audiences demand countless sequels, the call for encore in reality a request for "en-corps," to bring on more bodies,[17] testifies to this capacity.

Freud's own investigation of aesthetics in "The 'Uncanny' " (1919) extends aesthetics beyond the theory of beauty to "the theory of qualities of feeling."[18] In addition to its obvious connections to the subject of horror, "The 'Uncanny' " also offers implicit commentary on the paradigm of exile and return. Freud spends a great deal of space tracing cognate definitions for the German words *"unheimlich"* (rendered as "uncanny" in English) and its opposite *"heimlich." Heimlich* yields "homely," "cosy," "familiar" while cognates for *unheimlich* translate as "strange," "foreign," "daemonic," "gruesome." Freud also focuses on an alternative meaning for *heimlich*—"concealed"—and concludes,

> What interests us most in this long extract is to find that among its different shades of meaning the word *'heimlich'* exhibits one which is identical with its opposite, *'unheimlich.'* What is *heimlich* thus comes to be *unheimlich.* . . . Thus *heimlich* is a word the meaning of which develops in the direction of ambivalence, until it finally coincides with its opposite, *unheimlich.*[19]

The prefix "un" for Freud becomes "the token of repression." The familiar is alienated through the process of repression and returns as a double, "a thing of terror." Indeed, Freud states,

> Many people experience the feeling [the uncanny] in the highest degree in relation to death and dead bodies, to the return of the dead, and to spirits and ghosts. As we have seen some languages in use to-

day can only render the German expression "an *unheimlich* house" by "a haunted house."[20]

Freud links the uncanny to the compulsion to repeat, a principle he develops and ties to the death instinct in *Beyond the Pleasure Principle*, published a year later (1920). Impelled by the compulsion to repeat, the once familiar returns from its exile in the unconscious to appear as the uncanny, and in doing so renders dubious the distinction between imagination and reality.

We may extend Freud's discussion to speculate that this disturbance of the secure borders of the conscious world in turn causes the compulsion to repeat to be manifested in the conscious realm in the form of obsession with the disturbance. We can also speculate that the uncanny feeling dissipates upon becoming once again *heimlich,* in arriving at a satisfying explanation for its appearance by unveiling its source. Barring this occurrence, it ephemerally can be vanquished through another act of repression. However, such an act produces only the illusion of closure because the compulsion to repeat might again dredge it into consciousness. A third possibility is that it persists in the conscious realm as a fetish. Indeed, Freud tells us that uncanny effects are produced "when a symbol takes over the full functions of the thing it symbolizes."[21] Nor are these possibilities necessarily mutually exclusive. Our search for explanation motivates and is motivated by fetishizing, so that our explanations are often oblique or procrustean—intellectual forms of repression. What seems intellectually satisfying may in reality be yet another act of concealment (*heimliche*), providing occasion for another return of the repressed (*unheimliche*) as part of an ongoing narrative characterized by exile and return.[22]

Freud theorizes the construction of identity, and hence differentiation, as a defense against primary anxieties which he subsumes into castration anxiety. The anxiety, however, remains in a dialectic with the differentiated self produced to counter it. The desire for identity therefore becomes an act of concealment, since the perception of a unified and secure self is premised on a repression of that which initiated its construction and which continues to threaten it.

Lacan extends this view of the experience of identity as an act of concealment which is premised on a reaction to an Other. For Lacan, the awareness of the Self as a separate subject is effected through a recognition of Self as an object as if seen in a mirror, the mirror constituted by the looks of Others. The acquisition of identity depends upon the recognition of difference and marks the entrance into the Symbolic Order. Lacan's mirror phase effects a shift from an inner sense of total presence to an awareness of discrete subjectivity. However, this subjectivity is imposed from without so that the discovery of difference marks the onset of alienation from the innate capacity for spontaneous fusion and a movement toward cultural dependency. With the entrance into the Symbolic Order, the individual becomes a subject of language and will forever anticipate his own image in the images of Others.[23]

Just as the Symbolic is premised on difference, the Imaginary is premised on a quest for the state of undifferentiation from which it has been exiled into the Symbolic Order, to a condition preceding the mirror stage and its creation of dualism which is sustained by the social code. Prior to exile, the child is its own ideal and experiences no discrepancy between Self (as perceiving subject) and Other (as perceived object). However, once the individual has entered the Symbolic, the Imaginary is inextricably linked to it and can only be expressed through it. The quest for an undifferentiated sense of presence must work through the signifying system which constrains it, and therefore this quest is doomed to fail. We can never unknow completely, we cannot forget our fall. Impelled by the Imaginary to seek a sense of coherence, we look toward the Other and achieve a substitution for the feeling of coherence we seek to recover. However, since this substitution is mediated by the Symbolic, it can exist only incompletely before the threat of difference is reactivated. The ongoing dialectical relationship between Imaginary and Symbolic repeats the paradigm of exile and return where the impulse to return is perpetually encouraged and frustrated by the exilic condition.

Horror films encode the desire for the Imaginary and for the return to the archaic imago of the pre-mirror stage. The borders of the Symbolic are violently transgressed, projecting their rupture. The desire for the paradisal sense of fusion and presence before the fall into the Symbolic is manifested by the focus on mutilation or the concentration on a single body part as the emblem of horror. This attack on the body is an assault on the identities dictated by the Other and reinforced by the law of language and related social hierarchies; in effect, a refutation of the process of the subject's formation.[24] The transgressive opposition to the Law horror films encode can also be seen as an opposition to the Father and to the castration he threatens at the thetic threshold. By shattering the distinction between subject and object, these films perform an act of negation that paradoxically liberates viewers from, while imprisoning them in, the sources of repression. To elaborate on this attack upon subjectivity and social order, I wish to turn to the prototype of the postmodern horror film, Hitchcock's *Psycho*.

II

I'm full of fears and I do my best to avoid difficulties and any kind of complications. I like everything around me to be clear as crystal and completely calm. I don't want clouds overhead. I get a feeling of inner peace from a well-organized desk. When I take a bath, I put everything neatly back in place. You wouldn't even know I'd been in the bathroom. My passion for orderliness goes hand in hand with a strong revulsion toward complications. . . . One thing for sure: I never have any erotic dreams!—Hitchcock, interviewed by Truffaut

One way in which *Psycho* (1960) marks a first in movie history is that Hitchcock demanded audiences be kept out of the theatre once the picture had started. He did so because latecomers anticipating the appearance of Janet Leigh would have arrived after she had been killed in the film. In other respects, Hitchcock is not so considerate about his audience's possible dismay. In addition to the brutal murder of the protagonist less than midway through the film, a move which leaves Norman Bates as the only character in whom the viewer is emotionally invested, Hitchcock leaves the forty thousand dollars stolen by Marion as a red herring. He focuses his camera on the money several times to tease us about its importance until, like an afterthought, Norman tosses the newspaper wrapped around it into the trunk of Marion's car to be buried in the swamp with her body. About his game with the audience Hitchcock states, "I was directing the viewers. You might say I was playing them, like an organ." [25]

The viewer does indeed resonate to Hitchcock's cues. Beginning with the opening sequence in which, despite the precise date and time written on the screen, the camera appears to move aimlessly across the rooftops of Phoenix and, as if by random selection, tracks forward through a partially raised window into a darkened hotel room, Hitchcock maneuvers us into an encounter with our own illicit desires. Just as Marion tells Sam "you make respectability sound disrespectful" in the first conversation of the film and Norman proclaims to Marion "it's a dirty night" as she checks into his motel, the sympathies Hitchcock evokes in his audience contradict the morality with which it initially steps into the theater. The viewer reacts to the injustice of Sam's debts and alimony which force him to meet Marion secretly, not to the seedy hotel or, by the standards of 1960, to the inappropriate rendezvous. Cassidy's vulgar flaunting of his money, his boasts of spoiling his daughter, who in contrast to Marion will soon ease into marriage, make him an acceptable victim for theft. The voices Marion imagines as she drives and the inscrutable gaze of the policeman behind his dark glasses drives the viewer deeper into her beleaguered state of mind as she pointlessly exchanges cars under the policeman's scrutiny. The irony that she stops at the Bates Motel only fifteen miles from Fairvale is nothing but unfair after her exercise of will. In her conversation with Norman, Marion recognizes her own entrapment in his and rationally resolves to return the money the next morning. However, the veneer of ethics restored within the film is quickly rent when Marion's ritualistic rinsing of sin is invaded by the repeated thrust of a vengeful mother's knife. Nor does Hitchcock permit the spectator's outrage at this violation to be uncomplicated, for his camera work eroticizes Marion's body as it is slashed and punctured, extending the association with voyeurism established when Norman spies on Marion through the hole in his office wall. Drawing upon the tactics of pornography, Hitchcock titillates us by turning the woman on the screen into an object and then implicates us in her brutalization since we have already begun to violate her through our fantasies.[26] As a result, our attraction and repulsion to what we view clash. Norman's painstaking mopping up after his mother's misdeed then spirals attention from the vacant stare of Marion's corpse to Norman as sympathetic victim through his devotion.

With the sudden elimination of both Marion and the stolen money from the plot, which leaves the viewer reeling from the shock, Norman deepens from a curiosity to a source of possible stability in a world gone mad. However, the conjectured nobility of Norman's sacrifice eventually is destroyed along with any semblance of stability or wholeness in his character and, by extension, the viewer's. When Marion's sister, Lila, explores the Gothic house, the camera follows her, recording not just the crowded rooms of a stifling home, but the facets of Norman's mind. With eerie leisure, the camera presents the bed in which Norman murdered Mrs. Bates and her lover, now permanently indented with the shape of Mrs. Bates' body, Norman's attic room with its little boy's furnishings and unmade bed, and the cellar in which he has hidden the skeletal remains of his mother.

The stairs serve as transitions between the components of Norman's insulated mental world, and Hitchcock is careful to film them for maximum symbolic effect. When the detective Arbogast climbs them seeking access to Mrs. Bates's bedroom, his threatened intrusion into the secrets of the Bates home is brutally deflected as the murderous knife descends into his face, forcing him back down the stairway. Hitchcock moves the camera from the single shot of Arbogast ascending the stairs to a high angle shot when he reaches the top. Not only does the high angle permit the viewer to witness Norman's mother moving in for the kill, but it also abruptly splinters the viewer's perspective. Arbogast is converted from subject in the single shot to object in the high angle before the two merge in the sudden close-up of his head slashed by the knife. The sequence is repeated when Norman hides his mother in the fruit cellar. He climbs the stairs to her bedroom in a single shot; however, the camera does not follow him into her bedroom. Instead it turns and looks back down the stairs again in a high shot as Norman carries his complaining mother to the cellar. The specular movement of the camera, its mirrored advance and retreat, comments on the merger of subject and object, foreshadowing the climactic revelation of Norman's split personality. When Lila enters the bedroom to which the spectator previously had been denied access, she is startled by her reflection in a mirror, briefly thinking it to be the image of Mrs. Bates. Through these combinations of subject and object, Hitchcock stresses the viewer's complicity in the unmasking of Norman's mystery as a discovery of self.

The intricate subject/object permutations in *Psycho* lead Janet Bergstrom to pose a reading based on multiple identificatory positions:

> Wouldn't Norman's scenario have to read something like this? When he meets Marion, it is as the son to an available woman. When he watches her in the shower, Norman is the son watching the mother (Marion), imagining himself as the mother's lover ("the imaginary and ungraspable relation of the primal scene"). When Norman, impersonating his mother, kills Marion, it is as the mother killing a rival of her son's affection. . . . Each shift necessitates corresponding changes in the imaginary identifications of the other characters in the scenario.[27]

Bergstrom draws on Freud's discussion of the stages of fantasy in "A child is being beaten" (1919) to demonstrate the complexities of identification. In Freud's analysis, the patient progressively identifies with the father doing the beating, the child being beaten, and herself viewing the beating, with the latter stage providing a means for masturbatory satisfaction.[28] The identification then moves from subject to object to a conflation of the two that offers voyeuristic pleasure. Although Bergstrom's reading is important for suggesting the positional shifts within Norman's identity, it falls somewhat short in describing the process of viewer engagement.

While Freud's stages of fantasy are progressive, *Psycho* repeatedly dramatizes the annihilation of subject, arousing in the viewer the desire for and fear of this annihilation. In addition, the specular camera movement allows for a reversal of cause and effect and the frustration of logic so that objectification through analysis is also undermined. Although Mrs. Bates appears quite mobile in her rages, Norman carries her to the cellar like the invalid he claims she is. As viewers, we shift between the roles of analyst and analysand to discover that we are neither one nor the other but both.

However, neither the film nor the viewer permits the collapse of the distinction between subject and object to be conclusive. Just as the hysteric converts psychic disturbances to a somatic fixation, the viewer compensates for the absent subject by focusing on a new presence readily offered in the film.[29] Hitchcock's camera objectifies the subject during moments of threat, thereby mirroring the viewer's own defensive posture to that threat, before subject and object converge and a new subject must be projected. Each subject is cannibalized and dismissed, appropriated to be destroyed, like Norman watching Marion through the hole in his wall.

Psycho encourages hysteria in the viewer by continually stripping away our constructions of stability. In the same manner that the hysteric protects against loss by totalizing the body in a concentrated erotogenic zone, we react to the loss of our source of identification by searching for another subject on which to fixate so that we may deny absence. As Marion says of resolutions when comparing them to headaches, "You forget them as soon as they stop hurting." Or replace them with another resolution. However, the film subtly undermines this process by presenting an increasingly suspect succession of sources for the viewer's projections.

Because we seek an explanation to alleviate our dismay over the sudden absence of a center in the film, we indulge ourselves in Arbogast who, as a detective, offers the potential for discovery and revenge. With Arbogast's death, we are left with Lila and Sam. Not only are these characters thinly sketched by intention, but also we have learned to be more defensive. Because Lila is Marion's sister and intrudes in the house like Arbogast, she is safely distanced. The viewer is also placed on guard regarding Sam when, like Marion, he converses with Norman in the motel office. The unseen mother has become the active center of the film. In the same way that she controls her son, she has manipulated our responses. This parallel combines with our hysterical need for a physical presence to sharpen our identification with Norman and to set us up for the climactic negation.

The rude deletions and undercuttings of hysterical projections onto the bodies on the screen are finally allayed by the psychiatrist's explanation of Norman's condition. Hitchcock permits his viewer another transitory refuge by casting Norman as object rather than subject. Refusing to see ourselves when looking at Norman, our gaze becomes the inscrutable look of the policeman. Our distance is both salvation and threat as we fulfill Norman's statement to Marion concerning "the cruel eyes studying you." However, this is Hitchcock's final ruse. Now we fixate on language, using the word to kill the thing that haunts us. But the explanation, the apparent restoration of meaning, does not endure. The concluding image of Marion's car being dredged from the swamp works regressively as an emblem of all that has been dredged from beneath the viewer's repressions during the course of the film. Hitchcock's fascination with Freudianism as demonstrated in *Spellbound* and *Vertigo* turns back on itself at the conclusion of *Psycho* to question the efficacy of psychoanalytic explanation. By undermining the closure of the psychiatrist's assessment, Hitchcock reasserts the tension that has hystericized us throughout the film.[30]

Lacan's reworking of Freud's aphorism *"Wo Es war, soll Ich werden"* is instructive here. Unlike Freud, Lacan does not see the subject as an integrated whole but as merely an effect of a sliding signifier. Its construction is therefore fleeting, and it disappears as the signifier shifts to create another subject. Lacan uses the term *aphanisis* to describe this disappearance and stresses its applicability as a philosophical concept to Cartesian skepticism.[31] Regis Durand considers the relevance of *aphanisis* to postmodern narrative and, appropriating Lacan's words, concludes "Lacan's lesson is that not resolution but punctuation is what is required, and that a step toward it may be taken if texts are seen as existing 'around the living moment of the *aphanisis* of the subject.'"[32]

Psycho proceeds via a process of negation which encourages hysterical resistance in the viewer only to negate that resistance, thereby exacerbating the hysterical reaction. Freud defines the function of negation as "a way of taking cognizance of what is repressed; indeed it is already a lifting of the repression, though not, of course, an acceptance of what is repressed."[33] The horror film acts to lift repression while sustaining its effect. By forcing us to shift among multiple identities, *Psycho* implicitly exposes our constructions of Self as performances, like those of the actors on screen. In doing so, it reveals Self as a response to Other and reawakens the desire for the Imaginary. The demise of the subject, then, kindles conflicting responses of apprehension and yearning that intensify one another. As the exhibitions and concealments of *Psycho* demonstrate, it is in this demise and its repetitions that we must look for an understanding of viewer engagement with the horror narrative.

III

This horror of waking—this *was knowledge.*—*James, "The Beast in the Jungle"*

In "Instincts and their Vicissitudes" (1915), Freud discusses scopophilia. He attaches it initially to pregenital autoeroticism, after which the pleasure of the look is transferred to others by analogy, providing the erotic basis for looking at another person as object.[34] For Freud, scopophilia and exhibitionism are opposites, yet one of the four categories of vicissitudes Freud discusses in the essay is "reversal into its opposite."

In her application of Freud's essay to the psychodynamics of viewer engagement with cinema, Laura Mulvey applies this reversal to spectators' repression of their exhibitionism and the projection of the repressed desire onto the performer. However, Mulvey contends that contemplation of the female form evokes the castration anxiety it originally signified. Although pleasurable in form, the look may become threatening in content. Mulvey poses two means of escape from this anxiety: (1) a counterbalancing by the devaluation and/or punishment of the object capable of provoking the anxiety, or (2) the substitution of a fetish object.[35] David Lynch's *Blue Velvet* (1986) comments on the viewer's scopophilic obsessions and reveals our attempts at order to be acts of concealment. The film's parodic underpinnings depict the two means of escape from castration anxiety as reversals of each other, creating a circular pattern where the exile from anxiety inevitably leads to a return. In effect, *Blue Velvet* castrates its audience.

The blue velvet curtains that frame the film place the spectator in complicity with the voyeurism that is at its center. They allude to the title, the title song, a romanticized past and future posed within the story, the dominant fetish of the villain, and a self-reflexive commentary on the story and viewer involvement in the story as performance. The detective role that Jeffrey Beaumont and, by extension, the viewer assume discovers the mystery of the searcher as well as the objects of the search. "I'm seeing something that was always hidden," Jeffrey confides to Sandy. What is observed becomes autoerotic projection, a fantasized obsession to divert anxiety. Sandy tells Jeffrey, "I don't know if you're a detective or a pervert" as he goes to break into Dorothy Vallens's apartment. His subsequent experience demonstrates the two to be interchangeable. Jeffrey comes out of the closet, both literally and figuratively.

After watching through the slats in Dorothy's closet door as she undresses, Jeffrey is presented with both castration and seduction when his voyeurism is discovered. Holding the phallic knife, Dorothy usurps

Jeffrey's power as voyeur and forces him out of the closet to experience the role in which he had cast her. By commanding him to undress and then fondling him while holding the knife, Dorothy converts observer to observed, fetishizer to fetish, and renders voyeuristic pleasures ambivalent. Thus, the role reversal parodically dramatizes the classic dialectic of phallus and castration, the attribution to the woman of an absence in response to the anxiety created by the fantasized threat of this lack within the male's own body.[36] The parodic twist to the formula occurs when the fetish becomes potential punisher, inducing pleasure and threat simultaneously, thereby elevating the object to fetish while devaluating it to object of punishment. This specular shift collapses the difference between the two means of escaping castration anxiety while the threat is maintained through the presence of the knife. The voyeur is not permitted detachment, but is compelled to witness himself as spectator and object.[37]

When Frank Booth appears, Dorothy adopts Jeffrey's position as fetish and object of punishment while Jeffrey, relegated to the closet again, watches Frank perform as his doppelgänger. Frank commands Dorothy to expose her genitals for him and contributes to his arousal by tearing a piece of material from her blue velvet robe and putting it in his mouth as he rapes her. As Alice Kuzniar points out in her article linking *Blue Velvet* to E. T. A. Hoffman's *The Sandman* (the story which is central to Freud's "The 'Uncanny' "), Freud's essay "Fetishism" (1927) includes velvet as a typical fetish, one which fixates the gaze on the female pubic hair and covers the absence of the phallus, the sign of castration.[38] During the later joyride, Frank refers to Dorothy only as "Tits," another instance of his fetishizing. Kuzniar aptly analyzes his behavior:

> For Frank, the pure fetishist, sexual gratification can only come with the denial of the castration threat. He can only shoot when he drapes his "revulva" with blue velvet, associating the shot with ejaculation or, as he calls it, "a love letter." Afraid that Dorothy might see what he fears, his castration, Frank commands her not to look at him. When during the joyride Frank suddenly stops the car to ask Jeffrey, "What are you lookin' at," the dreaded answer "nothing" unleashes his wrath. The fetishist not only diverts his gaze, he wants others to do the same.[39]

But the audience's gaze is compounded rather than diverted. Disguises are removed to no effect—Dorothy's wig, Frank's well-dressed man costume, Gordon's use of his policeman status to cover his illegal activities. Instead, transgressive disguises accumulate. Even the temporal setting of the film is nebulous, combining characteristics of both the 1950s and 1980s. The progress of the narrative toward the self-conscious restoration of order at its conclusion is consistently halted by a retrogressive looping motivated by a confusion of roles. The boundaries distinguishing subject from object, sadist from masochist, observer from observed, male from female, and father from child are removed, permitting convertibility rather than difference.

Substitutions proliferate once Jeffrey trespasses on the bad side of town, Lincoln, and encounters the Booth who will assassinate the orderly pairings into which he has hitherto arranged his life. The apartment building in which Dorothy lives is named "Deep Rivers," and Jeffrey's entrance into it constitutes admission to his own hidden recesses. After Jeffrey and Dorothy exchange roles, Frank intrudes and announces his shift from playing Baby to Daddy opposite Dorothy's Mommy. Jeffrey later plays Frank in slapping Dorothy during their lovemaking. Ben's bisexual demeanor substitutes for Roy Orbison's body as he lipsyncs "In Dreams" while Frank also mouths the words to the song. At the conclusion of the joyride and after observing "you're like me," Frank "feminizes" Jeffrey, smearing his lips with lipstick and kissing him. He then places the blue velvet from Dorothy's robe in Jeffrey's mouth as he beats him to the accompaniment of Orbison's song.

The status of fatherhood also undergoes numerous permutations, signifying an assault against the stability of the Symbolic and its governance of the Self through the Law of the Father. Jeffrey comes home from college after his father's heart attack to assume the position of man of the house.[40] He also attempts to play Dorothy's comforter and guardian against the brutality of "Daddy" Frank, although he slips into Frank's sadism at Dorothy's masochistic urging. At one juncture, Dorothy even calls him by her husband's name. As agent of the law and replica of the ideal father from 1950s TV, Sandy's (a variance of Sandman?) father, Detective Williams, opposes Dorothy's (Sandy's shadow self) "Daddy," Frank, as another agent to initiate Jeffrey into fatherly knowledge. Indeed, the inhaler Frank places over his face to enhance his sensations during rape and murder replicates the iron lung in which Jeffrey finds his father in his visit to the hospital.

Jeffrey's killing of Frank and emergence from the closet as Detective Williams says "it's all over" should therefore constitute his eradication, or repression, of his dark side and his embrace of the Symbolic Order. Indeed, Jeffrey's father has miraculously returned to health and joins Detective Williams for a joint family idyll in suburbia at the end of the film. Sandy's robin returns with her vision of harmony and love. And Dorothy is reunited with her son in a world restored to white picket fences and blue skies. However, the conclusion is as obviously mechanical as the robin on the Beaumonts' window sill.

The repetition of the opening sequence, complete with friendly fireman and crossing guard, is again framed by the blue velvet curtains that opened the film, signalling the end of a performance and mocking the desire for artificial closure. We cannot emerge from the closet with Jeffrey and accept Detective Williams's assurance that everything is all right without deliberately ignoring the heavy-handed parody with which Lynch derides our desire to do so. By undermining the scopophilic wish to control narrative, to exert phallic power in the power of the look, *Blue Velvet* returns us to the very anxiety from which we sought escape. It castrates us as viewers by reflecting our fetishizing back onto us and showing it to be both a sadistic quest at mastery and a masochistic need to be mastered. The distinctions that constitute our sense of order are erased and we plummet powerlessly into the deep river of the Imaginary and into a temporary return to a realm without mirrors.

IV

One tries to move forward but finds oneself glued to the spot.
—*Freud,* THE INTERPRETATION OF DREAMS

George Romero's *Night of the Living Dead* (1968) presents an unrelenting narrative of negation. Made on a shoestring budget with only two professional actors in the entire cast, the film hybridizes and twists many of the staples of classic horror films to produce an obsessive tale of loss. R. H. W. Dillard points to Hitchcock's *The Birds* as the artistic antecedent for *Night of the Living Dead*, and indeed the unpredictable assault by a horde is a typical ingredient of science fiction horror.[41] Unlike *The Birds*, however, a rational explanation for the disruption of the natural order—the destruction of a NASA satellite carrying high levels of radiation—is offered, but with little emphasis.[42] Instead, the paragons of reason and normality are repeatedly besieged, the fundamental categories of order frantically transgressed. The television announcers advise shooting the ghouls in the head to kill (or re-kill) them: "Kill the brain and you kill the ghoul." The film works on us in similar fashion, numbing our cognitive capacity to distinguish and systematize. The narrative, like the waves of the dead, permits no reprieve in its compulsive assault, and we respond to this devouring of our sense of order with paradoxical obsessions.

A farmhouse, emblematic foundation of American culture and values, provides the setting for most of the film. However, its furniture and large portions of its structure are systematically dismantled to convert it into a fortress against the onslaught of the dead. The traditional values it symbolizes—family, cooperation, the efficacy of hard work—are likewise decimated as the film progresses.

As *Night of the Living Dead* opens, Barbara and Johnny's dutiful visit to their father's grave is accompanied by Johnny's cynical banter. However, the revenge of the dead is swift when a ghoul old enough to be the siblings' father kills Johnny and chases Barbara to the farmhouse. At the farmhouse she is joined by Ben, who becomes the film's ostensible protagonist. Single and black, he is an outsider who ironically assumes the role of father-guardian of the farmhouse and its inhabitants. Without Barbara's aid, Ben begins a diligent effort to survive that persists throughout the film. They are joined by a young couple and a family who had been hiding in the cellar. As Dillard notes, the young couple, Tom and Judy, would have been the romantic leads had *Night of the Living Dead* been a 1950s teenage horror film.[43] They work hard, following Ben's directions without question, and sacrifice themselves in an attempt to save the group. However, their sacrifice, like most of the efforts in the film, is futile and, as Romero's grisly close-ups show, results in nothing but food for the ghouls.

The only nuclear family in the farmhouse, the Coopers, invert any ideal conception of family. Harry is mean and selfish, Helen obviously detests him, and their daughter Karen eventually feeds on her father and repeatedly stabs her still protective mother with a garden trowel. Barbara is also victimized by family. Recognizing her brother among the undead who break into the house, she embraces him only to be carried off for eating by the clamoring swarm of ghouls.

In the same manner that the family unit disintegrates, cooperation by the group for purposes of survival cannot be sustained. Tom and Judy's efforts are in vain. Ben and Harry fight for territorial control and, at one point, Harry locks Ben out of the house and is later shot by him. Once she reaches the farmhouse, Barbara remains in a state of shock, completely dependent on Ben. She does revive to rescue Helen from the clutches of the undead, but consequently is destroyed by them. Despite their activities, the flesh-eaters themselves are never sufficiently altered in appearance to negate their uncomfortable resemblance to the living. As Romero states in an interview, they are "the neighbors."[44]

Ben's desperate hard work ultimately fails to save him. Refuting his own logic, he takes refuge in the cellar he had previously labeled a deathtrap and emerges after the night of horror to the sounds of the posse. Romero duplicates the ghouls' assault on the living in the random and unemotional destruction of the living dead by the sheriff and his men. In both cases, the mob advances deliberately and dispassionately to fulfill a basic need, whether it is nourishment or the elimination of a threat. The final irony is Ben's death at the hands of the rescuers who mistake him for a ghoul. After shooting him, they fling his lifeless body in a pyre to be burned with the rest of the undead (now dead again). The mob makes no distinctions among outsiders.

Engagement with a narrative that dissolves normative distinctions, even the border between life and death, evokes profound anxiety and the need to counter that anxiety. The source of anxiety is the threat of absence to the objects of desire represented through the Symbolic and therefore the threat of absence of self-definition. Like the constant parade of ghouls who mangle and devour the socially constituted personalities within the film, destroying them as recognizable presences with identifiable purpose, *Night of the Living Dead* attacks and cannibalizes the Symbolic for its viewers. In doing so, it also cannibalizes its own narrative, stifling linear advancement with compulsive repetition and inducing a parallel response in us. As a result, we suffer a tropological affliction in that the reactions we proffer to counter our anxiety contain their own undoing.

The psychological reaction induced by such a film can be characterized as obsessional neurosis. In his famous Rat Man case (1909), Freud calls obsessional neurosis "a dialect of the language of hysteria." He goes on to distinguish it from hysteria because of its lack of a conversion from mental process to somatic innervation. This distinction is certainly appropriate for a film which literally consumes the body or, in the case of the consumers, renders it merely a decayed and extraneous shell for the voracious appetite within. Unlike hysteria, in obsessional neurosis the trauma is not countered by amnesia but is deprived of its affective cathexis. Like screen memory, what remains of the trauma in consciousness is only "ideational content" and, despite its capacity to possess the subject, seems unimportant. The resultant defensive struggle against obsessional ideas is characterized by hybrid thinking in that the premises of the obsession being combatted are accepted. Attempts at reasonable reactions are therefore constructed on a foundation of pathological thinking. The uncertainty of memory contributes to the preponderance of doubt in the psychological processes of the obsessional neurotic. Doubt produces uncertainty about the subject's defenses and leads to a continual repetition of them in an attempt to exorcise that unbanishable doubt. However, the attempt to compensate for doubt produces only more generalized inhibition. As Freud states, "By a sort of *regression*, preparatory acts become substituted for the final decision, thinking replaces acting, and, instead of the substitutive act, some thought preliminary to it asserts itself with all the force of compulsion."[45] Monique David-Menard elaborates:

> The obsessional neurotic, to be sure, returns unceasingly to this dimension of absence associated with a symbolization of desire, but his incessant return is produced within the element of representation, that is, of meaning. The obsessional neurotic attempts, through his symptoms, to turn the symbolic back on itself . . . and through his contradictory rituals he tries to cancel out that element of symbolization in which his thoughts and acts continue, however, to circulate. Obsessive representations and actions attempt to reveal that the symbolic . . . is not as symbolic as it is thought to be, but in the process of forming such representations and performing such acts the obsessional neurotic resorts to the means of the symbolic. . . . The obsessional neurotic never stops trying to undo this, to act as if it were not the case, but his efforts can only end in frustration, for the means he uses in his thinking . . . belong to the symbolic order and presuppose the recognition of what he is struggling not to recognize.[46]

In *Night of the Living Dead*, the obsessional neurosis is induced in us through our dual identification with Ben and Barbara. Trapped in the farmhouse as the living dead, the return of the repressed, threaten to devour them, they react contradictorily to their uncertain fate, mirroring the alteration between centered and displaced ego involved in obsessional neurosis. Ben, the centered ego, perceives the intrusive threat as alien and enlists reason to withhold it. Despite his own alienation from mainstream values as a single black man, his actions express these values. As head of the household, Ben furiously conjures schemes for the survival of the group, risks his life to protect the woman of the house, and attacks the member of the group who resists cooperation. He boards up the house to keep the threat outside, checks and rechecks his handiwork, yet his frenetic activity is directed entirely by his reactive anxiety. The threat controls his life even when it is not currently intruding. His logic, born of pathological reaction to trauma, inverts itself, and he finally descends to the cellar against the dictates of his reason. At the opposite extreme, Barbara, the displaced ego, is overwhelmed by the threat and made incapable of decision or action. Indeed, an extension of her blood, her brother, has already been consumed by it, and ultimately what has possessed her mind will also ingest her body.

Freud explains that compulsive behavior is constructed in successive stages in which one stage attempts to neutralize its predecessor.[47] Indeed, to portray the obsessional behavior of the Wolf Man whose neurosis he describes as "at the level of cannibalism," Freud borrows the term "ambivalence" from Eugen Bleuler, who had introduced it in 1910.[48] By alternating between the perspectives of Ben and Barbara, *Night of the Living Dead* engages us in this ambivalence. We shift between paralytic anxiety produced by incessant threat to compulsive endeavors at reasonable responses that are revealed to be parodies of the process of reason.

The epistemological dis-ease that haunts contemporary life and is underscored by the postmodern horror film is anticipated by Freud in a footnote within his case history of the Rat Man:

> It must therefore be admitted that in an obsessional neurosis there are two kinds of knowledge, and it is just as reasonable to hold that the patient "knows" his traumas as that he does *not* "know" them. For he knows them in that he has not forgotten them, and he does not know them in that he is unaware of their significance. It is often the same in ordinary life.[49]

Freud's last sentence expresses the universal frustration that compels our engagement with narrative. Unable to forget yet incapable of remembering what is forgotten, our attempts to master narrative are endeavors to become our own narrators. Our attraction to fantasy is a profound response to mnemonic traces of the Imaginary which persist in the unconscious. In its transgressions of the established order, fantasy presents cognitive anomalies which paradoxically seduce us through menace. On the one hand, we need to assimilate the disruptive anomalies and adapt them to the integrity of the Symbolic Order through which we define ourselves. On the other, we are enticed *because* of their threat to that order. We attach to them our concealed but omnipresent desire to return to the ideal Imaginary and to its state of undifferentiation which existed prior to our exile into the Symbolic.

Postmodern horror films overtly announce their menace and orchestrate our responses of attraction and repulsion. They compel us to preserve what we think we are by repressing or reconfiguring the threat, then restore the repressed and expose our reconfiguration as fragile illusion. They rekindle our yearning for a return to the Imaginary while reminding us that our sense of the Imaginary is knowable only through the signifying system of the Symbolic. Postmodern horror films therefore offer knowledge about how we perform and engage the narrative of ourselves. We return to them repeatedly both to confirm that knowledge and to struggle against it.

4 Narrative Masking: Hermetic
Messengers *in* Ulysses

I

Wittgenstein once said that a serious and good philosophic work could be
written that would consist entirely of jokes (without being facetious).—
Malcolm, LUDWIG WITTGENSTEIN: A MEMOIR

In *Ulysses*, Joyce presents a narrative combatted by its narration. A
domestic novel, written by an exile, modeled on an epic, it roams between literary forms as Leopold Bloom and Stephen Dedalus meander
through the physical and mental topography of Dublin. As excava-
tors of the text's messages, we can look at the messenger figures that Joyce
adroitly places in *Ulysses* as they shift perspective and radiate meaning
in alternative directions. These messenger figures function as signposts in
the narrative to call attention to the reader's double motivation to create
and to suspect order, thereby directing us to become meta-readers. In his
discussion of hermeneutics as polarized opposition, Paul Ricoeur explains
this position:

> According to one pole, hermeneutics is understood as the manifesta-
> tion and restoration of a meaning addressed to me in the manner of
> a message, a proclamation, or as is sometimes said, a kerygma; ac-
> cording to the other pole, it is understood as a demystification, as a
> reduction of illusion.[1]

In *Ulysses*, these contradictory poles converge so that the narrative deconstructs any hierarchical privileging which it also might have advanced. The
reader's experience becomes a dialogue with the text, where point of view
consistently shifts so that reductive authority is rendered ephemeral. By

exposing their own masks, *Ulysses*'s messenger figures reveal the narrative masking by which Joyce's parody operates.

In his discussion of reversal and discovery in the *Poetics*, Aristotle uses Oedipus as his example of how discovery (*anagnorisis*) and reversal (*peripeteia*) combine to arouse pity and fear. He considers the Messenger in Sophocles's play the catalyzing agent for reversal and discovery:

> A reversal of fortune is the change of the kind described from one state of things within the play to its opposite, and that too as we say, in the probable or necessary sequence of events; as it is for instance in *Oedipus*: here the opposite state of things is produced by the Messenger, who, coming to gladden Oedipus and to remove his fears as to his mother, reveals the secret of his birth.[2]

The various messenger figures in *Ulysses* also signal reversal and discovery; however, Joyce's deliberate accent on the internal structures of the text resists both the climax and the closure found in a work like *Oedipus*. Joyce's poetics enlarges reversal beyond a central narrative turn and renders *Ulysses* polytropic so that multiple reversals occur and some are themselves reversed.[3] Instead of an explicit dramatic insight, discovery occurs implicitly in principal characters as well as in the reader. The tracing, retracing, and expansion of the tributaries of memory in which the characters engage mirror the reader's activity as demonstrated by the blur of penciled notes and crosslistings in most of our copies of *Ulysses*. The numerous synchronicities in Stephen's and Bloom's thoughts and peregrinations enhance the identity between reader and character, inviting the reader to posit symbolic judgments and to project scenarios for the characters. However, reversal and discovery are also conjoined. Reader traps, intentional errors, narrative omissions, and the general relativism encouraged by the text reverse the privileging of any discovery and subvert the authority of any single point of view. The "Circe" episode, for example, violates rational ordering by collecting many of the characters, objects, statements, and events which exist in the narrative memory to that point in the novel and radically rearranging them. In this manner, *Ulysses* performs as tease, encouraging and checking the reader's impulses for telos and identification.

What is constant in the conjunction of reversal and discovery is transformation. Just as the mythological messenger Hermes, or Mercury, foments change in his role as trickster, just as mercury or quicksilver catalyzes alchemical operations, messenger figures in *Ulysses* function as agents of transformation. I wish to consider the messenger's influence on character transformation and to suggest links between this transformation and the messenger's disruptive and restorative effect on narrative direction. The imposition of messengers signals narrative transformation, and performs a kind of narrative thievery by robbing authority from the preceding voice and inserting substitute and transitional voices. As navigators of narrative, messengers pilot it in both subversive and restorative directions.

The Homeric analogue which Joyce cleverly knitted into the interstices of *Ulysses* applies when considering the restorative capabilities of the messenger in both Homer's and Joyce's texts. Twice when Odysseus is stranded, in the realms of Calypso and Circe, and the narrative falters, Hermes appears to break the spells that hold him. In doing so, Hermes negates the authority of the captors. Odysseus is able to escape his entrapment; both he and the narrative resume their voyages. In *Ulysses*, Bloom offers Stephen an escape from his psychological entrapment by replacing Buck Mulligan as Stephen's symbolic messenger, a transference over which Bloom's daughter, Milly, presides as cosmic messenger.

By cancelling Mulligan's presence from the remainder of the plot, however, Joyce turns the narrative toward another trap. The derisive energy Mulligan embodies frequently intrudes, like a poke in the ribs, to adjust the reader's perspective from its intensive focus on Stephen's brooding and Bloom's troubles. The removal of Mulligan eliminates an identifiable character as a source of these playful disturbances and places mockery exclusively within the purview of a sequence of parodic narrators. Locating ludic power primarily in the tellers rather than allowing it to proliferate to the characters as well exposes authorial authority but tempers the reader's participation in it. Joyce resolves this problem by introducing a character at the beginning of the "Nostos" section who, like a narrator, performs chorically. Like Mulligan, D. B. Murphy, the sailor in the cabman's shelter, is storyteller, trickster, and messenger. Like Mulligan, he possesses the mythological Hermes's power to imitate, to adopt a series of masks. Joyce names Murphy "Ulysses Pseudangelos"—the false messenger—in his schemas for "Eumaeus," and the tattoo the sailor wears that can be manipulated to both smile and frown indicates his duplicity.[4]

When Homer's Odysseus returns to Ithaca to reclaim his authority, his disguise fools the swineherd, Eumaeus, and indicates Odysseus's descent from Hermes. Odysseus's grandfather, Autolycus, was the son of Hermes and was himself a thief and dissembler. In his "Eumaeus" episode, Joyce splits Odysseus's attributes. As a character, Murphy serves as a foil for Bloom, against whom Bloom asserts his paternal authority. As a Hermes figure, Murphy also serves as an incarnation of the trickster author, whose multiple transformations and disruptions convert readers to the mask of *hermēneus*. Indeed, *Ulysses* teaches its readers what Michel Foucault describes as the author's double function—a person designated by a proper name as well as a mask for the reader:

> a projection . . . of the operations that we force texts to undergo, the connections that we make, the traits that we establish as pertinent, the continuities that we recognize, or the exclusions that we practice.[5]

One of Murphy's masks mirrors the authorial posture that readers learn to wear. Another reveals readers as wanderers in the text, whose efforts to find stasis and closure, like Murphy's (and Bloom's) return home, result in confirmation of their perpetual exile.

The role of the Hermes figure in *Ulysses* therefore extends from signifier of character and narrative transformation to signifier of reader response. In the latter case, Hermes is expanded from mythological analogue to philosophical influence as Joyce brings his covert fascination with Hermetic thought to bear on the mask he fashions for his readers. Richard Ellmann's biography details the young Joyce's rejection of the theosophical movement, which involved Yeats and several prominent Irish writers. It also offers numerous instances of Joyce's private indulgence in similar interests. In a letter to Harriet Shaw Weaver regarding these interests, Joyce writes, "I would not pay overmuch attention to these theories, beyond using them for all they are worth, but they have gradually forced themselves on me through circumstances of my own life."[6] Not only did Joyce's library contain numerous works on mysticism, but his allusions to Hermetic writings and concepts steadily increased with each book he wrote.[7]

Although Joyce once referred to Aristotle as the greatest thinker of all times, he also maintained a lifelong interest in the Renaissance Hermetic philosopher, Giordano Bruno, who zealously attacked the dualism of Aristotle's philosophy.[8] In his insistence on correspondences and mirrored inversions, Joyce employs Hermeticism and its conflict with the fundamental principle of Western metaphysics, Aristotle's law of non-contradiction— "the most certain of all principles . . . it is impossible for anyone to believe the same thing to be and not to be. . . ."[9] Bruno sees the universe not as a finished product but as an eternally changing unsymmetrical world of process. His opposition to the Thomistic world denies the boundaries of contradiction, embracing instead the Neoplatonic conceit of *concordia oppositorum* realized in an infinitely shifting constellation of relationships between self and other, higher and lower. The satirical attack on the logical categories of Aristotelianism in Bruno's works as well as his use of dialogue form attracted Joyce's interest as a complement to the didactic absolutes that structured much of his Jesuit education. Bruno's advocacy of natural religion and his pantheistic view of the universe as a living creature pervaded by an immanent divine soul also appealed to Joyce's syncretic impulses.

I wish to argue that the continuous play of transformations within the concordance of *Ulysses* offers a message to read the work Hermetically. I also wish to qualify my thesis by acknowledging that Joyce was no unswerving devotee of Neoplatonic ideals, or of any totalizing principles. Instead, his interest was eclectic and gravitated toward what he could appropriate to undermine authority, including the authority he himself constructed. Hermeticism's emphasis on the simultaneity of opposites obviously appealed to Joyce's attraction to the contradictory. The message to read Hermetically is itself a philosopher's stone, found not at the conclusion of a search, but in the discovery that the search is its own purpose.

II

we must vaunt no idle dubiosity as to its genuine authorship and holusbolus authoritativeness—Joyce, FINNEGANS WAKE

The contradictions that the mythological Hermes embodies and resolves certainly appealed to the author who employed the Hermetic *concordia oppositorum* as a thematic design in *Ulysses*. As guide to travelers and god of commerce, Hermes possesses affinities with Bloom's symbolic attributes; and his accoutrements of hat, sandals, and staff link him with Stephen. Hermes is also the god of orators and of thieves, two functions which Michel Serres yokes in his development of the metaphor of the parasite. Serres points out that the parasite takes while giving nothing concrete in exchange, and uses the example of Odysseus eating at Alcinous's table and paying for the banquet with words.[10] In *Ulysses*, we witness the notorious parasitism that Ellmann has characterized in Joyce's life transferred to Stephen, whose rhetorical skills bring him offers of drink and employment in "Aeolus" and whose conversation, limited though it appears to be in the early hours of June 17th, is sufficient payment for Bloom's hospitality.

In a letter to Frank Budgen, Joyce wrote "Hermes is the god of signposts: i.e. he is, specifically to a traveller like Ulysses, the point at which roads parallel merge and roads contrary also."[11] Joyce was referring to Hermes's function as the god of the boundary-stone, the site of demarcation which must be transgressed for economic and cultural exchange to occur. Indeed, Norman O. Brown points out that the name Hermes was derived from the Greek word for "stone-heap," primitive boundary markers placed at entrances to houses and at crossroads.[12] Given two of his other divine duties, god of trade and conductor of travelers, Hermes governs both the signification and the breaching of distinctions. While aiding the preservation of discrete identities, he encourages interactions which will disrupt them. Joyce's stylistic intentions in *Ulysses* follow a similar duplicitous path. As Karen Lawrence argues, Joyce's stylistic conception is "regressive" in making presentations that are subsequently "denied by the rest of the book." [13] What is established is only to be refuted; borders are created so that they may be traversed.

Hermes's appearance as cosmic messenger in *Ulysses* is initially suggested through an allusion to his golden-winged sandals with which he traverses the sea in Book 5 of the *Odyssey*. It occurs in the context of a conversation between Stephen and Mulligan during which Mulligan expresses his allegiance to mockery. Mulligan's messenger status is underscored by specific links with his mythological counterpart. In "Telemachus," he is referred to as "Mercurial Malachi" (1.518)—"Malachi" is Hebrew for "my messenger"—and, as he plunges into the sea for his morning ablution, "Mercury's hat" is described "quivering in the fresh wind that bore back to them his brief birdsweet cries" (1.601–2). Stephen's mercurial hat and sandals are either handed to him by or borrowed from Mulligan, and Mulligan also comes to control the key to his domicile. When Stephen confronts Mulligan regarding the latter's cavalier dismissal of Stephen's mother's death, Mulligan responds,

> ... It's a beastly thing and nothing else. It simply doesn't matter. . . .
> To me it's all a mockery and beastly. (1.206–10)

Although his comment does little to prop up Stephen's mood, it demonstrates Mulligan's rejection of Stephen's maudlin obsessions and of his inscriptions of indelible meaning. Like Hermes the trickster, Mulligan shifts roles continuously, and beguiles his overly serious companion by endorsing none of them. While Stephen, as Telemachus, searches for a father, Mulligan derides all authority. As he does with Stephen's Shakespeare theory in "Scylla and Charybdis," Mulligan burlesques solutions, and thereby steers the narrative to evade closure and to sustain mystery.

As Mulligan descends from the top of Martello Tower with a partial recitation of "Who Goes with Fergus," a song of comfort in the first version of Yeats's *The Countess Cathleen*, Stephen's interior monologue initially picks up the comforting, positive images from Fergus's song. His associations with the name shift from Fergus mac Roich to Fergus mac Leti, whose gift from the fairies of sandals with which he could walk on or under the water, suggest the link with Hermes:[14]

> Woodshadows floated silently by through the morning peace from the stairhead seaward where he gazed. Inshore and farther out the mirror of water whitened, spurned by lightshod hurrying feet. (1.242–44)

Stephen's intertextualizing is spurred by images of freedom: Fergus mac Leti receives the sandals as a ransom for freeing the king of the little people, Hermes carries Zeus's instructions to Calypso to free Odysseus, and Fergus's song offers to free Stephen from his obsessive brooding on "love's bitter mystery." However, the reference to the song takes a turn when Stephen recalls singing it while his mother lay dying. His dark memories of her death and his vision of her as a vampiric ghost coincide with the appearance of a morning cloud which covers the sun, until they are interrupted by Mulligan's voice from within the tower. The narrator tells us, "Stephen, still trembling at his soul's cry, heard warm running sunlight and in the air behind him friendly words" (1.282–83). The "warm running sunlight" can again be taken as a reference to Hermes's golden winged sandals. The friendly words which unwittingly initiated Stephen's lugubrious meditation also conclude it, imposing circularity on this section of the narrative. The appearance of the Hermes reference shifts the narrative voice, creating a fold in the text which becomes one of many such registers of the sources of Stephen's psychological discontent and creative paralysis. The transition back to the narrative proper is again accompanied by a Hermes reference, thereby demonstrating the dual disruptive and restorative functions of the messenger figure.

The synchronicity between Stephen and Bloom is strengthened by narrative parallels. The first Bloom chapter, "Calypso," also contains a morning cloud (presumably the same one that passes over Stephen) at about the same distance into the episode that it appears in "Telemachus."[15] Like Stephen, Bloom plunges into a despairing meditation on death and decay at this point in the narrative. Like Stephen's, his depressive soliloquy ends with a Hermes reference: "Quick warm sunlight came running from Berkeley road, swiftly, in slim sandals, along the brightening footpath" (4.240–41). Bloom reenters 7 Eccles Street, where he will be cuckolded later that day, to discover messages, two letters and a card, on the hall floor. The letter from Blazes Boylan to Molly will in large part dictate his physical and mental evasions for the rest of the day, and inadvertently will result in his meeting Stephen and in the consequent merger of jewgreek and greekjew

(15.2097–98), Blephen/Stoom (17.549–51). The two messages from Milly, a letter to Bloom and a card to Molly, suggest the inequality with which she views her two parents.[16] Molly abruptly acknowledges her daughter's message before demanding that Bloom expedite his preparation of her tea, while she tucks Boylan's letter beneath her pillow. Her action, however, does not escape Bloom's notice and somehow he acquires knowledge of the letter's content, for his dread over their four o'clock appointment recurs throughout the day.

By sharing thoughts and possessing complementary personality traits, Bloom and Stephen are implicitly posed as psychological messengers to each other. An example of this connection occurs in a link between "Aeolus" and "Ithaca." J. J. O'Molloy, speaking of Seymour Bushe's rhetorical prowess in the Childs murder case, pauses dramatically before quoting from Bushe's oration. At this point a vignette appears to form in Stephen's mind:

> Messenger took out his matchbox thoughtfully and lit his cigar. I have often thought since on looking back over that strange time that it was that small act, trivial in itself, that striking of that match, that determined the whole aftercourse of both our lives. (7.762–65)

The vignette appears to be picked up again in Bloom's home after the keyless couple enters and Bloom, Stephen's messenger, kneels to kindle the hearth. The lighting of fires is revealed to be a touchstone in Stephen's mind for acts of kindness. He thinks of several such incidents and the narrative ironically posits domestic peace within a household where Molly has just cavorted with her lover (17.134–47).[17]

However, the "Aeolus" passage, with its mention of "Messenger," is troublesome. It intrudes stylistically and one cannot place it with certainty in Stephen's mind. Don Gifford separates the two sentences, linking "Messenger" with O'Molloy, who is about to deliver a message, and with a major figure in Bushe's speech, Moses, who was God's messenger. He identifies the second sentence as a parody of a passage in *David Copperfield* in which David comments on the wedding of Peggoty and Barkis.[18] Robert Spoo argues that the Dickensian parody announces proleptically a more extensive parody of teleology and monocausality which is situated in the problematic status of marriage in the novel. Spoo reminds us that marriage is a common source for teleological metaphors and states, "though the novel jokes about Stephen and Bloom going off to be married by Father Maher [16.1887–88] and taking nuptial communion together, in reality the later episodes hold off resolution and closure by putting styles and irony between the bride and the bridegroom."[19]

The mention of "Messenger" in "Aeolus" interrupts the narrative flow to create another fold which invites the reader to assign meaning while undercutting that meaning. Teleological order is both promulgated and transgressed, the mystification of narrative links is both enhanced and demystified in a convergence of contrary intentions.

Although never appearing as a physical presence in *Ulysses*, Milly Bloom functions as a messenger figure. For her mother, she serves as a link with the past. Molly takes pride in her daughter's attractiveness and, during the course of her soliloquy, mentions parallels with her own youth. Bloom considers their connection, calling Milly "Marionette" (15.540), thinking "Molly. Milly. Same thing watered down" (6.87), and reflecting on the fact that they often menstruate at the same time (13.785). But she also functions on a Hermetic level, connecting the cosmic with the earthly, and is linked with Hermes in a narrative shift reminiscent of those discussed in "Telemachus" and "Calypso."

The De Quincey parody in "Oxen of the Sun" consists of a parade of constellations which begins as an apocalyptic vision, the zodiacal forms serving as "murderers of the sun" (14.1095). Again the narrative content is transformed from negative to positive with the appearance of a Hermes reference. The harbinger of the day star, "the bride, ever virgin" is named Millicent and arises *"shod in sandals of bright gold"* (my italics) before metamorphosing into "Alpha, a ruby and triangled sign upon the forehead of Taurus" (14.1101, 1103, 1108–9). The pattern of constellations presented in the De Quincey parody replicates Bruno's allegory of cosmic renewal in his *Expulsion of the Triumphant Beast*.[20] Its concluding phrase also signals earthly renewal, for the next section of "Oxen of the Sun," the Walter Savage Landor parody, concludes with Mulligan pointing out to Stephen Bloom's trance-like staring at the scarlet triangular label of a bottle of Bass's ale. Bloom is himself a Taurus, and the Bass label perhaps reminds him of the red-labeled bottle of poison with which his father committed suicide (cf. 6.359). The Macaulay parody informs us that he contemplates transactions which occurred during his boyhood (14.1188–89), and he is so engrossed in his contemplation that he is initially oblivious to Mulligan's request that he pass the ale. The metamorphosis in the sky, prefigured by the Hermes reference, signals the potential for a parallel transformation on earth. Bloom's despairing preoccupation with losses of father, son, and wife is modified by his meeting Stephen who becomes a psychological

messenger to him. Bloom's wandering acquires a purpose other than evasion, and his mental scheming develops increased breadth and relevance to
his personal affairs. When he finally acknowledges Mulligan's request and
passes the ale to him, he also acquires the status of Stephen's messenger, a
position adumbrated at the conclusion of "Scylla and Charybdis" when he
came between Mulligan and Stephen on the library steps. Bloom rids himself of the red-labeled emblem of failed fatherhood and unwittingly usurps
the role of the usurper Mulligan by assuming care for Stephen, substituting
his human concerns for Mulligan's cynicism as a complementary message
for his adopted son.

Mulligan's whistle of call on the first page of the novel is answered by
the two strong whistles that pierce the calm of the morning (1.26–27); it is
also paralleled by two less professional whistles as Bloom attempts to hail
a coachman for Stephen and himself at the beginning of the Nostos section (16.28–30). Again this correspondence occurs at about the same point
in the narrative of the two episodes. Bloom's whistles also answer Simon
Dedalus's two shrill whistles at the beginning of the final chapter of *A Portrait of the Artist as a Young Man* as Stephen prepares to take flight from
home, further signifying Bloom's substitute paternity.[21] In "Eumaeus,"
Bloom will unmask another false messenger, one D. B. Murphy, an unmasking that Murphy's status as substitute Mulligan will simultaneously
undercut. Mulligan's mockery and abuse initiate Stephen's departure from
home, Bloom's angelic ministration offers light to this particular gentile
and effects a temporary domestic alternative.

The actual meeting of Stephen and Bloom has long germinated in the
reader's expectations due to the series of near-meetings prior to "Oxen
of the Sun." However, this climactic encounter achieves no particular dramatic resonance in the protean style that constitutes this episode. Indeed,
the narrative presentation linking the development of the English language
to embryonic development, itself a demonstration of the limitations of imi-
tative form,[22] obscures the dramatic significance of the first sustained encounter between the novel's two main characters. In the same manner, the
narrative voices of "Circe," "Eumaeus," and "Ithaca" distract the reader
from Bloom's paternal custody of Stephen. Through their exhibition of
perceptual and interpretive constraints, they qualify the very connections
they have encouraged the reader to make. In doing so, *Ulysses*'s messengers
conspire to embrace contradiction.

III

The origin lies at the place of inevitable loss, the point where the truth of things corresponded to a truthful discourse, the site of a fleeting articulation that a discourse has obscured and finally lost.—Foucault, "Nietzsche, Genealogy, History"

While promulgating his aesthetic theory to Lynch in *A Portrait*, Stephen states, "Aristotle's entire system of philosophy rests upon his book of psychology and that, I think, rests on his statement that the same attribute cannot at the same time and in the same connection belong to and not belong to the same subject" (*A Portrait* 208). After linking his theory of the process of apprehension to Aquinas, he adds, "when we come to the phenomena of artistic conception, artistic gestation and artistic reproduction I require a new terminology and a new personal experience" (*A Portrait* 209). This new language and experience become Joyce's style, an integrated cluster of changing elements that resist reduction to a generative first principle. Witness Joyce's parody of the law of non-contradiction in *Finnegans Wake*:

> . . . I cannot now have or nothave a piece of cheeps in your pockets at the same time and with the same manners, as you can now nothalf or half the cheek apiece I've in my mind unless Burrus or Caseous have not or not have seemaultaneously systentangled themselves, seldear or soldthere . . . [23]

In his pretentious dialect the speaker postulates the distinction between the twins Shem and Shaun, yet the Wake language inherently refutes the principle of non-contradiction. By substituting the prefix "sys-" which means "together" for "dis-" as the speaker attempts to say "disentangled themselves," Joyce paradoxically undercuts Aristotle's principle by simultaneously promoting and negating it.[24]

In "Scylla and Charybdis," Stephen ponders Aristotle's principle of identity during his rendition of his Shakespeare theory.[25] While the rumor of George Russell gathering a sheaf of younger poets' verses, a sheaf that would exclude Stephen, is discussed, Stephen looks at his hat and thinks,

> Aristotle's experiment. One or two? Necessity is that in virtue of which it is impossible that one can be otherwise. Argal, one hat is one hat (9.297–99).

Unlike Bloom, who typically employs material considerations to escape unpleasant thoughts or circumstances, Stephen relies on abstract ones. However, the larger context in which this aside is employed negates the aside, for Stephen's theory poses Shakespeare as father and son consubstantial, a sundering which becomes a reconciliation. Although Stephen later states that he does not believe his own theory, the context is again one of personal frustration. The theory ultimately offers more information about Stephen's situation than it does about Shakespeare's. Stephen's identification with his fictional biography both equates and separates him from his subject, an equation that offers him insight and a separation that gives him pause.

Nietzsche, who hammered with the philosophy of perspectivism, states of Aristotle's law of non-contradiction:

> The conceptual ban on contradiction proceeds from the belief that we are able to form concepts, that the concept not only designates the essence of a thing but comprehends it—In fact, logic applies only to fictitious entities that we have created.[26]

Indeed Joyce operates through contradiction, through implicit revisions that are in a constant state of becoming through self-aware fiction and fictional self-awareness. As Umberto Eco states, his work is a continuous dialectic "between Chaos and Cosmos."[27] His references to the law of non-contradiction and the principle of identity, in *A Portrait*, *Ulysses*, and *Finnegans Wake*, occur amid professorial diatribes, by Stephen in the first two instances and by Shaun in the last. While Joyce, with Aristotle, would attack Plato's celebration of eternal immutable forms, he would accept Plato as a defender of dialogue, dialogue which is always open to novel turns and which knows no finality. The attraction to Bruno also relates in some measure to Bruno's use of dialogue form. In contrast, Joyce's education via catechism, reflected in "Nestor" and parodied in "Ithaca," ultimately consisted of fixed precepts rather than an ongoing dialogic pursuit. For Joyce, the ontological condition of experience and of language is to be dialogical.[28] The quasi-monologues in which mention of the law of non-contradiction occur, are all undercut, whether by context, subtext, or the language through which they are represented.

As an exile, Joyce's fascination with the idea of return extends beyond geographical locality to metaphysical principle. The Neoplatonic concept of epistrophe, the principle of reversion of phenomena back to their archetypes, informs the appeal of Hermeticism to Joyce, for the search for unity is essentially a return. However, Hermetic thought poses no distinction between unity and multiplicity. Instead of the Cartesian cogito, where unity is achieved by reducing things to a common denominator, the Hermetic principle of oneness is experienced simultaneously as cosmic unity and plurality. The philosophy of signatures functions through analogy to expand rather than contract. Sympathetic relationships between plants, places, stars, and the human situation oppose the Cartesian logic of hierarchical exclusion through difference.[29] These sympathetic relationships within the primacy of chaos posited by Hermeticism allow for infinite imitation and substitution, a multiplicity of interchanging masks, when subsumed into a literary text. The worlds of *Ulysses* and *Finnegans Wake* consist of correspondences, from the thought fragments that Stephen and Bloom mysteriously share and the elaborate schemas that Joyce constructed linking time, color, and anatomy with episodes of *Ulysses* to the animistic view of *Finnegans Wake*. Joyce's preference is for the analogical, an attempt to knit together the world. His works grow increasingly encyclopedic, increasingly inclusive, explicitly transgressing the boundaries of identity in "Circe" and in *Finnegans Wake*. As master parodist, he is also supreme imitator, a Hermes himself who exchanges masks in his passage between opposites—a magician, shape-shifter, *pharmakeus*.

IV

. . . a system is like the tail of truth, but truth is like a lizard; it leaves its tail in your fingers and runs away knowing full well that it will grow a new one in a twinkling.—Turgenev, Letter to Tolstoy, 1857

Oscar Wilde once said, "man is least himself when he talks in his own person. Give him a mask, and he will tell the truth."[30] Like the messenger figure in narrative, masks are invariably related to transition and to the transgression of boundaries.[31] In primitive societies their purpose is to establish an equivocal frontier between man and beast by incorporating their differences. By offering the possibility of selective personification, masks have a therapeutic function. They objectify the repressed or unknown, and thereby impute ontological status to emotional states. In the tradition of classical theater and myth, infused with polytheistic preferences, masks as personae testify to the ambiguity and ambivalence central to mutability. Both the Satyr and the Gorgon, which A. David Napier labels the two archetypal mask types,[32] express this ambiguity and ambivalence in their hybridization of human and beast. The very function of the Gorgon is ambivalent. Although it is horrific and deadly, Perseus uses the Gorgon's head to rescue Andromeda and to save his mother from a siege by Polydectes. Indeed Perseus has affinities with Hermes. In addition to the wallet for hiding the

Gorgon head and avoiding its lethal stare, he obtains winged sandals and a helmet of invisibility from the nymphs so that he may flee the remaining Gorgons.

In "Circe," an appropriate episode for masking due to its dramatic form and protean character roles,[33] Joyce explicitly mentions masks four times. The initial two instances occur within a theatrical context (15.424, 1690). The third blends mirrored opposites as the Siamese twins, Philip Drunk and Philip Sober, appear masked with Matthew Arnold's face (15.2512–14), foreshadowing the imminent conjunction of the complementary personalities of Stephen and Bloom reflected in the mirror with Shakespeare's face (15.3821–23). The fourth explicit mention of a mask occurs as a stage direction, personifying a transition in time:

> (The night hours, one by one, steal to the last place. Morning, noon and twilight hours retreat before them. They are masked, with daggered hair and bracelets of dull bells. Weary they curchycurchy under veils.) (15.4081–84)

"Daggered hair" can be seen as a reference to Medusa, particularly in light of the transitional context and as a foreshadowing of the next scene where Stephen confronts his ghoulish mother. The masked noon and twilight hours wearily retreat, their morris dancing signifying change,[34] as the night hours plunge Stephen into his unconscious to therapeutically purge his obsession with his mother.

In "Plato's Pharmacy" Jacques Derrida discusses the Egyptian counterpart of Hermes, Thoth, as a signifier god, a joker capable of infinite substitutions with no fixed identity of his own. As a variable, Thoth/Hermes is capable of taking on the mask of his opposite, thereby opposing himself by taking shape from the very thing he resists and for which he substitutes.[35] Like a mask, the messenger figure translates into its opposite. Joyce's parody is essentially narrative masking. It takes shape from the thing for which it substitutes and conflates differences so that a new order emerges. The connotations of parody are in this sense paradoxical in being both disruptive and restorative.

The term parody is in part derived from "para-ode" in Greek tragedy, meaning the entrance from the side of the stage by the chorus. By offering a social or divine context for the preceding or succeeding actions, the Greek chorus imposes stability on the narrative. In doing so, it demonstrates the restorative function of the messenger figure which complements its transgressive purpose. René Girard has written on the sacrificial and restorative functions of the Greek chorus which operates as a collective voice, a voice of moderation and common sense that offers equilibrium in the face of the continual oscillations of the tragic situation. In effect, it dissolves differences to meet the threat of maleficent contagion and to reinforce the domestic status quo.[36] In *Totem and Taboo*, Freud considers how the chorus serves as a sympathetic presence for the tragic hero, warning him of impending disasters and mourning him when he meets his fate.[37] The incarnation of the messenger at the beginning of the Nostos—the return—section of the novel, D. B. Murphy, performs chorically.

Murphy is listed in the Gilbert-Gorman and Linati schemas as "Ulysses Pseudangelos"—the false messenger.[38] A sailor from the Rosevean, the threemaster that passed behind Stephen at the conclusion of "Proteus," Murphy returns after a seven-year voyage as mythic storyteller and liar extraordinaire. His return prefigures Bloom's uncomfortable return to 7 Eccles St. where, at the conclusion of the episode, the "Ithaca" narrator will simultaneously inflate his peregrinations through Dublin by linking them with the adventures of another mythic sailor—Sinbad—and deflate them with the final dot. As Bloom meditates on the fate of Parnell and Kitty O'Shea and considers the connections with his own marital situation, he thinks, "coming back was the worst thing you ever did because it went without saying you would feel out of place as things always moved with the times" (16.1402–3). His anxiety mirrors that of Stephen, who has returned to Dublin with his pretentions to poetic greatness punctured, and of Molly, whose soliloquy recaptures significant events in her life in an attempt to come to terms with the sexual transgression she has performed earlier in the day.

As Ulysses in modern guise, Bloom functions as counterpart to Murphy. The protean face of Murphy's tattoo marks its wearer as an adept at conjuring illusions. Bloom's unveiling of him has been read as the final triumph of this restored hero-patriarch over his Dublin adversaries. As protector of Stephen, Bloom's commonsensical warnings undercut Murphy's recreation of his wanderings. When Bloom asks him about the Rock of Gibraltar, he transforms Murphy from animated storyteller to sulking has-been who confesses to being "tired of all them rocks in the sea" (16.622). Bloom's "Sherlockholmesing" leads him to take the measure of Murphy and to impart a lesson to Stephen: "Our mutual friend's stories are like himself. . . . Do you think they are genuine? He could spin those yarns for hours on end all night long and lie like old boots" (16.821–23).

Although we see Bloom's victory on one level, we commit a misreading in not also seeing Murphy, like Mulligan, as an incarnation of the trickster author and as a mirror for the reader. The master labyrinth weaver also has tired of the fixed rocks of style and form and must fictionalize to truthfully tell the tale of narrative memory as the continual exchange of masks. We are also procrustean in our elevation of Bloom in not noting that Bloom's stilted speech and ostentatious commentaries are no more genuine than Murphy's postcard. Bloom's proffering of Molly's photograph as an enticement to Stephen uses visual fiction in an attempt to regain control of his household. In essence, Bloom and Murphy function as counterparts, contained singly in Odysseus.

Like the Man in the Macintosh, Murphy appears as an unsolvable conundrum, a gesture toward the uncertainty principle with which Joyce subtly infuses his work.[39] Murphies and Macintoshes continually create fissures in the narrative flow of *Ulysses* and are endlessly variable in their repetition. They comment on the unfolding plot of Bloom, Stephen, and Molly by intersecting with it and by offering an alternative to the privileging of that plot over another that contains an exposition of the texture and function of narrative. Their messages break the linear flow and cause us to become meta-readers who must reconstruct the text while reminding us of the revisionist tendencies of memory.[40] In our re-readings, we must reexamine our dismissal of Mulligan and Murphy as false messengers and our assured acceptance of Bloom's angelic ministration. In addition to involving us in Joyce's fictions, the messengers in *Ulysses* also cause us to step outside of those fictions.

Return becomes not just a theme in *Ulysses*, but a narrative structure as demonstrated by Joyce's fascination with chiasmus. The principle of return operates on the level of character, narrator, and reader. All read reflexively, repeating and reintegrating details and images captured through the paradoxical mask of memory. The genre that emerges is one E. D. Hirsch has termed "intrinsic," manifested not through an ideal model but through the reading process.[41] The impulse to return in the principal characters, the various narrative voices, and the reader stems from the search for unification, the mythic quest for *quinta essentia,* the signatures of the author god in the world of the book. Yet these illuminations are achieved via multiplicity, so that re-cognitions are illusory selections from experience, reconstructions infiltrated by mutability.

As Vicki Mahaffey contends, the narrative movement of *Ulysses* splits its readers' minds in two by promising to bring them home while progressively estranging them from what home represents.[42] Inevitably altered by the passage of time, home is rendered fictitious so that one returns to find oneself still in exodus. The destabilizing shifts that narrative masking coerce reveal readers to be exiles, unable to achieve the closure they seek.

In addition to attacking readers' sensibilities, however, Joyce's transgressions also liberate them from those sensibilities. As a proto-postmodernist, Joyce invites his readers into the authorial gesture by demonstrating to them their exilic status. Reading, like the quest for home, is displayed as an exercise in approximation rather than attainment, an ongoing dialogue between reader and text that involves selection and change.

When Murphy is unveiled as liar by Bloom, he exits center stage in the "Eumaeus" narrator's rendition of the events in the cabman's shelter. In this manner, Murphy as messenger also functions as scapegoat in the Girardian sense of the term. Girard argues that the original event that led to rite was murder, and that the objective of ritual is to keep violence outside the community. He advances the concept of mimetic rivalry as a universal model for the human psyche, one that logically leads to scapegoating. The surrogate victim, or *pharmakos,* initially functions as the Other and becomes the repository of violent projections and must be killed to restore order to the community. As such the *pharmakos* is like the *pharmakon,* both poison and antidote.[43]

Not only does Murphy offer Bloom the opportunity to prove himself before Stephen by serving as father-protector and wise man at the level of plot, but he also functions to restore narrative order after the violent disruption of "Circe." As scapegoat, Murphy is imbued with Otherness, an Otherness that is actually a projection of the reader's and narrative memory's anxieties over their own fictionalizing. By sacrificing the messenger, whose lies are in actuality reflections of the truth of misreading and narrative revisionism, these anxieties are temporarily allayed and the comfort of a linear plot about characters is ephemerally restored.

D. B. Murphy wears the mask of liar, but it is a monstrous face at which readers resist looking directly, afraid of seeing their own reflections. Instead, Joyce's narrative shifts implore his readers to play Perseus, whom Homer calls "preeminent among all men."[44] Because Perseus would perish by gazing directly at the Gorgons, he approaches them by peering into the mirror of Athena's shield and decapitates Medusa. Similarly, *Ulysses's* messengers permit its readers a deflection through which to approach their anxieties over the fictional nature of their recognitions. In "Eumaeus," Bloom's displacement of Murphy momentarily allows readers to slay these anxieties. However, Joyce remembers that once Medusa's head was severed her children sprang from her neck. Although the scapegoating and choric functions of the messenger figure restore the linear plot by reconciling the Other, the narration must oscillate toward another transgression in order to maintain its dynamism.

By transgressing non-contradiction, Joycean messengers spur us to read Hermetically. We move simultaneously backward and forward in the text, associatively replicating experience yet continuously revising those associations as we progress into new experiences. By containing opposites and incorporating the Other, messenger figures unify this multiplicity while providing clues to authorial signatures.

Joyce's narrative masking subsumes the reader into the text as interpreter or *hermēneus,* a diviner of its signatures, yet internal conflicts and implicit parodies render each reading transitory. The boundaries of interpretation are shown to require consistent redefinition and reinterpretation. Perception is showcased as a metonymic and synecdochic act, a combination of memory and forgetting.[45] Joyce forces his readers to make continual choices and changes that may shift with each reading. We move from part to whole, from fetish to allotropic state, in a dynamic discourse where paradigms become contingencies and contingencies paradigms. And in choosing, the reader is permitted to return to the original impulse involved in the creation of the work, to assume the authorial presence, while participating in polytropic enactments of that impulse. Like the satiric underpinnings in Bruno's works, Joyce's synthesis proceeds from and by parody, a gesture toward the limitations and imitations of comprehending based upon a selected order of appearances. As sorters of messages, we engage in infinite permutations and combinations of dialogue with the messengers of meaning in Joyce's text—a process that paradoxically creates unity through disruption and disruption through unity.

5 *Milan Kundera's* The Unbearable Lightness of Being: *Narrative Betrayal and the Ideology of Powerlessness*

I

On the surface, an intelligible lie; underneath, the unintelligible truth.
—*Kundera,* THE UNBEARABLE LIGHTNESS OF BEING

When Milan Kundera wrote *The Unbearable Lightness of Being*, he was a political exile from Czechoslovakia, living in France, whose books were banned in his native country. Thus, it is not surprising that his fiction addresses oppression and its instruments, particularly language. Since the novel's publication, Vaclav Havel, the country's leading playwright and dissident, has become President and Wenceslas Square is no longer the setting for police bludgeoning advocates of free speech. Yet Kundera remains in France and, as Janet Malcolm's recent *New Yorker* travelogue reveals, he is resented by many who comprise the Czech intelligentsia. Malcolm focuses on a foreign affairs journalist who, because he had signed the human rights declaration Charter 77 in 1978, was relegated to menial work for the next twelve years, most recently as a window-washer, until the political shift restored his position. In *The Unbearable Lightness of Being*, Kundera's character, Tomas, is converted from surgeon to window-washer for refusing to cooperate with the authorities. Unlike Malcolm's subject, however, Tomas comes to find this transformation a personal reprieve, a feeling which is aided by the numerous sexual dalliances his new position affords him. According to Malcolm, Kundera's portrayal of Tomas's fate and his book's success in the west "only exacerbated the sense of injury felt by those who had stayed in Czechoslovakia and had lived out the reality that Kundera 'improved on' in his fable of totalitarianism." Her journalist/window-washer comments,

"Actually, Kundera is not a Czech author anymore. He's become something like a French wit. He should write about France rather than about Czechoslovakia."[1]

Stung by what he considers Kundera's inconsistency, the fictional oasis he creates within an anti-totalitarian polemic, the journalist would exile the exile. He condemns Kundera for aestheticizing grim social realities, for foregrounding sensual pleasures when political persecution exists. However, the journalist's hostility is in part motivated by his own desire for better times, a desire against which he has had to harden himself and of which *The Unbearable Lightness of Being* reminds him. Some part of him wants to be Tomas while another part reminds him he is not. By denying Tomas his moments of pleasure, he risks imposing the very one-dimensionality he denounces as a practice of government.

Ironically, Kundera would sympathize with the journalist's feelings. His novel is acutely conscious of the aesthete's pernicious power and self-reflexively comments on itself for indulging in that power. It also recognizes the dangers of a singular perspective and compensates by generating an implicit dialogue between the fictional story and the metaliterary commentary on that story, both of which comprise the novel. This dialogue causes the reader's perspective to oscillate between the stories of Tomas, Tereza, Sabina, and Franz and the narrator's contextualizations of those stories. Each perspectival swing disrupts its predecessor, so that the reader's engagement with the novel becomes a series of renegotiations. In this manner, *The Unbearable Lightness of Being* continually betrays itself to tell the story of the reader's misreadings.

The novel's depiction of kitsch elucidates the cultural dissemination of oppression, the making of the Self in terms of the Other. For Kundera, the language of ideology is best defined as kitsch. Kitsch functions duplicitously to repress any signification that would challenge its monistic authority. Indeed, the domestic bliss that concludes the novel is intentionally contaminated by kitsch to underscore this point. Kundera traces the complicity of kitsch to its theological roots in the denial of divine defecation and of sexual excitement in Paradise. Given the contradiction between the incompatibility of God and shit and "the basic thesis of Christian anthropology, namely, that man was created in God's image," he concludes that "shit is a more onerous theological problem than is evil."[2] Shit becomes a metaphysical problem with a theodicy that results in kitsch as an aesthetic ideal. In this aesthetic ideal, the literal and figurative meanings of shit are repudiated: "kitsch excludes everything from its purview which is essentially unacceptable in human existence" (248).

Rather than locating totalitarianism strictly in material hardships produced by a political system, *The Unbearable Lightness of Being* considers it more broadly in manifestations of monolithic thought. For Kundera, kitsch pervades these manifestations as well as the methodologies and motivations which engender them. Kitsch regulates memory, infiltrating its revisionist capacities to imprint a repetitive program. As an aesthetic ideal, it substitutes fixation for flux.

Given the pervasiveness of kitsch as an instrument of monolithic ideology, a means by which the Symbolic Order perpetuates itself, Kundera plays with the term "betrayal." At points in the novel, he inverts it from its normally negative connotations so that it signifies an act of liberation. Kundera's narrative considers the ramifications of betrayal, betrayal not only of communist brainwashing but of all ideological monomania. The narrator defines betrayal as "breaking ranks and going off into the unknown" (91), and the narrative demonstrates it to be both emancipating and imprisoning. I would like to argue that *The Unbearable Lightness of Being* functions in terms of betrayals on the level of plot and narrative structure. These betrayals operate by negating or shifting authority, by refusing to endorse or to sustain the endorsement of philosophical petitions in both literary and metaliterary contexts. They constitute a revisionist aesthetic, attacking any teleological assumptions the novel simultaneously advances. In doing so, they recapitulate our role as exiles in our engagement with the text.

The narrative structure of *The Unbearable Lightness of Being* implicitly attacks its own illusion of unification. As Terry Eagleton states, "Kundera constantly interrupts himself in order to give the slip to the totalitarian drive of literary fiction."[3] Indeed, genealogies deteriorate with the convergence of differences. The metaphors of lightness and weight establish two teleological thrusts to the narrative, each of which acquires positive or negative connotations depending on the immediate situation. Lightness versus heaviness occurs as freedom versus responsibility, uniqueness versus eternal return, Parmenides versus Beethoven. At times lightness seems ephemeral and superficial, at others liberating and significant. Heaviness too is seen both as a burden and as a valued necessity. What is heavy becomes light, and what is light becomes heavy. The sexual excitement of difference becomes the stultifying repetition of sameness, although the novel concludes with the pastoral happiness of sameness, itself undercut by our awareness that it is a prelude to death.

The alternating poles of lightness and heaviness organize the novel's structure and motifs, demonstrating ideologies to be monistic traps that inhibit aesthetic and human freedom. Some chapters present dictionaries of misunderstood words, suggesting that meaning is relative to cultural and temporal context. Kundera's table of contents reveals his revisionary intentions. The titles of chapters one and two, "Lightness and Weight" and "Soul and Body" respectively, are repeated in chapters four and five, "Soul and Body" and "Lightness and Weight," suggesting a mirror effect. The Nietzsche/Parmenides opposition established in the opening pages, where Nietzsche views weight as positive and lightness as negative while Parmenides holds the inverse to be true, is applied to the plot of these mirror chapters. Lightness and heaviness, positive and negative are reversed as dualistic poles become interchangeable. Kundera, the ironist, is necessarily a relativist, since irony is essentially practiced through an adjustment of perspective, a shift of the lens (or lenses) through which the world is exposed. This adjustment of perspective is always toward a more distant view, which diminishes individual characters and makes their behavior seem more comparable and less distinct. Of course, receding mirror images have the same effect.

The chapter that separates these mirror chapters also joins them. Appropriately entitled "Words Misunderstood," it shifts our attention to the power of naming and causes us to add the resulting perspective to the previous and subsequent chapters. Ironically, it is a perspective marked by the inevitability of distortion. The namer arranges the mirror's angle of reflection. An image is conjured in one chapter that is reflected, with differences due to the new situation in which it appears—the angle of reflection—in its mirror chapter and that mirror image is then projected back through the narrative memory. Each shifting of opposites carries with it the history of its prior incarnations in the text. Differences and samenesses merge and names mutate. Since there are numerous surfaces of meaning, which operate obliquely to one another, synthesis is undermined.

Chapter six, "The Grand March," argues against the pernicious power of kitsch while Chapter seven, "Karenin's Smile," is infused with kitsch. By negating decay and promoting sentiment, kitsch functions to curtain off death and to unify the multitudes by transforming personal memory into a shared illusion. It derives "from the basic images people have engraved in their memories: the ungrateful daughter, the neglected father, children running on the grass, the motherland betrayed, first love" (251). The heart dictates responses to these images, and "when the heart speaks, the mind finds it indecent to object" (250). The model of communist kitsch is the May Day ceremony, but its appropriated slogans and parade of identically smiling citizens transfer readily to any political ritual that garners and solidifies support through the appeal of manufactured abstractions. We witness this most poignantly in the Grand March scene of the novel where democratic idealism is subject to the same withering cynicism with which Kundera discusses Czech oppressors.

Kundera permits the literary (the characters' story, exclusive of explicit commentary) level of his novel to descend to kitsch and to exemplify an ideology. The betrayal of the literary by the narrator then frees the reader into the irony of the metaliterary (the narrator's commentary), though even that freedom needs to be disenchanted. Although Tomas and Tereza domi-nate the literary plot of *The Unbearable Lightness of Being*, Sabina is the character who transfers most readily to the metaliterary sphere.[4] "Charmed more by betrayal than by fidelity" (91), even when concretely absent from the immediate plot, her looming presence connects substantively to the metaliterary context, and her role as artist mirrors Kundera's. Sabina de-scribes the theme of her paintings as "the meeting of two worlds. A double exposure" (22): "On the surface, there was always an impeccably realis-tic world, but underneath, beneath the backdrop's cracked canvas, lurked something different, something mysterious or abstract" (63). Like Kun-dera, Sabina is an exile who challenges social and artistic convention. In this respect, she mimics the reader as well as the author.

Sabina's bowler hat, a memento from her grandfather, functions in ludic fashion to undermine narrative and cultural authority during its multiple appearances. Sabina betrays the legacy of her fathers by perching the mas-culine hat atop her naked female form, thereby transgressing sexual bound-aries as a means to seduction. Tomas, himself a violator of decorum, is attracted. Franz, who likes his illusions more secure, is confused. Tereza extends the gender playfulness associated with the hat when she uses it as a prop in the photographic session with Sabina. In doing so, she assumes Tomas's role, boldly suggesting that Sabina pose nude. However, Sabina re-verses the situation by commanding Tereza to strip, thereby playing Tomas herself while casting Tereza in her role.

The bowler hat also introduces the first dictionary of misunderstood words (89), a dictionary that discusses obliteration of memory as an inten-tion of cultural labeling. The hat as prop and motif excites and unites the seducer and seducee, *mutatis mutandis* the narrator and the reader. Sabina admires the effect she creates by posing for Tomas and herself before a mirror. Likewise, the narrator repeats and suggestively modulates the ap-pearance of the bowler hat to reveal a motif. Our cognizance of this motif constitutes seduction by the narrator, yet interpreting the arrangement of appearances pulls our own image into the narrative mirror. Like Tomas, we watch ourselves watching.

In "The Grand March" section of the novel, the narrator amends the tale he told in Part Three of Sabina standing naked before the mirror with the bowler hat on her head and Tomas at her side. He tells us that her self-denigration excited her and she fantasized "Tomas seating her on the toilet in her bowler hat and watching her void her bowels" (247). For Sabina, this fantasy leads almost immediately to orgasm; however, a narrative link with Tereza presents an inverse reaction. After Tereza's sexual encounter with the engineer, she voids her bowels in his water closet to appease her desire for humiliation, "to become only and utterly a body, the body her mother used to say was good for nothing but digesting and excreting" (157). Her memory of the liaison with the engineer becomes a paranoiac obsession in which Tereza believes him to be an agent of the State who has gathered data that may potentially compromise her. The narrator neither affirms nor denies her belief. The materialism of the body therefore functions doubly as lightness and weight. It is a source of ecstasy as well as shit, a trap and a vehicle for liberation.

Sabina's performance before the mirror pulls differences together in one body; Tereza uses her reflection to establish difference. By staring at her image in the mirror, she wishes away the signs of her mother's features in her face and focuses on what is hers alone. Seeking escape from her mother's view of bodies as infinite sameness, Tereza battles to be a body unlike other bodies:

> It was not vanity that drew her to the mirror; it was amazement at seeing her own "I." She forgot she was looking at the instrument panel of her body mechanisms; she thought she saw her soul shining through the features of her face. She forgot that the nose was merely the nozzle of a hose that took oxygen to the lungs; she saw it as the true expression of her nature. (41)

For Tereza, difference converts body to soul, weight to lightness.

Body as material sameness becomes body as cage, an object for emotional and political oppression as theorists like Foucault and Elaine Scarry have shown. Foucault reverses the influence of Christian theology by teaching that the soul is the prison of the body:

> This real, non-corporeal soul is not a substance; it is the element in which are articulated the effects of a certain type of power and the

reference of a certain type of knowledge, the machinery by which the power relations give rise to a possible corpus of knowledge and knowledge extends and reinforces the effects of this power. On this reality-reference, various concepts have been constructed and domains of analysis carved out: psyche, subjectivity, personality, consciousness, etc; on it have been built scientific techniques and discourses, and the moral claims of humanism. But let there be no misunderstanding: it is not that a real man, the object of knowledge, philosophical reflection or technical intervention, has been substituted for the soul, the illusion of the theologians. The man described for us, whom we are invited to free, is already in himself the effect of a subjection much more profound than himself. A 'soul' inhabits him and brings him to existence, which is itself a factor in the mastery that power exercises over the body. The soul is the effect and the instrument of a political anatomy, the soul is the prison of the body.[5]

The unique "I" Tereza perceives in the mirror in her awakening to difference Foucault would consider a misrecognition, an adaptation to the look of the Other. Lacan would agree with him. Kundera multiplies Tereza's experience with her reflected image within the story and structure of his novel to suggest his readers' own duplicity in the process of imposing themselves on the face of the text.

II

As soon as psychology has finished with anxiety, it is to be delivered to dogmatics.—Kierkegaard, THE CONCEPT OF ANXIETY

Whether or not Kundera is aware of Lacan's work, Tereza's perception of her unique self in the mirror illustrates Lacan's mirror stage. Like the child in Lacan's mirror stage, Tereza's sense of a total gestalt and consequent *jouissance* constitutes a recognition of her own bodily unity and anticipates a mastery of that unity. As Lacan points out, however, this imaginary and ideal perception guarantees subsequent alienation of the real subject from this imaginary construct. Lacan terms the anxiety over losing this image of unity the fantasy of the "body-in-pieces" (*le corps morcele*).[6] Ellie Ragland-Sullivan expands on this concept in terms that touch on Kundera's intentions:

Denial, objectification of others, and illusory ideals of the ego all play their part in making consciousness an irremediably limited principle of "self"-idealization and misrecognition (*meconnaissance*). By *meconnaissance* Lacan means the original mirror-stage putting on of another's image and Desire as our own, which we repress as knowledge and repeat as process.[7]

In her reading of Lacan, Jane Gallop states,

> The mirror stage is a decisive moment. Not only does the self issue from it, but so does "the body in bits and pieces." This moment is the source not only for what follows but also for what precedes. It produces the future through anticipation and the past through retroaction. And yet it is itself a moment of self-delusion, of captivation by an illusory image. Both future and past are thus rooted in an illusion.[8]

Intersubjective relationships which are largely characterized by identification and projection are therefore extensions of this formative phase, and the alienation of subject from ego ideal is translated to an aggressive tension between Self and the Other onto whom the imaginative ego has been projected. Just as the ego becomes an Other, the Other metamorphoses to alter ego.

As Gallop points out, the decisive moment of the mirror stage begins the oscillation that is the making and unmaking of the Self. In the same manner, readers as exiles interact with the text in a reenactment of the attempt to return to the imaginary ideal, an attempt that a self-conscious text like *The Unbearable Lightness of Being* exposes and undermines. Shifting between literary and metaliterary discourses in a constant rearrangement of perspective, we are seduced and distanced while our interpretive constructs are rendered transitory. We therefore re-read while reading, possessed by anxiety over misreadings we have committed and ineluctably will commit.

Kundera's anti-totalitarianism, his deflation of singular perspectives, is realized by maintaining his readers' oscillation through irony. He describes this process in an interview:

> Between what we think about ourselves and what we actually are there exists an infinite distance, just as there is an infinite distance between what we wish things were and what they are, or between what we think they are and what they are. To apprehend this distance, this abyss, means to destroy the poetic illusion. This is also the essence of the art of irony. And irony is the perspective of the novel.[9]

Kundera's approach confirms Friedrich Schlegel's definition of irony as a "permanent parabasis."[10] Paul de Man rejects some of Schlegel's earlier commentators who see irony in terms of an organic temporality, "a preliminary movement toward a recovered unity, as a reconciliation of the self with the world by means of art." Instead, de Man asserts irony works in terms of repetition, as "a self-escalating act of consciousness":

> Irony divides the flow of temporal experience into a past that is pure mystification and a future that remains harassed forever by a relapse within the inauthentic. It can know this inauthenticity but can never overcome it. It can only restate and repeat it on an increasingly conscious level, but it remains endlessly caught in the impossibility of making this knowledge applicable to the empirical world. It dissolves in the narrowing spiral of a linguistic sign that becomes more and more remote from its meaning, and it can find no escape from this spiral.[11]

De Man's ironic spiral portends in our recurrent discovery of the act of reading as mnemonic performance, infiltrated by displacement and endlessly rehearsed in the dialectic of desire and loss. Returns are disclosed as counterfeit, a revelation that is unable to terminate the process of returning. Irony heightens anxiety because it dislodges hegemonic imperatives and refuses the comfort of totality. It reminds us we are exiles by forcing us to wander back and forth in the text. In that wandering, we seek a means of resisting the eternal oscillations. We take solace in illusory feelings of possession and control that seem to still the anxious flux. Kundera calls these feelings our *es muss seins,* a phrase he in turn manages to ironize.

Kundera uses *"es muss sein,"* a pronouncement which inspired Beethoven to compose his last string quartet (No. 16, Opus 135), as a leitmotif in the novel. Beethoven converted its context from that of a joke to a serious philosophical inquiry, from light to heavy. Beethoven introduced the last movement of the quartet with *"Der schwer gefasste Entschluss"* (the difficult resolution). Kundera uses *"es muss sein!"* for metaliterary discourses on necessity and on chance, and it occurs within the story of Tomas and Tereza in instances both of necessity and of chance. Thus, the same motif occupies two opposite vectors within the text, each of which occurs in both positive and negative contexts. The narrator informs us that human lives, like music, are "novelistic":

> They are composed like music. Guided by his sense of beauty, an individual transforms a fortuitous occurrence (Beethoven's music, death under a train) into a motif, which then assumes a permanent place in the composition of the individual's life. Anna [Karenina] could have chosen another way to take her life. But the motif of death and the

railway station, unforgettably bound to the birth of love, enticed her in her hour of despair with its dark beauty. Without realizing it, the individual composes his life according to the laws of beauty even in times of greatest distress (52).

Tomas's personal imperative, his *es muss sein!*, is rooted in controlling the body of the Other. He does this through sex and surgery:

> Surgery takes the basic imperative of the medical profession to its outermost border, where the human makes contact with the divine. . . . When Tomas first positioned his scapel on the skin of a man asleep under an anesthetic, then breached the skin with a decisive incision, and finally cut it open with a precise and even stroke (as if it were a piece of fabric—a coat, a skirt, a curtain), he experienced a brief but intense feeling of blasphemy. Then again, that was what attracted him to it! (193–94)

Both sex and surgery involve penetration of the Other's body, a volitional union with a yielding unknown. The anxiety of the discoverer confronted with the unknown is allayed by this totalizing activity. Penetrating the body reveals its secrets so that the penetrator can appropriate those secrets for his own, thereby conquering the Other by assimilating its dissimilarity within the Self. The "blasphemy" is the betrayal of difference, a volitional quest born from the acknowledgment of that difference and from the anxiety attendant to that acknowledgment. The need for unity motivates the betrayal; the search for difference is the pursuit of sameness:

> Only in sexuality does the millionth part dissimilarity become precious, because, not accessible in public, it must be conquered. As recently as fifty years ago, this form of conquest took considerable time (weeks, even months!), and the worth of the conquered object was proportional to the time the conquest took. Even today, when conquest time has been drastically cut, sexuality seems still to be a strongbox hiding the mystery of the woman's "I." So it was a desire not for pleasure (the pleasure came as an extra, a bonus) but for possession of the world (slitting the outstretched body of the world with his scapel) that sent him in pursuit of women (200).

"Possession of the world" occurs when the world is a mirror of the ideal Self. Desire for such possession is reactive rather than innate. It arises from the need to eradicate the anxiety caused by the recognition of difference, a perception that mirrors back a fragmented rather than a unified identity.

What is recognized yet not contained within the image of the ideal Self is threatening in its mystery and must be solved, must be penetrated, must be possessed to extinguish the threat. In this respect, the functions of Tomas's penis and his scapel, of libertinism and surgery, are identical. Both penetrate the mysterious Other to appropriate its mystery and to make it one with the totalizing Self.

Kundera's betrayal of the reader consists of the various mirrors he implants into the text, mirrors which he ultimately shatters to convey his aesthetic as the preservation of anxiety and the ideology of powerlessness. Tomas's desire to possess the world mirrors our desire to understand rationally, and thereby possess, the world of the text. The organized construct, the system, that emerges permits closure and assimilation into the ideal totality of the Self. What is organized and unified prohibits violation, and it is potential violation with which we tease ourselves. Our engagement with the text, an attraction to the mystery of difference, is erotic in that it promises us the opportunity to play both violator and violated. Encountering difference reflected in the mirror of the novel, we risk a displacement of the ideal image we bring to the text. However, we also seek to penetrate the mystery, to conquer difference and to make it our own. The Lacanian model indicates that these two stages are mutually dependent, and that the anxiety (violated) phase is reactive to the mirror (violator) phase. Imagining the Self is immediately followed by anxiety over the loss of that image, an anxiety that in and of itself may fragment the image. Kundera accepts the mutuality of the duality and continuously shifts its poles to maintain the dynamics (or erotics) of the text. The metaliterary sphere penetrates the literary one and is penetrated by it. By mirroring the reader's interpretive quest, it seduces us with the jubilation of comprehension. But the interactive nature of these two dimensions hybridizes the novel, rendering comprehension a monolithic illusion, and returns again and again to the realm of anxiety. What we have taken for consummation remains continual foreplay.

III

The pleasures of interpretation are henceforth linked to loss and disappointment, so that most of us will find the task too hard, or simply repugnant; and then, abandoning meaning, we slip back into the old comfortable fictions of transparency, the single sense, the truth.—Kermode, THE GENESIS OF SECRECY

The first mention of the title in the plot occurs during a discussion of Sabina by the narrator when she departs Geneva for Paris: "Her drama was a drama not of heaviness but of lightness. What fell to her lot was not the burden but the unbearable lightness of being" (122). He goes on to consider the oxymoronic quality of the title—how one becomes trapped by flight: "One could betray one's parents, husband, country, love, but when parents, husband, country, and love were gone—what was left to betray? . . . What if that emptiness was the goal of all her betrayals?" (122). The narrator then betrays our immersion in the story of Tomas and Tereza by jumping ahead three years to Sabina's receiving word of their accidental deaths, thereby imposing a frame of death around our reading of their subsequent exploits. Light moments are rendered heavy within this context, mirroring the "double exposure" of Sabina's paintings.

The unbearable lightness of being, then, constitutes a definition of Kundera's aesthetic, a flirtation with the inevitability of loss and an exposure of the anxiety that accompanies this flirtation. His narrator informs us that "the novel . . . is an investigation of human life in the trap the world has become" (221).[12] Traps in the novel stem from choices and from the losses that accompany choices. Tomas is asked to choose between his honor and his profession, his son and his refusal to publicly endorse a political petition, Tereza and the lightness of libertinism. Yet it is when these choices are imposed from without, as social or cultural interdicts, that they become ideological imperatives, *es muss seins*. Because these imperatives sculpt the self as a representation of the Other, the most profound loss is that of self-definition. The unbearable lightness of being occurs in those fleeting moments when one is most oneself rather than oneself as defined through the Other, when one refuses the choices posed from without and acts on what spontaneously flows from within, when one resists the obsessive pull of *es muss sein*. So powerful are the influences of cultural imperatives, however, that their absence creates the pervasive sense of emptiness upon which Sabina meditates. Betraying them renders the betrayer apprehensive regarding the tentativeness of the pristine self. Each ephemeral entrance into a self-contained Eden therefore includes a retrospective and a proleptic Fall.

Tomas is incarnated looking outward for identity. The narrator tells us he first envisioned him "standing at the window of his flat and looking across the courtyard at the opposite walls, not knowing what to do" (6). We might imagine him transfixed, watching the play of his own reflection in the window against the courtyard walls he views. This image of Tomas returns in the fifth chapter, the mirror of the one in which it first occurs. We are told, "characters are not born like people, of woman; they are born of a situation, a sentence, a metaphor containing in a nutshell a basic human possibility" (221). These metaphoric possibilities tentatively transcend the trap of the world by creating links among its situations and by suggesting the possibility of a totality through additional connections. Although kitsch also promises totality, it is an unimaginative fundamentalism that binds images together through superficial emotional appeal. Rather than possibility, it offers limitation. Instead of a verticle and veridical excavation of physical and metaphysical strata of meaning, kitsch's operations are exclusively horizontal repetitions, its tropes reductive rather than expansive, metonymic rather than metaphoric.[13]

The desire to escape reductive repetition coalesces with the acceptance of loss and the relinquishment of the pursuit of control. "*Einmal ist keinmal*," says Tomas to himself (8), what happens but once might as well not have happened at all. The narrator repeats this statement in the mirror chapter, and extends its application from an individual life to history. History, like life, is a sketch rather than a finished picture: "History is as light as individual life, unbearably light, light as a feather, as dust swirling into the air, as whatever will no longer exist tomorrow" (223). In other words, history is a story; its characters representatives of human possibility. It is possibility that motivates the characters, engages the reader, and remains always unrealized so that the telling does not cease. The finished picture is an end to possibility. The acknowledgment of the loss of totality takes us beyond the mirror stage and provisionally beyond the rule of the Other. As the fragmentation that accepts anxiety and thereby eludes its domination, the unbearable lightness of being is the freedom from the finished picture, from the ideological system. The inversion of the concluding chapters betrays the reader to simulate this freedom.

"The Grand March" chapter contains Kundera's exposition on kitsch. Using the death of Stalin's son as an introduction, Kundera weaves his metaliterary commentary with Franz's participation in the perverse vanity of the Grand March. He concludes the chapter with Franz's funeral and his wife's appropriation of his memory for her own glorification. "Before we are forgotten, we will be turned into kitsch," the narrator tells us. "Kitsch is the stopover between being and oblivion" (278).

In the course of this chapter, the narrator presents a brief essay on "the look," a concept that parallels Lacan's Gaze:[14]

We all need someone to look at us. We can be divided into four categories according to the kind of look we wish to live under. The first category longs for the look of an infinite number of anonymous eyes, in other words, for the look of the public. . . . The second category is made up of people who have a vital need to be looked at by many known eyes. . . . Then there is the third category, the category of people who need to be constantly before the eyes of the person they love. . . . And finally there is the fourth category, the rarest, the category of people who live in the imaginary eyes of those who are not present. They are the dreamers (269–70).

Into the first category, the narrator places the American actress who ostentatiously participates in the Grand March; into the second, "the tireless hosts of cocktail parties"—Franz's wife, Marie-Claude, and her daughter. Tereza and Tomas fit the third category and Franz and Tomas's son, Simon, are placed in the fourth. Sabina is strikingly absent from all four categories. Nor is the hierarchy of these categories clear. What is clear is the illusory sense of unity gained through the look, a personal kitsch that keeps fragmentation at bay.

Jean-Paul Sartre's aphorism, "*L'enfer, c'est les autres,*" more readily applies to the philosophy Sabina embraces and, ironically, to the point of view toward which Kundera guides the reader. I use "ironically" because the reader defines himself through the author's Gaze while he is led to reject the totalizing illusion self-consciously presented and undercut by the author. Kundera himself comments, "Irony irritates. Not because it mocks or attacks but because it denies us our certainties by unmasking the world as an ambiguity." [15] *The Unbearable Lightness of Being* shifts the look beyond the realm of kitsch by destroying the embellishments by which kitsch cloaks anxiety. Rather than repressing anxiety over the destruction of the unified mirrored Other, Kundera releases the reader from repression by celebrating fragmentation. Sabina reveals this in her epiphany concerning the meaning of beauty:

> From that time on she had known that beauty is a world betrayed. The only way we can encounter it is if its persecutors have overlooked it somewhere. Beauty hides behind the scenes of the May Day parade. If we want to find it, we must demolish the scenery (110).

Kundera betrays his metaliterary conclusions with his literary ending while implicitly calling upon his reader to betray his literary ending by invoking his metaliterary conclusions. By accepting the ending, we accept the kitsch that is a repression of the imminent deaths of Tomas and Tereza. After shedding sentimental tears at the death of the dog, Karenin, we embrace the happy conclusion complete with its nocturnal butterfly. The narrator informs us that "the sadness was form, the happiness content. . . . Happiness filled the space of sadness" (313–14).

But, like Sabina, we have learned that form and content are not opposite sides of a duality. When we are courageous enough to shatter the mirror and find beauty and jubilation not in the projected image but in examining the resultant shards, we discover that form is content and content form. In his concluding chapter, Kundera teases us with kitsch, betraying his own Gaze, to offer us the possibility for self-assertion by assuming the authorial stance and demolishing the scenery of kitsch. Through this assertion, we exile ourselves from the comforting totality of closure and accept the anxiety of the continual search. In doing so, we enact and reenact a personal version of Nietzsche's "mad myth" (3) of eternal return; in effect, returning to the beginning of the novel through the idea with which it began.[16] Return, in this sense, contravenes Freud's view in *Beyond the Pleasure Principle* of repetition as death instinct. Instead, return functions in a Kierkegaardian sense, as re-creation and, as in Kierkegaard, repetition creates identity.[17] Without certitude imposed from without, the reader's choices, his re-creations, constitute assertions of identity. However, these assertions are replete with anxiety regarding their lack of constancy. In his own religious context, Kierkegaard clearly describes this situation:

> Anxiety is a desire for what one fears, a sympathetic antipathy; anxiety is an alien power which grips the individual, and yet he cannot free himself from it and does not want to, for one fears, but what he fears he desires.[18]

The identity toward which Kundera directs the reader is not power in the sense of control. Like Nietzsche's eternal return, it is in a continual state of becoming. Nor is it controlled, for the reader who has absorbed the lessons of narrative betrayal has learned that freedom lies in betraying the *es muss seins* imposed by the Other. Learning to read Kundera means learning to read with "sympathetic antipathy," a condition that fosters return and re-creation. Like Tomas, as revealed through Tereza's final dream in which he is a helpless rabbit, we realize the unbearable lightness of being in our powerlessness.

6 D. M. *Thomas's* The White Hotel: Mirrors, Triangles, and Sublime Repression

I

When Discord has fallen into the lowest depths of the vortex concord has reached the center.—Empedocles

The horror of D. M. Thomas's *The White Hotel* is also its passion. Its narrative structure propels the reader backward and forward in an obsessive quest to explain the convergence of contraries that constitutes the novel's motifs. Sex and violence parallel and coalesce as the narrative movement conflates the pleasure of the text with its terrifying vision. The reader moves through the dizzying succession of narrative voices, each undermining its predecessor, and seeks an authoritative interpretation through repetitive clues. However, the notions of authority and repetition become attached to a death force, culminating in the Babi Yar chapter which defies the closure of each of the previous chapters and is in turn defied by the concluding chapter. The prologue invites us to read the text as psychoanalytic detectives, drawing on events and images from the past in our epistemological search. Freud's last letter in the prologue advises a dispassionate attitude toward analyzing Anna G.'s poem and journal. Yet the voice of Anna's documents, matter-of-factly describing the rain of corpses over the landscape while the pleasures of prolific sex are tinged with violent imagery, is disconcerting. Although the scenes and events are fantastic, the tonality with which they are rendered seems strangely flat— like that of a mind in shock. This sense is reinforced in Freud's case history when he remarks that his initial encounter with Anna reminded him of the faces of victims of battle trauma.[1]

Ferenczi's letter in the prologue depicts Freud teasing Jung for his Christian mysticism, a fate he regards the Jews as having escaped (4).[2] However, Lisa's clairvoyance becomes the epistemological vector of the text that counters rational analysis. Rather than symptoms of past causes, Anna/Lisa's present torments predict the future. Here the terror of the text replicates and magnifies the terror of the events it depicts. The interpretive direction is reversed as deduction gives way to prescience and future revelation replaces a deterministic past. We discover the flat tone of Anna/Lisa's initial documents to be a repression not only of the anti-Semitism of the past but of the holocaust of the future. These are repressed in her present consciousness and disowned through the substitution of an obsessive sexuality which only partially masks, because of its place in, Lisa's persistently intrusive vision of the future.

The text itself operates within a similar psychic duplicity. Thomas directs us into Lisa's past in Freud's case history and in Lisa's modification in "The Health Resort" chapter, allowing us to reach intellectual resolutions at the conclusion of each as Freud's brilliant deductions are extended and metamorphosed through Lisa's revelations. Lisa's life appears to have reached a stable and healthy center; however, the Babi Yar chapter shatters this semblance of security. The inability of the Jews to discern the implicit meaning in the signs directing them to evacuate mocks us as readers leaning on our rational crutches. The "demon of repetition" (129) is revealed as truly demonic as the images from Anna's poem and journal are horribly realized. Repression is disclosed to be proleptic as well as historical. As Lisa indicates in the final chapter, *anagnorisis*—recognition—is what is wrong (261). It breaks through the metaphoric defense of repression but leaves us buried in the void.

The author's note defines myth as "a poetic, dramatic expression of a hidden truth." In plot and narrative structure, *The White Hotel* is about ways of discovering truth. By directing the reader through various revisions, it traces the mythic resonance of archetypal images. The novel functions as palimpsest where we read backward as we move forward. Through repetition of images we experience no erasure; instead we have memory and revision of memory. Mirrors and doubling imply dualities which in turn create choices for the reader. We are presented with the conflicting epistemologies of Freud and Jung, the oppositions of rationalism and mysticism, Eros and Thanatos, analysis and prescience, myth and history, Jew and Christian, Medusa and Ceres. However, the novel never comes down completely in endorsement of either side of a duality. Such absolute authorities become red herrings. Like Anna's gesture which accompanies her lies to Freud, they are the stroking of a crucifix.

In his letter in the prologue Hanns Sachs terms the white hotel Eden before the Fall (10), a timeless realm, and goes on to say that meaning depends on time. Although the poem and the journal are set in timelessness, as documents they enter the realm of time in Freud's and the reader's act of interpretation. By forcing the mythic into the historical we simultaneously establish the authority of interpretation and reenact the Fall. Authority is proleptically undermined in the prologue when Ferenczi's letter recounts Freud's refusal to risk his authority by revealing personal feelings that would confirm or deny Jung's hypothesis regarding his sister-in-law (5–6). The author's footnotes to Freud's case history, which quote Freud against himself, continue to erode his authority. In contrast, the postcards from the white hotel, the excerpts from Anatoli Kuznetsov's Babi Yar, and Dina Pronicheva's appearance invite multiple perspectives. We are shown the limitations of the mono-myth, whether Freudian, Nazi, or hermeneutical. Essentially, the narrative structure of the novel is intentionally decentering and ultimately regenerative. Enclosures are collapsed so that expressions of truth proliferate. Through the reimposition of metaphor in the final chapter, the aesthetic transcends the historical and the text revises itself again. Repression is restored as metaphor, and the novel reveals its sublime underpinnings, igniting the reader in the purifying fire of pleasure and terror.

II

Dying each other's life, living each other's death.—Heraclites

Two dominant motifs, mirrors and triangles, define the narrative structure of *The White Hotel*, underscoring the Hermetic reflection of macrocosm in microcosm at the thematic heart of the novel.[3] The novel continually presents patterns of repetition and paralleling, an interweaving of details, images, and motifs. Lost or left luggage appears in Anna's journal (45), in Lisa's account of traveling by train (151), in her meeting with Victor in Milan (171), all prefiguring the confiscation of her suitcase at Babi Yar (230). The shroud of Turin is mentioned in Father Marek's sermon in the journal (71) and accounts for Lisa's rejection of Christ's resurrection in "The Health Resort" chapter (167–68). The vision of Christ with hands placed delicately over genitals is replicated in the Babi Yar chapter as Lisa views the naked Jews going to their deaths with their hands covering their genitals in a pathetic gesture at modesty (243).

The fire at the white hotel is personalized as Anna realizes that her hair is on fire (37), is picked up again when Lisa reports to Freud that Alexei singed her hair with his cigar (126), again when Anna confirms that her mother and uncle died in a hotel fire when on an illicit rendezvous (137), and is repeated in Lisa's letter to Freud when she tells him of the sailors molesting her while she viewed the burning waterfront (187). This destructive image is temporarily rendered positive when Lisa makes love with Victor and "the flashes of the lighthouse lit up her husband's white hair" (211).

Lisa's honeymoon with Victor takes place on a boat as did the incidents with Alexei, with the sailors, and with Lisa's youthful discovery of her mother, aunt and uncle in three-way sex. These mirrorings conflate the fire/water imagery and pick up the motif of traveling which is repeated in the various train journeys throughout the novel. This conflation attains sinister proportions in the Babi Yar chapter when the Jews are told that they will be evacuated by train, itself a gruesome reminder of the thousands of Jews who were evacuated by train to death camps. In a further conflation, after the massacre the Nazi stokers construct a pyre of bodies and set the fire by igniting the hair of the dead (251). At the conclusion of the chapter, the narrator reports the continuous efforts to annihilate the dead. A dam is erected across the ravine of bodies, transforming the emerald lake of Anna's poem, which is also depicted as a red sheet, into a putrid one (252). Eventually the dam bursts, burying Kiev in mud and corpses. Again historical events coalesce, for we are reminded of Ferenczi's letter detailing Jung's fascination with mummified bog corpses, a fascination which led Freud to faint because he was convinced that Jung wished his death (5).

Blood imagery pervades the novel. Anna's lover states "I want your blood" as they make love while she is menstruating (46). He asks her, "can you feel the blood falling?" and she responds, "I fall ill every autumn" (45) —autumn being when her mother died and when the massacre at Babi Yar occurs. Their lovemaking is immediately followed by Anna's lover cutting his steak, an image repeated when Victor cuts up his beefsteak "tenderly and expressively" (153), and recalling the "rare and beautiful" steaks with their natural juices that the jolly chef in "Don Giovanni" cooked (28). The Düsseldorf murderer, Peter Kürten, kills because he needs to drink blood and, out of frustration at not finding a victim one night, he cuts off the head of a swan and drinks its blood (178). Kürten desires to remain alive moments after he is executed by guillotine so that he can hear his own blood gush. The purity and innocence of the swans that conclude Chapters one and two are contaminated by blood and death, an image prefigured when Victor writes of his swan song (204). The image of Kürten's killing the swan and his wish to hear his own blood gush haunts Lisa, causing her head to spin (178). She prays that he will not be the same Peter Kürten when he enters the afterlife, but believes that "somewhere—at that very moment—someone was inflicting the worst possible horror on another human being" (179). Her prayer and belief are prophetic. Kürten is seen playing with children in the final chapter, though under the careful watch of armed guards (262–63). When Lisa looks into the ravine at Babi Yar, her head swims upon viewing the sea of bodies before she too falls into the "bath of blood" (248).

Other recurring images include oranges in the context of trees, groves, nipples, and with water Anna's sole source of nourishment at the white hotel, crows and ravens (symbolically birds of prophecy), corsets, cats, whales, plums, peaches, stars, and cedar and pine trees.[4] Narrative detail and inversions of detail find revelatory expression in the motif of mirrors. Freud's letter to Ferenczi characterizes Anna's hysteria as if "Venus looked in her mirror and saw the face of Medusa" (8). Freud later terms Anna's mother Medusa as well as Ceres (142).[5] In "The Health Resort" chapter, Lisa's letter to Freud introduces new facts that modify Freud's analysis. We learn that as a young girl Lisa discovered her mother (Mary) and her mother's twin (Magda)—mirrors of each other as archetypal Virgin and Whore—in a ménage à trois with Lisa's uncle. In her revision of her night on the yacht with Alexei, she recalls waking to see her reflection in the wardrobe mirror which resurrects this traumatic discovery of "the grimacing woman, joyful; and the smiling woman, sad. Medusa and Ceres" (192). Lisa distinguishes the twin sisters by the crucifix that only her aunt wears. Her mother had removed hers due to the anti-Semitic protests of her family over her intention to marry a Jew, a situation replicated in Vogel's anti-Semitic comments in Anna's journal and foreshadowed in the Freud/Jung, Jewish rationalism/Christian mysticism duality reported in Ferenczi's letter. We learn in "The Health Resort" chapter of Lisa's marriage to a Jew-hater which causes her to deny her identity, to secretly wish that her uncle was her father, to hallucinate catastrophes when having sex with her husband, to induce a miscarriage, and ultimately to withhold significant information from Freud because he is Jewish. Lisa's suppression of her Jewish identity alters Freud's interpretation as we revise the previous chapters which have attained the status of documents within the text. However, her repression also catapults us forward to the incident at Babi Yar where she initially denies her Jewishness to escape the slaughter.

Lisa's mirror phobia coincides with her reading of Freud's case of the Wolf Man who was obsessed with intercourse *more ferarum*. Intertextual connections suggest themselves when we review this case. The Wolf Man's wife is referred to as "Tatiana" from *Eugene Onegin*, his sister is named

Anna, and the color white recurs in his wolf dreams. Freud believed that evidence from this case would confirm his argument for the primacy of infantile prehistory as opposed to Jung's contention that ancestral prehistory was most influential.[6] The combination of human and savage captivates Lisa and finds expression in her attribution of Medusa/Ceres, "good and evil coupling, to make the world" (192), to her mother and aunt's mirroring. Characteristically, it also refers us backward and forward in the text. In the "Don Giovanni" poem, Anna writes:

> your son impaled me, it was so sweet I screamed
> but no one heard me for the other screams
> as body after body fell or leapt
> from upper storeys of the white hotel
> I jerked and jerked until his prick released
> its cool soft flood. Charred bodies hung from trees.
>
> (19–20)

In the Babi Yar chapter, these images are parodically paralleled as thousands of people are shot by the Nazis and fall into the ravine. Lisa jumps with Kolya before the bullets strike them. Lying amidst the carnage, her muffled movements are detected and her breast is kicked in before she is raped with a bayonet: "very gently, Demidenko imitated the thrusts of intercourse; and Semashko let out a guffaw, which reverberated from the ravine walls as the woman's body jerked back and relaxed, jerked and relaxed. . . . Demidenko twisted the blade and thrust it in deep" (249–50). Lisa's belief that the source of her breast and ovary pains was organic in opposition to Freud's contention that they stemmed from her rejection of her lesbian impulses finds disturbing confirmation in this scene. The fearful interdependence of good and evil, Eros and Thanatos, which is *The White Hotel*'s thematic design, is synedochically expressed in the mirroring of plot details established in the poem and journal of Anna—whose name is itself chiasmic.

Triangles dominate the sexual relationships in the novel. In a version of the Oedipus conflict in which the father usurps the child in the mother's affection, Madame R's mothering of Lisa ends when she marries. Lisa later forms a harmonious triangle with Victor and Vera, both of whom are Jews, and eventually takes Vera's place as Victor's wife and as mother to Kolya. She writes to Freud that she has just sung an oratorio called *Oedipus Rex*, and she performs with Victor in *Eugene Onegin*, at the center of which is a love triangle. She later accepts Victor's marriage proposal in a letter which mirrors that of Tatiana to Onegin. The initial letter of the prologue has Ferenczi writing to his mistress Gisela whose ex-husband will commit suicide on their wedding day. And in that letter Ferenczi mentions Freud's dream regarding his sister-in-law Minna working like a peasant while his wife looks on idly, which causes the rift between Jung and him regarding his refusal to risk his authority (5). In her letter in "The Health Resort" chapter, Lisa reveals that Freud had been to Bad Gastein on vacation with Minna when Lisa, at this point a former patient, met them (182), a replication of the liaison between Lisa's mother and uncle which culminates in the hotel fire. In Anna's poem and journal, we see a triangle with Anna, her lover, and Madame Cottin, prefiguring Anna's report to Freud of Alexei's having sex with another woman on the yacht. Both events are based on Lisa's repression of the ménage à trois that she witnessed as a young girl. Anna's duplicitous report concerning Alexei has him taking the girl doggy style, replicating Anna's being mounted from behind in her poem and journal, and based on Lisa's repression of viewing her mother with Lisa's uncle behind her and her aunt stroking her breast. The repression of the past also attains a universal dimension when linked with the Wolf Man's compulsion for intercourse with animals.

In this magic web of a novel, mirrors and triangles occur as plot details, character relationships, motifs; and triangles also define the structure of *The White Hotel*. The six chapters break down into two triangles, the details, motifs, and themes of which interlock chiasmically as mirror images—emblematically a Star of David.

The "Don Giovanni" poem, written between the staves of the libretto of Mozart's opera, implicitly warns us to read between the lines if we are to discern meaning. As Sachs indicates in his letter, we are in a timeless realm, Eden before the Fall. Freud refers to Anna having "given birth" to this material (9), a loaded image, as we later learn, for Anna has induced a miscarriage so that she will not give birth to the child of her anti-Semitic husband. Biblical images of flood and catastrophic fire occur in a dreamscape overflowing with breast milk and the honey of continual sex. Internal and external occurrences coalesce as the flames of the hotel fire merge with Anna and her lover's sexual passion. Sex and catastrophe coincide, yet we witness magically restorative, regenerative, and nurturing powers. The chapter concludes affirmatively with the white purity of the swans and the snow covered mountains as we are told that "no one was selfish in the white hotel" (28).

Like the poem, "The Gastein Journal" is a subjective fantasy which becomes a documentary object. The movement in the novel from individual to general is indicated by the shift from first to third person and from poetry to prose. The chapter begins with Anna dreaming the vision of Dina Pronicheva from Kuznetsov's account of Babi Yar, which will be realized in its mirror chapter, Chapter five. The juxtaposition of sex and violence continues as do the magical restorative powers. The white hotel is completely rebuilt ten days after the devastating fire, and guests continue to pour into its premises despite the flood, fire, landslide, and bodies falling to earth—the mirrored inversion of the sequence in which these catastrophes will occur in Chapter five. Within the ahistorical frame of this chapter, Vogel's anti-Semitic remarks and Bolotnikov-Leskov's comments regarding violence and terrorism seem out of place except when considered as a foreshadowing of Chapter five. The disembodied flying breast and the womb gliding over the lake also attain a realistic dimension in the mirror chapter. What emerges more clearly in "The Gastein Journal" is a sense of the community of the white hotel. The postcards provide various perspectives on the mundane and the fantastic events that occur within the hotel, often focusing on the romantic escapades of Anna and her lover. This sense of community will be reflected in the tragic community of martyrs at Babi Yar, and the statement that "the spirit of the white hotel was against selfishness" (86) will be recapitulated in Lisa's ethical decision to proclaim her Jewishness and die with Kolya.

The third chapter, "Frau Anna G.," provides Freud's case history, his analysis of the poem and journal and his attempt to locate the source of Lisa's breast and ovary pains.[7] It pulls Chapters one and two into one vision and concludes the first triangle of the novel with the authority of Freud's masculine, rational interpretation. Freud's position as a patriarchal authority is later underscored when Lisa acknowledges that he was the priest—a Father—in her poem and journal. Freud's psychoanalytic method assumes that knowledge offers release. By locating repression and by sharing repressed aspects with others, these aspects become real and unburden the Self. In the final chapter Lisa will tell the young doctor that it is *anagnorisis*—recognition—that is the source of her pains. As Freud's epistemology moves backward, the reader reads backward, pulling together images from the poem and journal and connecting them to Anna's autobiographical revelations. White, equated with innocence in Chapters one and two, now becomes equated with guilt. Using Lisa's stroking of her crucifix as a lie detector, Freud analyzes the source of her pains as her hatred of her disturbed femininity and comes to equate the white hotel with the womb.

However, Freud's authority, already called into doubt in Ferenczi's letter, is further undercut by the documentary footnotes that the author adds to the case history. We learn that "Freud's unusual emphasis on the mother's role may have owed something to the recent death of his own mother" (142 note). The initial footnote tells us that one of Freud's favorite quotations was Charcot's dictum "Theory is good, but it doesn't prevent things from existing" (122 note). Besides revealing Freud's capacity for self-parody, this quote ironically adumbrates the direction of the rest of *The White Hotel*, a confirmation of mystical prescience rather than rational analysis of the past. We also learn that Freud had completed about half of *Beyond the Pleasure Principle* at the time of Lisa's analysis. This work, which focuses on the death instinct, was to substantially revise Freud's view of the unconscious. In essence then, Freud's case history of Anna G. contains the germs of revision of its own conclusions.[8] Freud's words to Lisa, that she is "cured of everything but life," turn out to be prophetic. They propel the novel into its second triangle where we move from the realm of documents for analysis (Anna's poem and journal) and a published document (Freud's case history) into an overtly novelistic treatment of Lisa's future life, the climax of which draws from Kuznetsov's document on Babi Yar.[9] The narrative voice, supplanting Anna and Freud's personal voices, becomes omniscient so that the meaning of the white hotel in Lisa's life can be universalized.

The second triangle of the novel proceeds to revise the reader's memory of the first triangle. In effect, we have sane Lisa rereading and revising the first half of the novel which is partially written by and partially in response to the writings of crazy Lisa. As a mirror to Chapter three, the feminine perspective that dominates Chapter four rivals the authority of the father offered by Freud's theories. Lisa's letter to Freud reveals her source for Don Giovanni, revises her story of Alexei, reports the incident with the sailors, and reveals her husband's anti-Semitism. We learn that her sexual escapades had been more extensive than she had admitted, and this fact and her interpretation of the girlish incident with her Japanese chambermaid counter Freud's homosexual interpretation. In response, Freud again offers a quotation that contradicts his methodology, this time from Heraclites, "The soul of man is a far country, which cannot be approached or explored" (195–96). However, Lisa's approach has paralleled Freud's, the past is dredged up and the resolution is again historical.

The white hotel becomes the health resort, and the chapter concludes with a sense of peace and resolution. Lisa marries Victor and becomes surrogate mother to Kolya. The trauma instilled by her previous experiences on boats seems rectified by the domestic haven she enters on her honeymoon voyage with Victor. Inspired by the scent of a pine tree, Lisa enters a joyful epiphany in which she envisions her own perpetuity within the continuum of time (213–14). Feminine peace derives from nature, not in the timeless sense of the white hotel, but as part of time. Lisa's embracing of repetition revises Freud's view that it is a demon to be quelled. She couples male deduction with a female telluric connection to put the pieces of her life and, consequently, of the narrative memory together. Like Chapter three and like each of the subsequent two chapters, Chapter four offers a sense of closure which, like all authority, is rendered ephemeral by the thematic and narrative design of *The White Hotel*. Even in this chapter, which culminates in emotional health and intellectual resolution, the death instinct haunts in Lisa's obsession with Peter Kürten who, like the Wolf Man, incarnates the universal coupling of savage and human and, like Lisa's epiphany, is replicated backward and forward across the continuum of time.

In "The Sleeping Carriage" chapter, the positive resolution of "The Health Resort" is revised. Paradise in this context is only rumor, an illusory reading of signs. Sex and death are once again joined as the unconscious images of Chapter two are realized in catastrophic history. The attention to community suggested in Chapter two is extended to the rich human complex grotesquely massacred and buried at Babi Yar—a quarter of a million white hotels. The lack of selfishness that characterizes Anna's phantasm becomes an ethical choice, a proclamation of identity and concern in the midst of savage indifference. Again we observe the attempts of history to devour the romantic richness and complexity of the individual. The dam built over the ravine bursts as if the victims of the annihilation refuse to have their victimization repressed. Although no memorial was erected at the ravine (instead a road, a television center, and an apartment building were constructed), the novel presents a revisionist history from the inside, a commemoration of the white hotel of Lisa and of all those murdered at Babi Yar.

Lisa's mystical prescience, confirmed by the events of the chapter, is endorsed by Thomas as a viable epistemology. Tellurically centered, it presents a humanistic alternative to the material reality of linear history and to the over-reliance on rational design. The epigraph of *The White Hotel*, from Yeats's "Meditations in Time of Civil War," reads:

> We had fed the heart on fantasies,
> The heart's grown brutal from the fare;
> More substance in our enmities
> Than in our love . . .

Lisa's ethical choice, redeemed in her dream of Dina Pronicheva, counters the brutality of the heart that pervades the chapter. Following the direction espoused by the Heraclites quote, the last sentence of "The Sleeping Carriage" prepares us to transcend the enmity of history and the limitation of rational interpretation: "But all this had nothing to do with the guest, the soul, the lovesick bride, the daughter of Jerusalem" (253).

The title of the final chapter, "The Camp," plays on the historical concentration camp. However, the timeless realm of the first chapter is presented in this, its mirror. In opposition to the conclusion of the first triangle, this conclusion is aesthetically inclusive rather than rationally exclusive. Generally, things are benign. Memory is sweet, peace and congeniality pervade, the camp is non-denominational despite the implication that this is the destination the Jews at Babi Yar had hoped for. The camp is not by the Dead Sea, but is fed by the Jordan River; its water is always pure and fresh. Lisa makes contact with her father and exchanges nurturing breastfeeding with her mother. Her mother offers the final piece of the puzzle regarding the love triangle that Lisa witnessed as a young girl—that Magda was homosexual. Even Peter Kürten appears playing with children. Contrary to the interpretive direction with which the first triangle concludes, Lisa tells her mother, "it's the future that counts, not the past" (271).

Although violence and destruction have apparently ceased in this rejuvenated, albeit post-lapsarian, world, the effects of Thanatos are not repressed.[10] People are still scarred and maimed, Freud's cancerous jaw continues to hurt him, and, despite Kürten's playing with children, armed guards accompany him. During her conversation with her mother, Lisa's statement, "wherever there is love, of any kind, there is hope of salvation" (271), is interrupted by her mental image of a bayonet flashing over spread thighs. She corrects herself with "wherever there is love in the heart." Implicitly we are returned to the epigraph from Yeats which explains the manner in which Chapter six revises its mirror Chapter one. Instead of Eden before the Fall, we have Eden after the Fall—more purgatory than paradise. Rather than feeding the heart on fantasies which include tragedy but repress response, the love that proceeds from the heart contains a healing impulse that both acknowledges and reacts against Thanatos. The indiscriminate breastfeeding that occurs in the first chapter is here put into context. Lisa's ethical choice in the preceding chapter is extended to the final image that we have of her in the novel as she hurries to join a group of nurses who are attending to the wounded. The telluric significance of her name, Erdmann ("Erd" is German for "earth"), and of her pseudonym, Anna G. ("G" pronounced in German becomes one of the names of the Greek earth mother, Ge),[11] are realized in Lisa's nurturing. As she goes to perform this function, she realizes that her pelvis and breast have ceased to hurt. Smelling the scent of a pine tree, her epiphany of human and temporal connection from "The Health Resort" returns. Without a system of clarity, *anagnorisis,* she is incapable of placing her memory of the scent, but her heart is not obscured. The pine scent "troubled her in some mysterious way, yet also made her happy" (274).

III

As soon as writing, which entails making a liquid flow out of a tube onto a piece of white paper, assumes the significance of copulation, or as soon as walking becomes a symbolic substitute for treading upon the body of mother earth, both writing and walking are stopped because they rep-resent the performance of a forbidden sexual act.—Freud, "Inhibitions, Symptoms and Anxiety"

In his review of *A Secret Symmetry: Sabina Spielrein between Jung and Freud* in the *New York Review of Books,* Thomas again turns his attention to a triangular relationship.[12] Sabina Spielrein was a patient of Jung's with whom he had sex. Jung excused his breach of professional ethics on the basis that Spielrein had never paid him and was therefore technically not his patient. Spielrein went on to gain a degree in medicine and formed an intellectual alliance with Freud. Thomas writes that "Freud attempted to draw Spielrein into their shared Jewishness, against the blond Aryan" Jung. Apart from the biographical interest that this book generates, Thomas re-veals that Spielrein's essay on the balance of creative and destructive forces in passion, published in 1912, was the germ of Freud's theory of the death wish, published as *Beyond the Pleasure Principle* in 1920. As already has been mentioned, Freud's fictional treatment of Anna G. occurs while he is composing this treatise. As a discourse haunted by images of catastrophe and as a movement from the authority of the empirical to that of the meta-psychological, Freud's vision in *Beyond the Pleasure Principle* dovetails with that of *The White Hotel.*

Harold Bloom's discussion of Freud in *Agon: Towards a Theory of Revisionism* is helpful for applying Freud's psychological theories to the function of language. Bloom argues that in *Beyond the Pleasure Principle* Freud equates literal meaning to Thanatos and figurative meaning to Eros.[13] Since the relationship between figurative and literal meaning in language is always a crossing over, Eros and Thanatos take the shape of a chiasmus. In his book on Freud, Paul Ricoeur stresses that Thanatos as a drive is allied to compulsions to repeat.[14] As a consequence of chiasmus, repression be-comes a fantasy of Eros to mask the repetitive urge within the procreative.

The White Hotel counters the repetitive urge with a proleptic one, linking it to Eros. The dispassionate narrative voice of Chapters one and two represses the horror of the future. However, the fantasies of proliferating sexual love ultimately are solipsistic and self-referential—taking on the repetitive dimension of Thanatos. It is only through desire of or union with another that Eros can emerge unencumbered to fight against the death instinct. *The White Hotel* presents Lisa's decision to accompany Kolya and her nurturing role in "The Camp" to counter Thanatos. The repressed narrative voice of the poem and journal is now imbued with ethical direction. Eros is restored as love from the heart and joins with reason to heal the effects of Thanatos.

After the historical documents of Anna's poem and journal and Freud's case history, the events at Babi Yar become another context of historical discourse, another form of closure. An Oedipal conflict of sorts is enacted within the narrative structure as the umbrella of male, rational authority concludes the first triangle of the novel, negating female telluric and prescient powers and foreshadowing the violation of generativity in Chapter five. This is modified by the female interpretation that begins the second triangle before the historical dimension of Chapter five universalizes the private history of Lisa, again undercutting Freud's individual, patriarchal interpretation. In giving us "The Camp" as future, Thomas asks the reader to reject the father and to embrace the female perspective at the conclusion. In doing so, he offers an aesthetic defense against his own created image, a restoration of metaphor to combat the demon of repetition that is the death instinct of history and of language.

However, this concluding female perspective is a mythic one, part of the landscape of hysteria the author's note calls "the 'terrain' of this novel" which is shaped by a male discourse. In his *History of Sexuality*, Foucault has demonstrated the hysterization of woman, how the female body has been perceived as womb in moral, emotional, and medical senses. *The White Hotel* adopts this perspective in the aesthetic vision with which it concludes; however, the narrative proleptically and reflexively comments on this conclusion. Like the appropriation of Sabina Spielrein by Jung and Freud, Thomas assigns Lisa her vision and uses it to advance his own design.[15] We see this prefigured when she writes her poem between the staves of a score of *Don Giovanni*, thereby containing her text within a text that expresses the molding of the feminine form through masculine will. The prevailing corset imagery in the poem and journal extends the idea of imposition on the female form. We also witness Lisa's desire to please Freud, like a little girl posing for her father. She writes for him in a "child's exercise book" (11), gives him gifts, and, with his encouragement, reads his previous cases (120).[16] No doubt the latter instance colors her own reports to Freud, another example of his control over her discourse. The mythic capacity for nurturing assigned to the feminine in *The White Hotel* also involves a vision of woman as fillable vessel, as pliant and sympathetic space awaiting a male presence around which to conform. In her poem, Anna/Lisa describes herself "with a great gape of wanting" (18).

Like a palimpsest, the narrative writes over itself. The reader's engagement with the narrative is no less a process of rereadings. We wander in search of meaning, sometimes finding it compressed and then discover it to be dislocated. Driven by the death drive of repetition, we are also driven by our anxiety over the outcome of that drive. Thus, like the narrative, we repeat and defer repetition, discover meaning and then dislocate it, return to become exiles.

Again Bloom is helpful in his linking of the sublime to *Beyond the Pleasure Principle*. He labels Freud a poet of the sublime, a thinker more inspired by imaginative literature than science, who, in *Beyond the Pleasure Principle*, "abandoned the empirical for the daemonic."[17] In doing so, Bloom draws on the Burkean notion of the sublime which shifted the definition from loftiness of vision to terror allied with pleasure.[18] In Part II, Section I of *A Philosophical Inquiry into the Origin of our Ideas of the Sublime and the Beautiful* (1757), Burke asserts,

> the passion caused by the great and sublime in nature, when those causes operate most powerfully, is Astonishment; and astonishment is that state of the soul, in which all its motions are suspended, with some degree of horror. In this case the mind is so entirely filled with its object, that it cannot entertain any other . . . Hence arises the great power of the sublime, that far from being produced by them, it *anticipates* [italics mine] our reasonings, and hurries us on by an irresistible force.[19]

Bloom discusses Vico's argument that the sublime poet discovers his rhetorical drive in divination, the process of foretelling the dangers to the Self's survival, and equates this drive to what Freud terms the primal instinct of Eros.[20] *The White Hotel* operates as a sublime text through its combination of terror and pleasure that both contributes to and is realized in its proleptic vision. As a sublime text, it defends itself against its own created image by continuously revising that creation.[21] In terms of psychoanalytic and linguistic congruence, it undergoes a process of unnaming akin to Freud's *Verneinung*, or what Lacan has called *méconnaissance* or

Bloom misprision—a psychic disavowal. Through repetition, the reader notices patterns of images that signal a center from which the reading must proceed simultaneously backward and forward, a collapsing of time and hierarchies which makes the text both horizontal and vertical. However, the shifting context in which these images are presented renders our interpretive centers no more than a stroking of the crucifix, another imposed and self-imposed duplicity.

Ricoeur equates repression with metaphor and, paralleling Bloom, puts repression in the realm of Eros.[22] The proleptic vision that lurks through the repressions of the first four chapters of *The White Hotel* is realized in the Babi Yar chapter which offers *anagnorisis*. The death force of history eradicates all metaphoric readings of signs and annihilates figurative complexity with its monomania. To end the novel at this point would be an implicit endorsement of this nihilistic vision and a negation of the narrative multidimensionality that Thomas has built. In Chapter six, Thomas acknowledges Thanatos but restores metaphoric repression to the text so that Eros may again prosper. Through the scent of a pine tree, fictional depth is reinstated in the imaginative life of the text. This does not negate, however, the possibility that the repressed may return.

In his "Note upon the Mystic Writing Pad" (1924), Freud uses a common dime store toy, often referred to as a "Magic Slate," as a metaphor for how the unconscious works. Impressions strike the conscious mind like the writing implement on the slate, but their manifestations are eventually removed like the lifting of the plastic sheet on which the impressions register. However, the waxen slate that is underneath the plastic sheet functions like the unconscious in retaining all the marks elicited by the pressures of the writing implement.[23] *The White Hotel* functions in a similar fashion. Each chapter is so revisionary that it superficially wipes the slate clean; however, the imprints registered by all the narrative details remain in the reader's mind, sometimes superimposed on one another. The chiasmic triangles of the narrative structure constantly comment on each other as our backward and forward reading invites repetitive transformation, a combination of Eros and Thanatos. Psychical duplicity becomes the duplicity of fiction which is paradoxically liberating through its repressions in its sublime merger of terror and pleasure.

7 Exiling the Feminine: Engaging Abjection

I

She writes in white ink.—Cixous, "The Laugh of the Medusa"

I n posing readers of narratives as exiles, this study has been concerned with the psychodynamics of their entrapment and their wish to return to a preexilic state which persists in the convolutions of memory. It also has investigated how some narratives, particularly postmodern ones, advertise the problematic nature of this return. They encourage their readers' desire, but simultaneously estrange them from their sense of this preexilic "home" by demonstrating the products of memory to be fictitious. In these contexts, narrative engagement consists of a dialectical relationship between desire and loss. Driven to seek escape from their exilic status, readers approach home only to discover its illusory nature, and find themselves cast once again as exiles yearning to elude that role.

By characterizing and authorizing readers, we punch large holes in the safety net of Aristotelian form and turn our attention to a poetics of transgression. By often problematizing memory and consequently resisting closure, narrative engagement may frustrate what initially motivated that engagement. It therefore undermines expectation and denies readers the pleasure of relieving the tension generated by their quest. Despite this denial, however, readers find themselves attracted to the transgressive by paradoxical impulses on both cognitive and emotional levels. The attraction to anomaly is an urge to discover and to make sense of what fails to fit, and therefore threatens, the established order of things. However, this attraction is no less stimulated by the pleasure of possession, by the expectation of assimilating something exterior and making it part of oneself. The transgressive also violates boundaries and shatters social strictures, possibilities that appeal to the Dionysian Self imprisoned within the Symbolic Order. Ruptures of this order permit readers a glimpse of the pre-Symbolic Imaginary to which they yearn to return, a glimpse which can only be interpreted within the parameters of the Symbolic Order that has subsumed it. Readers as exiles naturally gravitate toward the transgressive in an attempt to terminate their exilic status, only to find that status, like transgression itself, interminable.

I wish to manufacture a conclusion to this study which forces me to transgress some of my own Symbolic boundaries in order to engage issues addressed by feminist critics. These issues include an intense awareness of the exile of the feminine from the controlling phallogocentric domain except as identities constructed by and for that domain. The semiotic assessments that expose and attack these constructions poignantly express an awareness that even such exposures and attacks are typically practiced within the limitations of a discourse perpetrated by male-dominated interpretive communities. In advocating a "gynocriticism," for example, Elaine Showalter examines the hierarchical tiering of criticism and its associated gender polarity—a "hermeneutics and hismeneutics," and argues that feminist criticism should no longer be the Annie Hall of English studies, adorning itself in men's ill-fitting hand-me-downs.[1]

After addressing the canon of American literature in *Sensational Designs* and suggesting an "Other American Renaissance" which includes Susan Warner and Harriet Beecher Stowe, Jane Tompkins attempts to remove the straitjacket of accepted academic discourse in an essay entitled "Me and My Shadow."[2] Responding to the barring of emotion from epistemological inquiry, Tompkins ponders the exclusion of women, the bearers of emotion in Western culture, from such inquiry. Her essay resurrects her emotional shadow self from the obscurity to which the controlling rational discourse had condemned it, and asserts it as a viable interpreter of the world of ideas. But it is the commentators who approach the exile of the feminine from a psychoanalytic perspective, while self-consciously interrogating the duplicitous snares of that perspective, that accord more directly with the concerns of my study.

By choosing an iconoclast like Joyce as the subject of her first book, Hélène Cixous demonstrated her interest in writers and writing that speak of and with a feminine voice.[3] Joyce's testing of the rational limits of language and, more specifically, the dazzling stylistic innovation through which he attempts to mimic a woman's—and, by extension, Woman's—

mind in the "Penelope" episode of *Ulysses* provided appropriate spring-boards for Cixous's own projects. In "The Laugh of the Medusa," she explores the manner in which the history of writing has been complicitous with a phallogocentric history of reason.[4] Her essay is a call to action for woman's writing so that she may "forge for herself the anti-logos weapon." Cixous proclaims that women must write through the body, the very body that men have repressed by considering it a "dark continent to penetrate and to pacify." Such language "does not contain, it carries":

> Though masculine sexuality gravitates around the penis, engendering that centralized body (in political anatomy) under the dictatorship of its parts, woman does not bring about the same regionalization which serves the couple head/genitals, and which is inscribed only within boundaries. . . . Her writing can only keep going, without ever inscribing or discerning contours . . .[5]

Cixous appropriates Derridean *différance* to defy the hierarchical binaryism of patriarchal thought and to proclaim an open-ended discourse that is as lyrical as it is anti-essentialist. In "The Laugh of the Medusa" and other works, she writes in a voice which she urges her readers to discover within themselves. It is the long-buried but primal and nurturing voice of the mother and the mother's body:

> The Voice sings from a time before law, before the Symbolic took one's breath away and reappropriated it into language under its authority of separation. The deepest, the oldest, the loveliest Visitation. Within each woman the first, nameless love is singing.[6]

It is from the plenitude of the Imaginary that this voice wells up. For Cixous, returning to this utopian realm of *jouissance* precludes exile into the drama of desire and loss, Eros and Thanatos.

For all of the poetic seduction of Cixous's vision, however, she can be accused of practicing her own version of foreclosure by ignoring the inevitable persistence of the Symbolic once one has been tainted by it. Toril Moi invokes Herbert Marcuse's critique of Norman O. Brown's utopianism to address what she sees as this limitation in Cixous's thought:

> The roots of repression are and remain real roots; consequently, their eradication remains a real and rational job. What is to be abolished is not the reality principle; not everything, but such particular things as business, politics, exploitation, poverty. Short of this recapture of reality and reason Brown's purpose is defeated.[7]

Moi questions Cixous's insistence on the archetypal dimension of the feminine to the neglect of the social, and worries that a retreat into the Imaginary would permit males to continue to claim reason and rationality as their exclusive territory.

Cixous's positive vision of writing as liberation assumes the capacity to recapture an originary memory and, in doing so, to expunge memories of what has intervened between that originary experience and its resurrection. Her libidinal writing excites, and her call for self-discovery through such writing is exciting because it ruptures the prevailing empirical discourse and permits glimpses of a comforting homeland that predates the fall into difference. However, Cixous indulges in a mysticism that fails to recognize these glimpses as temporary approximations rather than a permanent residence in the promised land of *jouissance*. By foreclosing the exilic experience, Cixous promulgates an impossible forgetting, one that Moi suggests concedes power to the oppressors.

The theoretical models and methodology of Lacan and Derrida also figure prominently in the work of Luce Irigaray, but intentionally she seldom acknowledges their presence. Irigaray's doctoral thesis, *Speculum of the Other Woman*, led to her expulsion from Lacan's *Ecole freudienne* at Vincennes, so the oppressive force of the master discourse is a concrete as well as a figural topic for her. Her work may be seen as a self-conscious dramatization of the process of renaming through the divestment of the "Name of the Father," a process that is also its subject of investigation. For Irigaray, female sexuality is the "hole" in psychoanalytic theory and in the Western theoretical discourse that is its antecedent and legacy. Following in the footsteps of another investigator of holes, Alice, who becomes one of her protagonist/subjects in *This Sex Which Is Not One*, she enters the wonderland of female sexuality equipped with a specular looking glass that inverts unitary and teleological representations.

The first third of *Speculum of the Other Woman* takes caustic aim at Freud's statements about sexual difference, particularly his lecture on femininity in *New Introductory Lectures on Psychoanalysis*. For Freud, sexual difference is based on the fact that the male has an obvious sexual organ and the female does not. The female is therefore perceived from a male perspective as deficient, constituting an absence that the male fears.[8] Freud's theories of penis envy and castration anxiety follow from these assumptions. Irigaray challenges the father's authority, persistently demonstrating the female's position as "sexual proletarian" who functions as man's Other, his negative or mirror self. As she puts it in the title of one section in *Specu-*

lum, for Freud "The Little Girl Is (Only) a Little Boy," or, more pointedly, "an inferior little man." The little girl perceives her clitoris as an inferior penis, a perception which, Irigaray contends, Freud attributes as a remedy for castration anxiety:

> If *she* envies it, then *he* must have it. If *she* envies what *he* has, then it must be valuable. The only thing valuable enough to be envied? The very standard of all value. Woman's fetishization of the male organ must indeed be an indispensable support of its price on the sexual market.[9]

In addition to taking on Freud, Irigaray implicitly rejects another father, Lacan, who lingers as an absent presence throughout her work. The theme of Lacan's public seminar in 1972–73 was Freud's question *Was will das Weib* (What does Woman want?). Although he concludes "there is a pleasure [*jouissance*] beyond the phallus," he goes on to assert that women are unable to clarify this pleasure and states, "Women don't know what they are saying, that's the whole difference between them and me." [10] In assessing Irigaray's relationship to Lacan, Carolyn Burke writes,

> Lacan is like the *paterfamilias* of the psychoanalytic family who refuses to acknowledge the independent wisdom of his daughters. The daughter, in turn, seeks a way out of her overdetermined transference to this rejecting father-lover by turning upon the terms of her allegiance.[11]

Irigaray responds to the paternal authorities of psychoanalysis by exposing their debasement of the female subject. By depicting the female as a lesser male, psychoanalytic law situates her outside of representation, repressed within the confines of a male Other. Furthermore, this cultural definition creates for women a superego that "despises the female sex" and instills guilt and self-hatred:

> Mutilated, wounded, humiliated, overwhelmed by a feeling of inferiority that can never be "cured." In sum, women are definitively castrated.[12]

Irigaray combats phallogocentric discourse by mimicking it, a deconstructive maneuver designed to unravel its seeming coherence and to expose its repressive tactics. Moi characterizes this strategy:

Hers is a theatrical staging of the mime: miming the miming imposed on woman, Irigaray's subtle specular move (her mimicry *mirrors* that of all women) intends to *undo* the effects of phallocentric discourse simply by *overdoing* them.[13]

By turning her specular looking glass on the essentialism promulgated by patriarchal rationalism, Irigaray analogizes it to the phallus, viewing it as a monolithic form with which women are unwillingly penetrated.

Like Cixous, Irigaray calls for expression of a feminine language. In "The 'Mechanics' of Fluids," an indirect indictment of Lacan's denigration of the female subject, she equates fluids with female expression while using solids to describe the inflexible categories of male rationality, including psychoanalytic discourse as practiced by Freud and Lacan.[14] Irigaray links the language she proposes and in which she writes to the fluid currents of the body. It is a language which attempts to disentangle the subject from the dictates of binaryism and telos.[15]

In "When Our Lips Speak Together," she continues her summons to speak from the body and addresses her comments directly to her readers, inviting them to participate in the spaces she leaves in the text. Burke points out that this complicity between reader and writer is "not unlike that which may occur in the analytic situation, between a nonsubordinate analysand and a nonauthoritarian analyst."[16] The title essay of her collection *This Sex Which Is Not One* invokes a contrast between the plurality of the female sex organs with the unitary phallus:

> Woman "touches herself" all the time, and moreover no one can forbid her to do so, for her genitals are formed of two lips in continuous contact. Thus, within herself, she is already two—but not divisible into one(s)—that caress each other.[17]

The dialogue of "When Our Lips Speak Together" continues to return the focus of language and thought from the disruptive insertion of the phallic to the autoerotic *jouissance* to be rediscovered within oneself:

> Erection is no business of ours: we are at home on the flatlands. . . . Stretching out, never ceasing to unfold ourselves, we have so many voices to invent in order to express all of us everywhere, even in our gaps, that all the time there is will not be enough. . . . If you want to speak "well," you pull yourself in, you become narrower as you rise.[18]

Critics of Irigaray have suggested that the model of the female she asserts is composed of the very essentialism she has targeted. Monique Plaza writes, "To found a field of study on this belief in the inevitability of natural sex differences can only compound patriarchal logic and not subvert it."[19] Moi faults her ahistoricism, and claims that Irigaray's analysis of woman invokes the very idealist and metaphysical classifying techniques employed by the phallogocentric tradition she criticizes.[20] Burke, however, proposes that such criticisms are reductive in their disregard of the manner in which Irigaray's arguments are expressed. She argues that they ignore Irigaray's proposal that feminine writing does not simply flow *from* the body but emerges in analogy *with* it. In other words, her vaginal fable does not merely substitute for the phallic one, but suggests a pluralistic posture that is more expansive.[21]

Irigaray's figurative and fluid style, like Cixous's, resists the logical drive of "acceptable" reasoned exposition. This resistance, coupled with an overt recognition and welcoming of readers as participants in the dialogue of the text, redirects the text's appeal from the purely cognitive to the emotional as well. In doing so, Irigaray embraces the inner Self which has been exiled as Other. Whether or not the return she attempts is conceived as an essentialist ideal, and therefore participates in illusory hierarchizing, is a matter of debate. Despite her iconoclastic style, certainly the Symbolic lurks within the words and the arrangements of the words Irigaray chooses. And surely it asserts itself in the margins and in the blank spaces between lines where a substantial portion of the engagement between reader and narrative transpires. Although Irigaray teaches her readers to rejoice in and through the feminine, their exultation occurs by practicing a semblance of return while remaining exiled.

By broadly locating the feminine in that which is marginalized by the patriarchal Symbolic Order, Julia Kristeva manages to steer her definition away from an essentialist debate and toward questions of positionality. Rather than a consistent and readily identifiable presence, the feminine is situated amorphously on the other side of permeable barriers located at the edges of the Symbolic Order. It is in these permeable barriers, which Lacan and Kristeva term rims, that the continuous interplay between the Lacanian Imaginary and Symbolic, which becomes the Kristevan Semiotic and Symbolic, occurs. According to Kristeva, the Semiotic continually releases disruptive pulsions into the Symbolic which must be in turn rejected so the stable identity imposed by the Symbolic can be maintained. This process of expulsion, a process inseparable from the provisional sense of identity it acknowledges, Kristeva terms abjection.

Kristeva finds signs of abjection in disgust and horror as reactions to the inability to transcend the base associations of the corporeal. She presents three broad categories—food, waste, and signs of sexual difference—that signal bodily functions which impinge on Symbolic identity but which cannot be negated by it. The corpse, for example, is the most horrifying and cognitively disruptive indication of the body as waste:

> If dung signifies the other side of the border, the place where I am not and which permits me to be, the corpse, the most sickening of wastes, is a border that has encroached upon everything. It is no longer I who expel, "I" is expelled. The border has become an object.[22]

Awareness of the corpse confirms the fragility of identity, a disturbance of borders that threatens Symbolic integrity with a return to the emptiness which preceded it and which is its destiny. As Kristeva states, "the death that 'I' am provokes horror."[23]

Abjection is therefore neither subject nor object, but persists in the interface between these and other binary oppositions with which the Symbolic codes subjectivity and sociality. It manifests itself in ambiguous and transgressive states, and in representations that signify the perpetual threat to the sense of Self against which the subject consistently responds.

Kristeva claims that certain social and religious rituals function to displace abjection and, in her commentary on Kristeva, Elizabeth Gross points out that such a claim is similar to Freud's argument in *Totem and Taboo* and *Civilization and Its Discontents*.[24] Freud asserts that civilization is founded on taboos assigned to eradicate the threat of polymorphous pleasures and incestuous relationships. However, Kristeva departs from Freud's position by contending that the threats to identity are expelled rather than deleted. They remain as unsettling reminders just outside the delicate sense of unity constructed by the Symbolic. Thus, abjection can be located in the ongoing dialectical process between the illusion of Self and the subject's attempt to expel from itself what threatens this illusion.

As with her concepts the *semiotic* and the *chora*, Kristeva places the abject on the side of the feminine. Contrary to the rational distinctions formed by language and naming, it focuses attention on thresholds. It resists these distinctions by inscribing itself in sites of the body, particularly those bodily holes which confuse the boundary between inside and outside and therefore between Self and Other. At these sites, what is inside the body is expelled to the outside and what is outside can be taken in. These orifices for elimination also constitute erogenous zones and thereby function as the scenes of generation and negation, attraction and repulsion, Eros and Thanatos. The process of abjection therefore follows the psychoanalytic design by tying identity formation to experiences of and through the body and to repressions of those experiences. It describes a dialogue between desire and loss that resonates most intensely in the ambiguous and transgressive. Abjection appears where boundaries are traversed and unity punctured so that the resultant breach threatens to widen and overtake the whole.

II

"He put his disease in me."—Dorothy Vallens, *in* BLUE VELVET

I began this chapter with a brief survey of analyses of the feminine as exile or abject within the phallogocentric tradition. I now wish to bring these discussions to bear on narratives—pornographic narratives—that deliberately fetishize the corporeal sites wherein Kristeva locates abjection. Pornography's fetishization of these sites functions to incorporate the abject as object while expelling it as subject. Pornography thereby effaces the abject's power so that it serves rather than disrupts the overriding masculine perspective. With the incorporation of the abject, the permeable boundary of identity solidifies and the dialogue of exile and return ceases. In pornography, the phallus proclaims meaning and its proclamation is monolithic and uncontested.[25] Rather than presenting an alternative that provokes internal dialogue, the feminine has been absented as a force with a will or desire of its own and thus is represented as a hole—a vagina, mouth, or anus—to be filled by the phallus.

In hard-core pornographic films, the hole that is the feminine serves solely as receptacle for the phallus. Because she is only an object, her pleasure is inconsequential, and she is ultimately refused the product of her attentions. The come shot, in pornographers' parlance the money shot, shows the penis ejaculating after it has withdrawn from the orifice it has occupied. The literal and figurative climax of the narrative centers on this representation of male pleasure. In *The Film Maker's Guide to Pornography*, we are pointedly told, "if you don't have the come shots, you don't have a porno picture."[26] Although the impossibility of graphically portraying this action from inside the woman's body necessitates that it be filmed externally, such shots also deny possession of anything male to the female. She receives the ejaculate *on* rather than *in* her body, often on her face so that the male in effect covers her identity with his own. In her valuable investigation of pornography, Linda Williams combines Marxist and Freudian perspectives on fetishizing to discuss the money shot. For her, the term itself combines money and sex to embody "the profound alienation of contemporary consumer society."[27] Both Marx and Freud consider fetishizing to be a form of self-delusion and self-evasion. By investing the fetish object with intrinsic value, fetishizers allow that object to substitute for the complexities of social or psychic relations in which they play a part. Marx views capitalism as a system that encourages the fetishization of commodities so that inanimate objects are invested with human value. By focusing attention on the products of their work rather than on their connections to other producers of commodities, capitalism alienates members of society from each other. Freud ties his discussion of fetishizing to castration anxiety, seeing the fetish as a substitute phallus developed in the unconscious of a male child who is unwilling to accept that his mother lacks a penis. Like Marx, Freud considers the fetishizer as an idolater who invests in an inanimate object, but, as Williams points out, the Freudian idolater converts the woman into an object even before he focuses his desire on the penis substitute he has conjured for her.[28]

In fetishizing the spending penis, pornographic films separate it from the female who has stimulated and satisfied the male's desire. His ejaculate acquires value, not as a sign of interpersonal pleasure or procreative power, but in and of itself. This fetishization also compensates for the lack experienced by the viewer concerning the female's orgasm. If her orgasm testifies to the male's power and to her having been fully conquered by it, the fact that it occurs invisibly becomes a source of doubt concerning his potency. The obsession with the male's orgasm substitutes for this doubt. It declares his power while obscuring the intersubjective nature of desire.

The reader's or viewer's engagement with these narratives is also fetishized. Pornographic narrative typically exists for and in sexual action performed in infinite variations by individuals who are infinitely substitutable. The Sadean prototype portrays bodies as if they are machine parts, and enumerates the possible ways they can fit together. In her essay, "The Pornographic Imagination," Susan Sontag remarks on pornography's usual deadpan tone and on the underreaction of the erotic agents given the situations in which they are placed.[29] Such mechanical reproduction, to invoke Walter Benjamin, enhances our sense of these erotic agents as objects without "auras," and thus leaves our sexual response to them unencumbered by the complications of identification.[30] By devaluing or eliminating context, pornography reverses the taboos on polymorphous perversity and concentrates our attention on the unending variations of genital manipulation. It abandons the subject as Self in order to depict self-abandonment.

By self-consciously employing pornographic conventions, narratives like Georges Bataille's *Story of the Eye*, Jean de Berg's *The Image*, and Pauline

Réage's *Story of O* function as meta-pornography and have earned the critical attention of Sontag and others. Whether their intention is parodic, philosophical, or both, these works explicitly and implicitly comment on the formulas they narrate. Of the three works mentioned above, the most obvious example of this is *Story of the Eye*, to which Bataille appends an autobiographical essay. The horrible experiences he recalls from his childhood serve as obvious sources for the erotic darkness he depicts in the story proper. For Bataille, engaging extreme experiences offers an understanding of the link between Eros and death, and such understanding becomes a source of creative energy, a triumph over suffering through suffering.[31]

The pseudonymous and anonymous Pauline Réage ironically begins her preface of de Berg's *The Image* by asking "Who is Jean de Berg?"[32] Like de Berg's, Réage's identity, especially her sexual identity, has been a source of controversy since the 1954 publication of *Story of O*. Whether a serious or a mock-serious confession, *Story of O* is a history of its protagonist's extinction as a subject. Her name refers to the obliteration of her personality as well as to the bodily openings through which she is defined by others.

As the narrative begins, O is described only by a catalog of her clothing, clothing which is replaced when she gets to the isolated château with costumes that permit the Roissy members uninhibited access to her sexual orifices. Control is extended to valets and servants over all her bodily activities, she is not permitted to speak but is only spoken to, and she must look only downward toward the Roissy men's exposed penises rather than toward their faces. In other words, she becomes signified utterly in terms of phallic power, her body defined entirely by terms imposed on her:

> Your hands are not your own, nor are your breasts, nor, most especially, any of your bodily orifices, which we may explore or penetrate at will. You will remember at all times—or as constantly as possible— that you have lost all right to privacy or concealment, and as a reminder of this fact, in our presence you will never close your lips completely, or cross your legs, or press your knees together . . . This will serve as a constant reminder, to you as well as to us, that your mouth, your belly, and your backside are open to us.[33]

Since phallic meaning is ascribed to O by viewing her as a collection of openings, much of the narrative focuses on these openings, especially on their remaking. O is written through the penetrations of and inscriptions on the surface of her body. Her anus is widened for easier penetration through the insertion of a series of phallic objects of increasing size. A double ring with a medallion is attached to her labia, and her buttocks are branded with the initials of the man to whom her lover, René, has given her, Sir Stephen (the initials "SS" have, of course, Nazi connotations). Throughout the narrative, she is whipped and her costumes arranged to display the resultant marks on her flesh as if they were a system of writing to be read by her tormenters.

Kaja Silverman points to one passage in particular in which O is depicted lying among photos of another woman which become stuck to her body so that O's image is reconstituted by the images to which she is attached.[34] Indeed, meaning is imprinted on O's body by the objects or other bodies that connect themselves to her. Her profession as a fashion photographer indicts her as a purveyor of the type of victimization to which she is now subjected. However, her stay at Roissy extracts from her the victimizer's authority. Although she returns to her profession, she takes primarily photographs of women in bondage, photographs René and Sir Stephen use to find new playthings for the men of Roissy. Their gaze directs her's.

At the conclusion, O becomes aware that Sir Stephen plans to abandon her and informs him she would prefer to die. He reacts by giving her his consent. Having been created, or re-created, by men during the course of the narrative, O becomes but an extension of their will. Deprived of purpose, she still requires permission not to be.

Like the men of Roissy inscribing phallic meaning on O's body, readers of *Story of O* enter the narrative and repeatedly redefine its openings. Like all pornography, it invites their fetishizing, their deepening of textual creases in which they temporarily dwell. In doing so, they take control of the narrative flow and signify meaning according to the demands of their pleasure, thereby etching their names within these openings. In effect, *Story of O* tells the story of this process. However, it also stages a teller who causes the narrative to somersault back on itself. *Story of O* is a kind of bildungsroman of the pornographic object in that it is narrated through the point of view of that object. Although the narrative is presented in the third person, we are limited exclusively to O's perspective. The irony of this narrative stance, giving O the authorial power to tell the story of her total submission, signals the duplicity of the text. The work, then, becomes the story of its readers' narrative bondage. It reflexively exposes them as pornographers, subjugated by their own frenzied need to instill monolithic meaning on the play of discourses they engage.

How we define pornography and how it affects us are, of course, much debated moral and legal questions. Justice Potter Stewart eschewed offering a precise definition of hard-core pornography, stating instead "I could never succeed in intelligently doing so. But I know it when I see it."[35] Ever attuned to questions of intersubjectivity, D. H. Lawrence asserts that pornography is what turns one's desire back on oneself instead of toward another. The effect is masturbation rather than intercourse.[36] The 1986 Meese Commission report on pornography offers this assessment: "pornography is the theory; rape is the practice."[37] One of the Commission's witnesses, Andrea Dworkin, extends this assessment more broadly to heterosexual intercourse as the basis for sexual violence. For Dworkin, the male role in intercourse is inevitably aggressive and dominating, and forces women to become colonized victims.[38] To explain the proliferation in the consumption of pornography, Alan Soble contends that it is a response to the feminist movement. According to Soble, pornographic fantasies of power are masculine attempts to compensate for a decreasing sense of economic and political power.[39]

Susan Griffin considers pornography to be culture's revenge against nature. By humiliating women's bodies, Griffin argues, men exert their cultural authority over nature and sever the connection between mind and body. This calculated sadism enables them to displace their own hysteria onto the bodies of their female victims. Rather than the liberating force pornographers proclaim it to be, pornography strengthens oppression by promoting sex while censoring sexual knowledge.[40]

Williams, however, makes a case for a shift in the genre to an increased awareness of changing gender relations. She discusses a range of recent pornographic films as well as the heightened depictions of sex in mass market romance novels to demonstrate attempts to address women's desires. Rather than dwelling exclusively on goal-driven masculine sexuality where the narrative moves inevitably toward the come shot, recent pornographic narratives often include a variety of sexual discourses which do not culminate only in the discharge of the penis. In doing so, Williams suggests, they help to break down hierarchies and undercut the hegemony of male sexual pleasure.[41] These depictions of undirected sexual action, of sex viewed more from the perspective of consumption than production, present alternatives to the dominant male gaze that Laura Mulvey associates with sadism or fetishistic scopophilia in cinematic narrative.[42]

Despite these alternatives, as Williams admits and as Foucault has amply shown, power is inevitable in desire because of desire's intersubjective foundation. To promote the illusion of independent power, the male gaze fetishizes in an attempt to erase the Other on which its power hinges. Mary Ann Doane and Williams argue that female spectators also require a sense of mastery. They therefore engage in no absolute merger with the object of identification, for to do so would repudiate the distance necessary for control. Doane states that the female viewer of narrative cinema is offered two options: "the masochism of over-identification or the narcissism in becoming one's own object of desire." Her response to these two untenable options is to adopt the "masquerade of femininity," not a purely passive perspective but an oscillating one. She recognizes the contractual nature of the scenario, that the victim asserts her will to pleasure by agreeing to play victim.[43] Indeed, Williams declares, masochism as absolute passivity is overstated. Instead, the female spectator shifts between male and female subject positions, "an oscillation within sadomasochism which is not identical to pure passivity."[44]

Considerations of oscillation and a plurality of discourses return us to Cixous's and Irigaray's expressions of a female language linked to the fluid currents of the body. For them, feminine discourse can autoerotically slip the grasp of cultural codes. By associating the feminine with the Semiotic rather than the Symbolic, Kristeva approaches the same appraisal but sees this evasion more in terms of challenge than escape. Like Lacan, she considers the Symbolic an inevitable dictator once one is exiled in its domain. However, the desire to return is never vanquished and presents a continual threat against which the identity conferred by the Symbolic must respond. This abjection is a process pornography sets out to conquer and which it in turn incites.

Pornography exiles the feminine as subject and recreates her as a collection of bodily openings to be filled, thereby replacing her perceived lack with phallic meaning. Because such a perception of identity is literally one-sided, movement is always into rather than out of these openings. Rather than thresholds of exchange, they are fetishized as appropriations of the phallic will. As inscribers of monolithic meaning, pornographic narratives work to rigidify the boundary between subject and object and to reconfigure or annihilate the abject which softens this rigidity. The violent tendencies toward women expressed in these narratives testify to the latter desire and to its recurrent frustration.

Although pornographic fantasies serve the Symbolic, they are also reactions to it. By displacing their own exilic anxieties onto others, readers recreate their repressions within these narratives, this time in the guise of repressors. The pleasure generated by the illusion of controlling this reenactment of their own primary experience is countered by the pain of once again participating in that experience. They relive their own fall from the Imaginary and consequently respond to this pain by seeking to obliterate the Other who now embodies it. The voyeur thus oscillates between sadistic and masochistic positions, a dialogue of exile and return which paradoxically engages abjection while seeking to eliminate it.

III

To what extent can truth endure incorporation? That is the question; that is the experiment.—Nietzsche, THE GAY SCIENCE

This book has attempted to show that the narrative of Self Kristeva describes developing from the encounter with the body also emerges through engaging the body of the text. The identity drama of desire and loss continually played out in association with corporeal sites of abjection is reenacted in the reading process of exile and return. The dynamics which define both paradigms are shifting contingencies. In both, yearning becomes resistance and resistance yearning at bodily spaces, or narrative folds, which feature abjection. In their quest for the totality of closure, both attempt to reach origins through endings and therefore recapitulate the death drive which they in turn strive to thwart. And in both, the expulsion of the Other which propels the narrative and enables self-definition through difference is mitigated by recognitions that the Other is actually part of the Self. In these transgressive junctures, the narrative of Self is unwritten so it may be written again.

I have focused on narratives designed to induce psychic dislocation in their readers and to expose their readers' attempts at intellectual order as quests for power and possession. These dislocations excite the transgressor within us while spurring the guardian of order, also within us, to expel what it mistakenly considers the intruder. The self-reflexiveness of these narratives, however, calls attention to these reactions and therefore functions to edify while disturbing us. The borders of identity are shaken so they might be extended and rendered more inclusive.

Like the psychoanalytic theories that inform this study, the paradigm of exile and return is premised on a belief that we fervently desire to reclaim our lost origins. This desire, its displacements, and the impossibility of recovering a clear sense of origin combine to animate our engagement with narratives. Narratives become living forms onto which we project the shifting frame of our personal dialogue of desire and loss. We engage and are engaged by them so that we might re-create ourselves through them, thus ending our exile with the desired return. However, repressions and displacements of this desire also contribute to narrative engagement. Their resistance to ending preserves the Self against its own undoing and attempts to secure the boundaries of identity against disruptive pulsions.

In our desire to escape our exilic status, we are drawn to these pulsions, which manifest themselves in the transgressive, the anomalous, in fissures within the narrative order. At these points, our need to protect our sense of identity conspires to expel these pulsions and to heal the ruptures they have produced in us. In the ongoing tug-of-war between these conflicting impulses, we discover and refute who we were, who we are, and who we want to be. We find ourselves as exiles forever seeking return.

Notes

Introduction

1　I am referring to the three essential orders Lacan constructs for the psychoanalytic field: the Imaginary, the Real, and the Symbolic. The Imaginary constitutes a narcissistic relation of the subject to its ego. It evolves out of the mirror stage in which the infant first perceives its bodily unity through encountering its reflection in a mirror, thus forming the outline of what is to become the ego. This order extends into adult relations through fantasies and images. The Symbolic contains language and therefore is the order through which the subject can represent desires and feelings. These representations, however, are culturally conditioned and therefore become expressions of oneself through the Other. The Real is the domain outside the subject, a persistent and intrusive realm, that exists outside symbolization. Malcolm Bowie writes, "each of Lacan's orders is better thought of as a shifting gravitational centre for his arguments than as a stable concept; at any moment each may be implicated in the redefinition of the others;" "Jacques Lacan," *Structuralism and Since*, ed. John Sturrock (N.Y.: Oxford University Press, 1979), 132–33.

2　Trauma for Freud is not brought through the original event in isolation but through repetition. An event becomes traumatic retrospectively when it is recalled by a later event in trauma. In *Project for a Scientific Psychology* (1895), Freud writes: "Here we have the case of a memory arousing an affect which it did not arouse as an experience, because in the meantime the changes [brought about] by puberty had made possible a different understanding of what was remembered . . . We invariably find that a memory is repressed which has only become a trauma by *deferred action* [*nachträglich*];" *The Standard Edition of the Complete Psychological Works of Sigmund Freud*, trans. and ed. James Strachey, 24 vols. (London: Hogarth Press, 1953–74), 1:356. Hereafter abbreviated as *SE*.

3　*Selected Letters of Friedrich Nietzsche*, trans. Christopher Middleton (Chicago: University of Chicago Press, 1969), 347. Letter of January 5, 1889.

4　Said writes,

　　. . . the contemporary critical consciousness stands between the temptations represented by two formidable and related powers engaging critical attention. One is the culture to which critics are bound filiatively (by birth, nationality, profession); the other is a method or system acquired affiliatively (by social and political conviction, economic and historical circumstances, voluntary effort and willed deliberation). This movement from filiation to affiliation "can be considered an instance of the passage from nature to culture;" *The World, the Text, and the Critic* (Cambridge: Harvard University Press, 1983), 24–25, 20. For intelligent analytical summaries of recent trends in applications of narratology to historiography, see David Simpson, "Literary Criticism and the Return to 'History,'" *Critical Inquiry* 14 (1988): 721–47 and John Kucich, "Narrative Theory as History: A Review of Problems in Victorian Fiction Studies," *Victorian Studies* 28 (1985): 657–75.

5   Certainly Harold Bloom's work on revisionism, particularly *Agon: Towards a Theory of Revisionism* (N.Y.: Oxford University Press, 1982), is a primary influence on this model.

6   Here I am interested chiefly in Barthes's essay "The Discourse of History," trans. Stephen Bann, *Comparative Criticism: A Yearbook*, vol. 3, ed. E.S. Schaffer (N.Y.: Cambridge University Press, 1981), and in Ricoeur's three-volume *Time and Narrative*, trans. Kathleen McLaughlin and David Pellauer (Chicago: University of Chicago Press, 1984–89). In *The Philosophy of History*, Hegel states,

> In our language the term History unites the objective with the subjective side, and denotes quite as much the *historia rerum gestarum*, as the *res gestae* themselves; on the other hand it comprehends not less what has happened than the narration of what has happened. This union of the two meanings we must regard as of a higher order than mere outward accident; we must suppose historical narrations to have appeared contemporaneously with historical deeds and events. It is an internal vital principle common to both that produces them synchronously. Family memorials, patriarchal traditions, have an interest confined to the family and the clan. The uniform course of events which such a condition implies is no subject of serious remembrance; though distinct transactions or turns of fortune may rouse Mnemosyne to form conceptions of them—in the same way as love and the religious emotions provoke imagination to give shape to a previously formless impulse. But it is only the state which first presents subject-matter that is not only adapted to the prose of History, but involves the production of such history in the very progress of its own being;

> *The Philosophy of History*, trans. J. Sibree, (N.Y.: Dover, 1956).

7   My concern with textual erotics, with the view that narrative engagement constitutes an act of desire, leans heavily on the work of Jacques Lacan, particularly on Lacan's applications of Freud to narrative, and on Freud himself. I am also heavily indebted to Peter Brooks's applications of psychoanalysis to narrative, *Reading for the Plot: Design and Intention in Narrative* (N.Y.: Knopf, 1984), and to Hayden White's tropological readings of historiography, *The Content of the Form: Narrative Discourse and Historical Representation* (Baltimore: Johns Hopkins University Press, 1987), *Tropics of Discourse: Essays in Cultural Criticism* (Baltimore: Johns Hopkins University Press, 1978), and *Metahistory: The Historical Imagination in Nineteenth-Century Europe* (Baltimore: Johns Hopkins University Press, 1973).

8   Gabriel García Márquez, *One Hundred Years of Solitude*, trans. Gregory Rabassa (N.Y.: Avon, 1971), 53–54.

9   "The Psychotherapy of Hysteria," *Studies in Hysteria* (1895), *SE* 2:303. For the development of the concept of transference in Freud's works see J. Laplanche and J.B. Pontalis, *The Language of Psycho-Analysis*, trans. Donald Nicholson-Smith (N.Y.: Nor-

ton, 1973), 455–62. For a discussion relating the historian's disavowal of transference to Freud's suppression of the seduction theory, see Dominick La Capra, "History and Psychoanalysis," *The Trials of Psychoanalysis*, ed. Françoise Meltzer (Chicago: University of Chicago Press, 1987), 9–38.

10   Donald P. Spence argues that the psychoanalytic process is not one of archaeological reconstruction, but is rather an interaction between patient and analyst to construct a narrative about the patient's past; *Narrative Truth and Historical Truth: Meaning and Interpretation in Psychoanalysis* (N.Y.: Norton, 1982).

11   In "Analysis and Truth or the Closure of the Unconscious," Lacan writes:
it is in the space of the Other that the subject sees himself, and the point from which he looks at himself is also in that space. Now this is also the point from which he speaks, since in so far as he speaks, it is in the locus of the Other that he begins to constitute that truthful lie by which is initiated that which participates in desire at the level of the unconscious;
Four Fundamental Concepts of Psychoanalysis, trans. Alan Sheridan (N.Y.: Norton, 1981), 144.

12   "Fragment of an Analysis of a Case of Hysteria" (1905), *SE* 7:1–122.

13   Peter Stallybrass and Allon White convincingly explore the grotesque as transgressive and apply it to the concept of carnival:
Social historians who have charted transformations of carnival as a social practice have not registered its displacements into bourgeois discourses like art and psychoanalysis: adopting a naively empirical view they have outlined a simple disappearance, the elimination of the carnivalesque. . . . Part of that process was the disowning of carnival and its symbolic resources, a gradual reconstruction of the idea of carnival as the culture of the Other. This act of disavowal on the part of the emergent bourgeoisie, with its sentimentalism and its disgust, made carnival into the festival of the Other. It encoded all that which the proper bourgeois must strive not to be in order to preserve a stable and correct sense of self;
The Politics and Poetics of Transgression (Ithaca: Cornell University Press, 1986), 178. See also Allon White, "Pigs and Pierrots: The Politics of Transgression in Modern Fiction," *Raritan* 2 (1982): 51–70.

14   In "The 'Uncanny'" (1919), Freud writes,
In the first place, if psycho-analytic theory is correct in maintaining that every affect belonging to an emotional impulse, whatever its kind, is transformed, if it is repressed, into anxiety, then among instances of frightening things there must be one class in which the frightening element can be shown to be something repressed which *recurs*. This class of frightening things would then constitute the uncanny; and it must be a matter of indifference whether what is uncanny was itself originally frightening or whether it had some *other* affect. In the second place, if this is indeed the secret nature of the uncanny, we can understand why linguistic usage has extended *das Heimliche* ['homely'] into its opposite, *das Unheimliche*; for this uncanny is in reality nothing new or alien, but something which is familiar and old-established in the mind and which has become alienated from it only through the process of repression;
SE 17:241.

15   Indeed, Linda Hutcheon refers to postmodern fiction as "historiographic metafiction," *A Poetics of Postmodernism* (London and New York: Routledge, 1988).

I Exiling history

1 Judith Mary Weightman, *Making Sense of the Jonestown Suicides: A Sociological History of the People's Temple, Studies in Religion and Society*, vol. 7 (N.Y.: Edwin Mellen Press, 1983); Steve Rose, *Jesus and Jim Jones* (N.Y.: Pilgrim Press, 1979).

2 Rebecca Moore, *A Sympathetic History of Jonestown, Studies in Religion and Society*, vol. 14 (Lewiston: Edwin Mellen Press, 1985).

3 James Reston, Jr., *Our Father Who Art in Hell* (N.Y.: Times Books, 1981), 57. Subsequent references are noted parenthetically.

4 Fredric Jameson, *The Political Unconscious: Narrative as Socially Symbolic Act* (Ithaca: Cornell University Press, 1981), 35.

5 *The Content of the Form*, 149.

6 *SE* 18:3–64. In his analysis of the death drive, Jean Laplanche considers three recurring elements: (1) the reflexive phase in which "Eros, the force that maintains narcissistic unity and uniqueness, can be deduced as a *return to a prior state* . . .;" (2) "the priority of zero over constancy," in which Laplanche cites Freud's "economic principle" in *Beyond the Pleasure Principle*, the tendency of the psychical apparatus "to maintain as low as possible the quantity of excitation present within it, or at least to maintain it at a constant level;" and (3) "the necessity of inscribing the two preceding priorities within the domain of the vital;" *Life and Death in Psychoanalysis*, trans. Jeffrey Mehlman (Baltimore: Johns Hopkins University Press, 1976), 115–17.

7 In a letter to me, dated October 24, 1989, Dorfman writes

> . . . I wrote *Mascara* first in Spanish, then rewrote it in English, and then, with that English version, rewrote the Spanish version again. I had it edited by my (North) American editor, and then, with her corrections and my rewriting parts to make some things clearer, I worked over the Spanish text (which was published by Sudamericana in Buenos Aires under the title *Mascaras*, though it should have been called *Mascara* in Spanish as well). In a sense, then it is my first English novel—and I was able to do this because the material seemed so alien to me, so *exiled* [my italics] from my contingent reality as a Chilean. It is a step further than *The Last Song of Manuel Sendero*, in the sense that rather than dealing with exile directly, it does in fact project my experience of distance and evil and "transgression" in a different way. So I seemed to control the text hardly at all—or was, at least, extremely surprised as it made its way into the world (word).

8 Ariel Dorfman, *Mascara* (N.Y.: Viking, 1988), 16, 42. Subsequent references are noted parenthetically.

9 In a December, 1986 interview, Dorfman states,

> I see exile as a terrible loss, the pain of being distanced from everything that gives you a meaning. There are two basic myths that come out of humanity's experience of that loss. One is the foundational myth. You break the past, you rupture the umbilical cord of the past to found a new society. . . . And the other myth of exile, the other form of redemption that exile offers, is the opportunity to go back, to return and with what you have learned outside, to renew your original society. One myth speaks of birth, the other of rebirth.

> Peggy Boyers and Juan Carlos Lertora, "Ideology, Exile, Language: An Interview with Ariel Dorfman," *Salmagundi* 82–83 (Spring–Summer 1989), 142–63.

10 See Freud, "The Dynamics of the Transference" (1912), *SE* 12:97–108, and "Remem-

bering, Repeating and Working Through" (1914), *SE* 12:145–56. See also Lacan, *The Four Fundamental Concepts of Psycho-Analysis*, 49–50. Peter Brooks has elucidated and applied these principles in *Reading for the Plot*, especially 113–42, in a manner that has profoundly influenced my argument.

11 I have found Paul Ricoeur's explanation of Freud's text extremely useful for my analysis; *Freud and Philosophy*, trans. Denis Savage (New Haven: Yale University Press, 1970), 243–54.

12 For example, Yosef Hayim Yerushalmi's recent *Freud's Moses: Judaism Terminable and Interminable* (New Haven: Yale University Press, 1991) quickly dismisses the credibility of Freud's thesis from a factual or scholarly standpoint. Yerushalmi cogently presents *Moses and Monotheism* as Freud's celebration of the Jews as agents of civilization, and of psychoanalysis as an extension of Jewish monotheism.

13 *SE* 23:99.

14 Ricoeur develops this line of thinking in *Time and Narrative*. See especially 1:77–80 and 2:100–01. See also White's brilliant analysis of Ricouer's theory of narrative in *The Content of the Form*, 169–84. Louis O. Mink claims that the concept of universal history is as old as Augustine's *City of God* and was introduced in modern thought in Vico's *Scienza nova*. According to Mink, "Universal History did not deny the diversity of human events, customs, and institutions; but did regard this variety as the permutations of a single and unchanging set of human capacities and possibilities, differentiated only by the effects of geography, climate, race, and other natural contingencies;" "Narrative Form as a Cognitive Instrument," *The Writing of History: Literary Form and Historical Understanding*, ed. Robert H. Canary and Henry Kozicki (Madison: University of Wisconsin Press, 1978), 138. Furthermore, Mink states that the claim to historical objectivity presupposes the idea of a universal history. Ricouer writes of Freud's contention in *Moses and Monotheism*, "For Freud, 'the universality of symbolism in language' is far more a proof of the memory traces of the great traumas of mankind than an incentive to explore other dimensions of language, the imaginary, and myth," *Freud and Philosophy*, 247.

2 Disrupting the look

1 E. H. Gombrich, *Art and Illusion: A Study in the Psychology of Pictorial Representation* (Oxford: Phaidon, 1959), 5.

2 Lessing, *Laocoön: An Essay upon the Limits of Poetry and Painting* (1766), trans. Ellen Frothingham (1873; N.Y.: Farrar, Straus, and Giroux, 1969), x.

3 Chatman writes, "We may spend half an hour in front of a Titian, but the aesthetic effect is as if we were taking in the whole painting at a glance. In narratives, on the other hand, the dual time orders function independently;" "What Novels Do That Films Can't (and Vice Versa)," *Critical Inquiry* 7.1 (Autumn 1980): 122. Wendy Steiner points to this passage and to the fact that Chatman's book on narrative, *Story and Discourse*, derives its title from the Russian formalist distinction between *fabula* and *sjuzet; Pictures of Romance: Form Against Context in Painting and Literature* (Chicago: University of Chicago, 1988), 14.

4 Roland Barthes, "The Rhetoric of the Image," in *Image—Music—Text*, trans. Stephen Heath (N.Y.: Noonday, 1977), 38–39.

5 Nelson Goodman, *Problems and Projects* (N.Y.: Bobbs-Merrill, 1972), 31–32.

6   Nelson Goodman, *Languages of Art: An Approach to a Theory of Symbols* (N.Y.: Bobbs-Merrill, 1968), 37. W. J. T. Mitchell points out that Goodman's equation of realism with the "standard" fails to consider the ideological values behind the standard: "Realism" cannot simply be equated with the familiar standard of depiction but must be understood as a special project within a tradition of representation, a project that has ideological ties with certain modes of literary, historical, and scientific representation. No amount of familiarity will make Cubism or Surrealism "look" (or, more importantly) *count as* realistic, because the values that underwrite these movements work at cross-purposes with those of realism; *Iconology: Image, Text, Ideology* (Chicago: University of Chicago Press, 1986), 73.

7   Mitchell, 164.

8   Steiner, 42.

9   In *The Stateman's Manual* (1816), Coleridge writes, Now an Allegory is but a translation of abstract notions into a picture-language which is itself nothing but an abstraction from objects of the senses; the principal being more worthless even than its phantom proxy, both alike unsubstantial, and the former shapeless to boot. On the other hand a Symbol is characterized by a translucence of the Special in the Individual or of the General in the Especial or of the Universal in the General. Above all by the translucence of the Eternal through and in the Temporal; *The Collected Works of Samuel Taylor Coleridge*, ed. R. J. White (Princeton: Princeton University Press, 1972), 6: 30. In "The Rhetoric of Temporality," Paul de Man inverts the hierarchy of symbol over allegory that Coleridge has established, and contends that time exists in allegory as a structural effect; *Blindness and Insight: Essays in the Rhetoric of Contemporary Criticism* (1971; Minneapolis: University of Minnesota, 1983), 187–228.

10 De Man, 207.

11 J. Hillis Miller writes of allegory dramatizing the "eternal disjunction between the inscribed sign and its material embodiment;" "The Two Allegories," *Allegory, Myth, and Symbol: Harvard English Studies 9*, ed. Morton Bloomfield (Cambridge: Harvard University Press, 1981), 365. Maureen Quilligan discusses the linguistic function of allegory, arguing for a figural imperative in *The Language of Allegory: Defining the Genre* (Ithaca: Cornell University Press, 1979), 27–33. I am indebted to Wai-chee Dimock's analysis of these and de Man's positions in her own investigation of the social function of allegory in the first chapter of *Empire for Liberty: Melville and the Poetics of Individualism* (Princeton: Princeton University Press, 1989), 3–41. Dimock terms allegory a narrative of spatialized time.

12 A prominent consideration of the autotelic nature of viewing as part of the complex issue of representation is Michel Foucault's analysis of Velázquez's *Las Meninas; The Order of Things: An Archaeology of the Human Sciences* (1966; N.Y.: Vintage, 1973), 3–16.

13 In the "The Work of Art in the Age of Mechanical Reproduction," Benjamin writes, The authenticity of a thing is the essence of all that is transmissible from its beginning, ranging from its substantive duration to its testimony to the history which it has experienced. . . . One might subsume the eliminated element in the term "aura" and go on to say: that which withers in the age of mechanical reproduction is the aura of the work of art. Benjamin goes on to contend that the most powerful agent for the shattering of tradition is film; *Illuminations*, ed. Hannah Arendt, trans. Harry Zohn (N.Y.: Schocken, 1968), 221.

14 Goodman, 248.

15 David Freedberg, *The Power of Images: Studies in the History and Theory of Response* (Chicago: University of Chicago Press, 1989). As a summary of what he advocates in a theory of response, Freedberg quotes Roland Barthes's *Camera Lucida: Reflections on Photography*, in which Barthes concludes that in order to see a photograph in all its fullness, he must combine two voices: "the voice of banality (to say what everyone sees and knows) and the voice of singularity (to replenish such banality with all the élan of an emotion which belonged only to myself);" trans. Richard Howard (N.Y.: Hill and Wang, 1981), 76. Quoted in Freedberg, 430.

16 Freedberg, 317–44. See also Wendy Lesser, *His Other Half: Men Looking at Women Through Art* (Cambridge: Harvard University Press, 1991). As Chapter seven will discuss, some feminist film critics, particularly Mary Ann Doane and Linda Williams, dispute this point of view.

17 Susanne Langer, *Problems of Art* (N.Y.: Scribner's, 1957), 86.

18 Max Ernst, *Une Semaine De Bonté: A Surrealistic Novel in Collage* (N.Y.: Dover, 1976).

19 John Russell, *Max Ernst: Life and Work* (N.Y.: Abrams, 1967), 20.

20 Friedrich Nietzsche, *The Gay Science*, trans. Walter Kaufmann (N.Y.: Vintage, 1974), 121–22. Russell points to this passage on p. 50.

21 Max Ernst, "Beyond Painting," *Max Ernst: Beyond Painting and Other Writings by the Artist and His Friends*, trans. Dorothea Tanning (N.Y.: Wittenborn, Schultz, 1948), 16–17.

22 Surrealist artists celebrated Violette Nozières, whose parricide constituted for them a renewal of libido within the stagnant bourgeoisie.

23 "Inspiration to Order," *Beyond Painting*, 22. Earlier in the essay, Ernst writes, "I am inclined to say that it amounts to the exploiting of *the fortuitous encounter upon a non-suitable plane of two mutually distant realities* (this being a paraphrase and generalization of the celebrated Lautréamont quotation, 'Beautiful as the chance meeting upon a dissecting table of a sewing-machine with an umbrella') . . . ;" 21.

24 Margot Norris, *Beasts of the Modern Imagination: Darwin, Nietzsche, Kafka, Ernst, and Lawrence* (Baltimore: Johns Hopkins, 1985), 134–69. Norris refutes the Surrealist genealogy established by Herbert Read and Hugh Sykes Davies in Herbert Read, ed., *Surrealism* (N.Y.: Praeger, 1971) and Anna Balakian, *Surrealism: The Road to the Absolute* (N.Y.: Dutton, 1970).

25 *Beasts of the Modern Imagination*, 137.

26 M. E. Warlick, "Max Ernst's Alchemical Novel: *"Une Semaine de bonté,"* *Art Journal* 46.1 (Spring 1987): 61–73.

27 Evan M. Maurer, "Images of Dream and Desire: The Prints and Collage Novels of Max Ernst," *Max Ernst: Beyond Surrealism*, ed. Robert Rainwater (N.Y.: New York Public Library and Oxford University Press, 1986), 80.

28 Maurer refers to another collage Ernst made in 1934 that prophesies the fate of the Jews during the Nazi holocaust. In the untitled collage, a bird-headed man wearing a large six-pointed star of David puts the bound body of a screaming woman into an oven. Ernst's former wife, Luise Straus, was among the victims of the Auschwitz crematoria.

29 I owe many of the insights expressed regarding this and other collages to my fruitful debates with my colleague Larry Reynolds.

30 Steven Marcus, *Freud and the Culture of Psychoanalysis* (N.Y.: Norton, 1984), 42–86.

31 *The Complete Letters of Sigmund Freud to Wilhelm Fliess, 1887–1904*, trans. and ed.

Jeffrey Moussaieff Masson (Cambridge: Belknap Press-Harvard University Press, 1985), 427. Letter of October 14, 1900.

32 See Steven Marcus, *The Other Victorians* (N.Y.: Basic, 1966) and Peter Gay, *The Bourgeois Experience: Victoria to Freud*, 2 vols. to date (N.Y.: Oxford, 1984, 1986).

33 "Fragment of an Analysis of a Case of Hysteria" (1905 [1901]), *SE* 7:7–122. References hereafter cited parenthetically.

34 Renée Riese Hubert, "The Fabulous Fiction of Two Surrealist Artists: Giorgio de Chirico and Max Ernst," *New Literary History* 4.1 (Autumn 1972): 161. Hubert also points to Ernst's twists on other myths and legends: Venus and Cupid, Susannah and the Elders, and Snow White.

35 Thomas Laqueur notes that the *Reference Handbook of the Medical Sciences*, the major English language medical encyclopedia of Freud's day, cites the Viennese anatomist and philologist Joseph Hyrtl, "who derived the word 'clitoris' from a Greek verb meaning 'to titillate' and observed that these etymological roots are reflected in the German colloquial term *Kitzler* (tickler)." The anatomy of the clitoris is presented as the homologue of the penis, and *Kitzler* is further defined as a clitoris or female rod, "*weibliche Rute.*" Laqueur states that in 1612 Jacques Duval wrote of the clitoris: "In French it is called temptation, the spur to sensual pleasure, the female rod and the scorner of men: and women who will admit their lewdness call it their *gaude mihi* [great joy];" *Making Sex: Body and Gender from the Greeks to Freud* (Cambridge: Harvard University Press, 1990), 237, 240, 300 note 114.

36 Norris, 165.

37 Maurer, 85; Norris, 165. Norris suggests that by depicting this foreigner as a servant Ernst replaces the sexual victimizations of "The Lion of Belfort" with a racial element in this book.

38 Maurer mentions Ernst's fascination with the morbid eroticism and depictions of transformation in Bram Stoker's *Dracula*. As he had done with his copy of Matthew Lewis's *The Monk*, Ernst had his copy of *Dracula* bound in full calf; Maurer, 84–85.

39 *Beyond Painting*, 28–29. See also Russell, 14–17.

40 Russell, 197.

41 Maurer, 91. Maurer goes on to point out that, by the addition of an umlaut over the "o" and a final "n," the German word for bird (*Vogel*) can be transformed into the verb "to fornicate" (*vögeln*).

42 *SE* 5:369.

43 R. F. Gombrich, "The Consecration of a Buddhist Image," *Journal of Asian Studies* 26 (1966–67): 24–25. Quoted in Freedberg, 85–86.

44 I am again indebted to Margot Norris's book. In a footnote, she mentions the application of foreclosure to Ernst's work, 249 note 4.

45 "From the History of an Infantile Neurosis" (1918 [1914]), *SE* 17:84.

46 J. Laplanche and J. B. Pontalis, *The Language of Psycho-Analysis*, trans. Donald Nicholson-Smith (N.Y.: Norton, 1973), 168. The quotes from Lacan are drawn from "Réponse au commentaire de Jean Hyppolite sur la 'Verneinung' de Freud," *La Psychanalyse* (1956, 1:46), *Écrits* (Paris: Seuil, 1966), 531–83. See also Bice Benevuto and Roger Kennedy, *The Works of Jacques Lacan* (London: Free Association Books, 1986), 150–59, for a discussion of foreclosure.

3   Cannibals and clock-teasers

1   Paul Ricouer, *Hermeneutics and the Human Sciences*, ed. and trans. John B. Thompson (Cambridge: Harvard University Press, 1981), 143.

2   Freud uses the term "screen memory" to characterize an unusually sharp but seemingly insignificant childhood memory. Exploration of these screen memories leads back to impressionable childhood experiences, usually experiences which have been repressed so that the screen memory constitutes an alteration by defenses of the original experience; "Screen Memories" (1899), *SE* 3:301–22. In "Remembering, Repeating and Working-Through" (1914), Freud writes of screen memories: "Not only *some* but *all* of what is essential from childhood has been retained in these memories. It is simply a question of knowing how to extract it out of them by analysis. They represent the forgotten years of childhood as adequately as the manifest content of a dream represents the dream-thoughts;" *SE* 12:148.

3   See "Remembering, Repeating and Working-Through" (1914), *SE* 12:145–56.

4   I am indebted to Peter Brooks's positing of the transferential model for reading in "The Idea of a Psychoanalytic Literary Criticism," *Critical Inquiry* 13 (Winter 1987): 334–48. Brooks writes,

> A transferential model thus allows us to take as the object of analysis not author or reader, but reading, including, of course, the transferential-interpretive operations that belong to reading. Meaning in this view is not simply "in the text" nor wholly the fabrication of a reader (or a community of readers) but comes into being in the dialogic struggle and collaboration of the two, in the activation of textual possibilities in the process of reading. Such a view ultimately destabilizes the authority of reader/ critic in relation to the text, since, caught up in the transference, he becomes analysand as well as analyst. (345)

My title also borrows Brooks's term "clock-teasing" from this essay.

5   James B. Twitchell, *Dreadful Pleasures: An Anatomy of Modern Horror* (N.Y.: Oxford, 1985), 16. Drawing in part on Todorov, Terry Heller offers a more elaborate discussion of the categories of fantasy. His term "terror fantasy" accords with what I am calling postmodern horror in its fragmentation of the reader (viewer) and consequent elimination of aesthetic distance between the reader (viewer) and the work; *The Delights of Terror: An Aesthetics of the Tale of Terror* (Urbana: University of Illinois Press, 1987), 14–16.

6   Christian Metz maintains that although film functions like a mirror it differs from the mirror in not reflecting an image of the spectator's own body. Thus the spectator is cast in the role of absent subject who can ignore himself/herself as voyeur; *The Imaginary Signifier: Psychoanalysis and Cinema*, trans. Celia Britton, et al. (1977; Bloomington: Indiana University Press, 1982).

7   *SE* 14:146.

8   Bruno Bettelheim, *The Uses of Enchantment: The Meaning and Importance of Fairy Tales* (N.Y.: Vintage, 1977). In *Dreadful Pleasures*, Twitchell argues the attraction to horror may be understood in essentially three ways: (1) counterphobia, (2) the return of the repressed, and (3) a rite of passage from onanism to reproductive sexuality.

9   Tzvetan Todorov, *The Fantastic: A Structural Approach to a Literary Genre*, trans. Richard Howard (Ithaca: Cornell University Press, 1975), 168.

10   There are numerous studies of the Gothic and horror tradition in literature and film. I

have primarily relied on Elizabeth MacAndrew, *The Gothic Tradition in Fiction* (N.Y.: Columbia University Press, 1979); Joseph Grixti, *Terrors of Uncertainty: The Cultural Contexts of Horror Fiction* (London and N.Y.: Routledge, 1989); Gregory A. Waller, *The Living and the Undead* (Urbana: University of Illinois, 1986); Terry Heller, *The Delights of Terror*; and David Punter, *The Literature of Terror* (N.Y.: Longman, 1980). Punter disagrees with my analysis of the Gothic as an essentially conservative tradition. He sees Gothic fiction giving voice to what capitalism represses and opposing the bourgeois mores of the realistic novel. Although I agree that this voice and opposition are expressed, I consider them ultimately to be vanquished.

11 Noel Carroll most thoroughly examines the lure of horror as a cognitive attraction to anomaly. Although I find his assessment of the application of psychoanalysis to a philosophy of horror limited, particularly by his neglect of Lacanian thought, Carroll's book is one of the clearest and most informative discussions of horror available; *The Philosophy of Horror* (N.Y.: Routledge, 1990).

12 Hélène Cixous focuses on the works of E. T. A. Hoffman to describe fiction that unmasks character and undercuts the experience of character as a mirror for the reader, "The Character of 'Character,'" trans. Keith Cohen, *New Literary History* 5 (1974): 383–402.

13 See Tania Modleski, "The Terror of Pleasure: the Contemporary Horror Film and Postmodern Theory," *Studies in Entertainment*, ed. Tania Modleski (Bloomington: Indiana University Press, 1986), 155–66 and Carol J. Clover, "Her Body, Himself: Gender in the Slasher Film," *Misogyny, Misandry, and Misanthropy*, ed. R. Howard Bloch and Frances Ferguson (Berkeley: University of California Press, 1989), 187–228, for investigations of the process of feminizing the audience. According to Modleski, the projection of submission and defenselessness onto the female body enables the male spectator to attain distance from terror while the female spectator is both denied access to pleasure and scapegoated for seeming to represent it. Clover explores slasher films to demonstrate that the audience is in the end masculinized by the very figure through whom it was earlier feminized. The surviving female victim appropriates the phallic machinery from the slasher and destroys him in the manner in which he had destroyed his female victims.

14 *The Complete Letters of Sigmund Freud to Wilhelm Fliess*, 280. Letter of November 14, 1897.

15 *The Complete Letters of Sigmund Freud to Wilhelm Fliess*, 281. Monique David-Menard discusses Freud's theory of hysteria as an effort to describe an epistemology of disgust, *Hysteria from Freud to Lacan: Body and Language in Psychoanalysis*, trans. Catherine Porter (Ithaca: Cornell University Press, 1989).

16 Immanuel Kant, *Critique of Judgment* (1790), trans. J. H. Bernard (N.Y.: Hafner, 1966), 155. In Part IV, Section V of *A Philosophical Enquiry into the Origin of our Ideas of the Sublime and the Beautiful* (1757), Edmund Burke considers how terrifying objects can cause sublime delight as long as we are not in harm's way of these objects; ed. J. T. Boulton (1958; Notre Dame: University of Notre Dame Press, 1968). Noel Carroll links pain, which would negate the kind of distance Burke's sublime requires, to Kant's disgust; *The Philosophy of Horror*, 240 note 20. As Terry Heller points out, Kant's notion of the sublime "replaces Burke's stillness of astonishment with a mind in motion, specifically between attraction and repulsion;" *The Delights of Terror*, 204.

17 See Jacques Lacan, *Le seminaire*, Book 20, *Encore* (1972–73), ed. Jacques-Alain Miller (Paris: Seuil, 1975).

18 *SE* 17:219.

19 SE 17:224–26. An editorial footnote tells us "according to the Oxford English Dictionary, a similar ambiguity attaches to the English 'canny', which may mean not only 'cosy' but also 'endowed with occult or magical powers'; 225 note 1.

20 SE 17:241.

21 SE 17:244.

22 In her ingenious reading of Freud's essay, Hélène Cixous considers Unheimliche as a relational signifier which subverts representations of a unified reality. In this manner, it serves as "a rehearsal of an encounter with death which is pure absence." Cixous sees Freud's reading of Hoffmann's tale of the Sand Man as casting both Hoffmann and the readers of Das Unheimliche as his own doubles while fiction itself serves as the double of the Unheimliche; "Fiction and Its Phantoms: A Reading of Freud's Das Unheimliche (The 'uncanny')," New Literary History 7 (Spring 1976): 525–48.

23 Jacques Lacan, "The mirror stage as formative of the function of the I," Écrits: A Selection, trans. Alan Sheridan (N.Y.: Norton, 1977), 1–7. The most illuminating commentary on the mirror stage I have found is Ellie Ragland-Sullivan, Jacques Lacan and the Philosophy of Psychoanalysis (Urbana: University of Illinois Press, 1987), 16–30.

24 Studies of fantasy as a subversive genre which add to the structuralist approach of Todorov and the focus on the carnivalesque by Mikhail Bakhtin include Peter Stallybrass and Allon White, The Politics and Poetics of Transgression (Ithaca: Cornell University Press, 1986) and Rosemary Jackson, Fantasy: The Literature of Subversion (London: Methuen, 1981). Using Lacan, Jackson writes of subversive fantasies setting up possibilities for radical cultural transformation by making fluid the relations between the Imaginary and the Symbolic; 91.

25 François Truffaut, Hitchcock, rev. ed. (N.Y.: Simon & Schuster, 1985), 269.

26 Brian DePalma works variations on this scene at the opening of Carrie, the close of Dressed to Kill, and, in more pointedly ironic fashion, in the opening spoof of Blowout. In each case, he sets up a scene in a hazy atmosphere visually reminiscent of a pornographic magazine and then introduces a discordant element—Carrie's period, the hands grabbing the woman, the slasher. (I am indebted to Jeffrey Cox for pointing out this connection to me.) I am assuming the masculine look of possession as my model for the viewer and, more broadly, for the role of spectator within the western Symbolic Order.

27 Janet Bergstrom, "Enunciation and Sexual Difference," Camera Obscura 3–4 (1979): 57–58. Bergstrom is responding to Raymond Bellour's reading of Psycho in which he employs the Freudian model of active male gaze toward the female body as object as fetishistic disavowal of castration anxiety; "Psychosis, Neurosis, Perversion," Camera Obscura 3–4 (1979): 105–32. Constance Penley discusses the two commentaries as part of an argument against the standard theoretical assumption of a male spectator; The Future of An Illusion: Film, Feminism, Psychoanalysis (Minneapolis: University of Minnesota Press, 1989).

28 SE 17:179–215.

29 David-Menard argues that the hysterical symptom is not a representation (Vorstellung) but a presentation (Darstellung): "the hysteric posits the object of her desire in the element of presence—as if it were there . . . In hysterical symptoms and attacks, the subject uses plastic and figurative thought to try to achieve the presence of the desired object and to achieve a jouissance in which nothing will have to be represented—that is, acknowledged as absent;" 110–11.

30 As Lacan and others since him have argued, psychoanalysis is not immune from that

which it attempts to cure. Lacan describes psychoanalysis as the "hysterisation of discourse, . . . the structural introduction via artificial conditions of the discourse of the hysteric;" *Feminine Sexuality*, ed. Juliet Mitchell and Jacqueline Rose, trans. Jacqueline Rose (N.Y.: Norton, 1982), 161. In his foreword to Monique David-Menard's book, Ned Lukacher argues that Freud converted the discourse of hysteria into the discourse of psychoanalysis: "Freud's abandonment of his self-analysis, and his subsequent refusal to be analyzed by any of his disciples, marks the birth of psychoanalysis in the fall of 1897;" xii. In arguing that human sexuality is grounded in masochism, Leo Bersani contends "psychoanalytic truth can be analyzed—and verified—only as a textual distress" where Freud's narrativizing functions to repress the failures of his argument; *The Freudian Body: Psychoanalysis and Art* (N.Y.: Columbia University Press, 1986), 90.

31 Jacques Lacan, *The Four Fundamental Concepts of Psycho-Analysis*, trans. Alan Sheridan (1973; N.Y.: Norton, 1978), 216–29. Hereafter referred to as *Four Fundamental Concepts*.

32 Regis Durand, "On *Aphanisis*: A note on the Dramaturgy of the Subject in Narrative Analysis," *MLN* 98 (1983): 868. The Lacan quote is from *Four Fundamental Concepts*, 223.

33 "Negation" (1925), *SE* 19:235–36.

34 *SE* 14:111–40. Although such a discussion is beyond the scope of this chapter, the language of "Instincts and their Vicissitudes" offers some potential links to the dialectic between the Imaginary and the Symbolic as articulated by Lacan. For example,

An instinct, on the other hand, never operates as a force giving a *momentary* impact but always a *constant* one. Moreover, since it impinges not from without but from within the organism, no flight can avail against it. . . . Let us imagine ourselves in the situation of an almost entirely helpless living organism, as yet unorientated in the world, which is receiving stimuli in its nervous system. This organism will very soon be in a position to make a first distinction and a first orientation. On the one hand, it will be aware of stimuli which can be avoided by muscular action (flight); these it ascribes to an external world. On the other hand, it will also be aware of stimuli against which such action is of no avail and whose character of constant pressure persists in spite of it; these stimuli are the signs of an internal world, the evidence of instinctual needs. The perceptual substance of the living organism will thus have found in the efficacy of its muscular activity a basis for distinguishing between an 'outside' and an 'inside';

SE 14:118–19.

35 Laura Mulvey, "Visual Pleasure and Narrative Cinema," *Screen* 16.3 (Autumn 1975): 6–18; reprinted in *Visual and Other Pleasures* (Bloomington: Indiana University Press, 1989), 14–26. Paul Willemen points out that Mulvey does not allow that the object of scopophilic desire can be male. He comments, "if scopophilic pleasure relates primarily to the observation of one's sexual like (as Freud suggests), then the two looks distinguished by Mulvey are in fact varieties of one single mechanism: the repression of homosexuality;" "Voyeurism, The Look, and Dworkin," *Afterimage* 6 (1976): 40–50; reprinted in *Narrative, Apparatus, Ideology: A Film Theory Reader*, ed. Philip Rosen (N.Y.: Columbia University Press, 1986), 210–18. D. N. Rodowick disputes Mulvey's emphasis on aggressive male dominance to the exclusion of feminine spectatorship; "The Difficulty of Difference," *Wide Angle* 5.1 (1982): 4–15. Gaylyn Studlar argues that Mulvey has repressed the function of masochism in her assessment of the perversity of

narrative cinema; *In the Realm of Pleasure: Von Sternberg, Dietrich, and the Masochistic Aesthetic* (Urbana: University of Illinois Press, 1988).

36 Freud develops the theory of the castration complex in his analysis of Little Hans, "Analysis of a Phobia in a Five-Year Old Boy" (1909), *SE* 10:5–149. In discussing the scopic drive, Lacan considers castration as the signifier which determines the gaze of the Other, *Four Fundamental Concepts*, 73 ff. Adopting an alternative perspective, Luce Irigaray refutes the masculine predominance of the scopic drive, *This Sex Which is Not One*, trans. Catherine Porter (Ithaca: Cornell University Press, 1985).

37 In "Instincts and their Vicissitudes," Freud discusses the interchangeability of sadism and masochism, how the subject identifies with the object. In masochism, "satisfaction follows along the path of the original sadism, the passive ego placing itself back in phantasy in its first role, which has now in fact been taken over by the extraneous subject." Inversely, "the sadistic aim of *causing* pains can arise also, retrogressively; for while these pains are being inflicted on other people, they are enjoyed masochistically by the subject through his identification of himself with the suffering object;" *SE* 14:128–29.

38 *SE* 21:155.

39 Alice Kuzniar, " 'Ears Looking at You: E. T. A. Hoffman's *The Sandman* and David Lynch's *Blue Velvet*," *South Atlantic Review* 54 (1989): 14. Kuzniar also points to Freud's claim that, by taking the place of the phallus, the fetish protects its user from acknowledging his homosexuality; *SE* 21:154. In addition, this excellent article lists several instances of doubling in *Blue Velvet* and shows how Jeffrey's experience in and out of the closet is drawn from that of the child Nathanael in *The Sandman*.

40 Could the family name, Beaumont, be a nod to the archetypal father of 1950s television, Hugh Beaumont, who played Ward Cleaver on *Leave It to Beaver*?

41 R. H. W. Dillard, "*Night of the Living Dead*: It's not Like Just a Wind That's Passing Through," *American Horrors: Essays on the Modern American Horror Film*, ed. Gregory A. Waller (Urbana: University of Illinois Press, 1987), 26. Dillard also discusses the revealing differences between the two films.

42 Even Romero is not satisfied by the radiation explanation as indicated by the following response to an interview question:

> The radiation scenario that people feel is an explanation in *Night of the Living Dead* was actually one out of three that were advanced in the original cut of the film, but the other ones got cut out and people have adopted that radiation thing as the reason why the dead are coming back. I really didn't mean that to be;

Dan Yakir, "Morning Becomes Romero," *Film Comment* 15 (1979): 60.

43 Dillard, 20.

44 Yakir, 62.

45 "Notes Upon a Case of Obsessional Neurosis" (1909), *SE* 10:155–319. See Steven Marcus's excellent discussion of this case history and its cultural ramifications, *Freud and the Culture of Psychoanalysis: Studies in the Transition from Victorian Humanism to Modernity*, 87–164. Freud first distinguishes between hysteria and obsessional neurosis in "The Neuro-Psychoses of Defence" (1894), *SE* 3:45–68. He returns to the subject in "Obsessions and Phobias: Their Psychical Mechanism and Their Aetiology" (1895), *SE* 3:74–82 and "Further Remarks on the Neuro-Psychoses of Defence" (1896), *SE* 3:162–85.

46 David-Menard, 110–11.

47 *SE* 10:192.

48   "From the History of an Infantile Neurosis" (1918 [1914]), *SE* 17:26, 64. Freud previously uses "ambivalence" in "The Dynamics of Transference" (1912), *SE* 12:106–7 and in "Instincts and their Vicissitudes" (1915), *SE* 14:131. Bleuler introduces the term in "Vortrag über Ambivalenz," *Zentralblatt für Psychoanalyse*, 1:266.

49   *SE* 10:196 note 1.

4   Narrative masking

1   Paul Ricoeur, *Freud and Philosophy: An Essay on Interpretation*, trans. Denis Savage (New Haven: Yale University Press, 1970), 27. Ricoeur's version of hermeneutics goes beyond that of Gadamer to reject the notion that hermeneutics should restore the past's meaning in its own terms; indeed, he would argue that that meaning should be exposed as a lie of consciousness. William V. Spanos also argues for a destructive poetics, a new hermeneutics which requires a rethinking of Heidegger's existential analytic: "Heidegger's destruction of the Western ontotheological tradition discovers that its metaphysical orientation manifests itself in a coercive 'permanentizing' of being (*Bestandsicherung*), and that this discovery reveals the platonic reality to be appearance, *eidos* (Idea), to be, in fact an *eidolon*, an idol or image." However, Spanos sees the limitations of Heideggerean phenomenology and Derridean deconstruction in their tendency to read literary texts spatially, and contends that temporal reading is best suited to demystification; "Breaking the Circle: Hermeneutics as Disclosure," *boundary* 2 5 (1977): 421–48.

2   *The Complete Works of Aristotle*, ed. Jonathan Barnes (Princeton: Princeton University Press, 1984), 2:2324. The relevant citation in Immanuel Bekker's 1831 standard edition of the Greek text of Aristotle, whose format all scholars of Aristotle use, is 1452a22–26.

3   The seminal discussion of *polytropia* in *Ulysses* is Fritz Senn's "Book of Many Turns," *James Joyce Quarterly* 10 (1972): 29–46; reprinted in *Joyce's Dislocutions: Essays on Reading as Translation*, ed. John Paul Riquelme (Baltimore: Johns Hopkins University Press, 1984), 121–37. Brook Thomas develops Senn's discussion in *James Joyce's Ulysses: A Book of Many Happy Returns* (Baton Rouge: LSU Press, 1982).

4   James Joyce, *Ulysses: The Corrected Text*, ed. Hans Walter Gabler, et al. (N.Y.: Random House, 1986), 16.673–89. All references are cited parenthetically by chapter and line number.

5   Michel Foucault, "What Is an Author?," *The Foucault Reader*, ed. Paul Rabinow (N.Y.: Pantheon, 1984), 110; from *Textual Strategies: Perspectives in Post-Structuralist Criticism*, ed. Josué V. Harari (Ithaca: Cornell University Press, 1979). In her book on authority and unauthorized narratives in Joyce, Vicki Mahaffey quotes this passage and points out that "Foucault too argues for a reversal of 'the traditional idea of the author' rather than an appreciation of its contradictory nature and potential;" *Reauthorizing Joyce* (N.Y.: Cambridge University Press, 1988), 25.

6   *Letters of James Joyce*, ed. Stuart Gilbert (N.Y.: Viking, 1957), 1:241.

7   For analyses of Joyce's complex and paradoxical interest in Hermetic philosophy see William York Tindall, "James Joyce and the Hermetic Tradition," *Journal of the History of Ideas* 15 (1954): 23–29; Craig Carver, "James Joyce and the Theory of Magic," *James Joyce Quarterly* 15.3 (1978): 201–14; Barbara DiBernard, *Alchemy and Finnegans Wake* (Albany: SUNY Press, 1980); and Robert D. Newman, "*Transformatio Coniunctionis*: Alchemy in *Ulysses*," *Joyce's Ulysses: The Larger Perspective*, ed. Robert D. Newman

and Weldon Thornton (Newark: University of Delaware Press, 1987), 168–86.

8   George Borach reports Joyce saying in 1917,

In the last two hundred years we haven't had a great thinker. My judgment is bold, since Kant is included. All the great thinkers of recent centuries from Kant to Benedetto Croce have only cultivated the garden. The greatest thinker of all times, in my opinion, is Aristotle. Everything, in his work, is defined with wonderful clarity and simplicity. Later, volumes were written to define the same things,

"Conversations with James Joyce," *Portraits of the Artist in Exile*, ed. Willard Potts (Seattle: University of Washington Press, 1979), 71.

Bruno railed against Aristotle's failure to accept the unity of opposites:

Aristotle, among others, did not grasp the one, did not grasp being, did not grasp the true, because he never realised how being is one; and though he was free to adopt a significance for being common to both substance and accident, and further to distinguish his categories according to so many genera and species, so many differentiations, he has not avoided being any less ignorant of the truth, through a failure to deepen his cognition of this unity and lack of differentiation in constant nature and being. And, as a thoroughly arid sophist, by his malignant explanations and his frivolous persuasions, he perverts the statements of the ancients and sets himself against the truth— not so much perhaps through weakness of intellect as through force of jealousy and ambition.

"Concerning the Cause, Principle, and One," *The Infinite in Giordano Bruno*, ed. Sidney Thomas Greenburg (N.Y.: King's Crown Press, 1950), 139. Theoharris Constantine Theoharris quotes this passage and offers excellent readings of Joyce's applications of Aristotle and Bruno in *Joyce's Ulysses: An Anatomy of the Soul* (Chapel Hill: University of North Carolina Press, 1988), 1–87. See also Richard Ellmann, *Ulysses on the Liffey* (N.Y.: Oxford University Press, 1972), 53–56; Sheldon Brivic, *Joyce the Creator* (Madison: University of Wisconsin Press, 1985), 44–54; and Elliott B. Gose, *The Transformation Process in Joyce's Ulysses* (Toronto: University of Toronto Press, 1980), 3–91.

9   *The Complete Works of Aristotle*, 2:1588. Metaphysics 1005b23.

10   Michel Serres, *Hermes: Literature, Science, Philosophy*, ed. Josué V. Harari and David F. Bell (Baltimore: Johns Hopkins University Press, 1982), xxxv.

11   *Letters of James Joyce*, 1:147–48.

12   Norman O. Brown, *Hermes the Thief: The Evolution of a Myth* (N.Y.: Vintage, 1969), 33–46.

13   Karen Lawrence, *The Odyssey of Style in Ulysses* (Princeton: Princeton University Press, 1981), 204, 206.

14   Standish Hayes O'Grady, "The Death of Fergus mac Leti," *Silva Gadelica* (London and Edinburgh: Williams and Norgate, 1892), 269–82.

15   In the 1961 Random House text, in "Telemachus" "A cloud began to cover the sun slowly, shadowing the bay in deeper green;" 9, and in "Calypso" "A cloud began to cover the sun wholly slowly wholly;" 61. In the Gabler text, the two appearances of the cloud are a perfect rhetorical match with a "wholly" added to Stephen's vision and taken away from Bloom's, so that for both "A cloud began to cover the sun slowly, wholly;" 1.248, 4.218. Jean Kimball points this out in " 'Lui, C'est Moi': The Brother Relationship in *Ulysses*," *James Joyce Quarterly* 25 (1988): 232. Sheldon Brivic offers a list of synchronicities in *Joyce the Creator*, 145–53.

16   For Molly's reaction to this slight see *U* 18.717–18.

17 I previously suggested the connection between the stylistic intrusion in "Aeolus" and the scene in "Ithaca" in "*Transformatio Coniunctionis*: Alchemy in *Ulysses*," 180–81.

18 Don Gifford, *Ulysses Annotated* (Berkeley: University of California Press, 1988), 146. The passage in *David Copperfield* is "I have often thought, since, what an odd, innocent, out-of-the-way kind of wedding it must have been! We got back into the chaise again soon after dark, and drove cosily back, looking up at the stars and talking about them" (chapter 10).

19 Robert Spoo, "Teleology, Monocausality, and Marriage in *Ulysses*," *ELH* 56 (1989): 439–62. Spoo notes another connection between the striking of a match and the marriage motif in Circe when Stephen asks Lynch for a cigarette and, immediately prior to lighting it, states "And so Georgina Johnson is dead and married" (15.3619–23).

20 See Michael Seidel, *Epic Geography: James Joyce's Ulysses* (Princeton: Princeton University Press, 1976), 55–59, and Robert D. Newman, "Bloom and the Beast: Joyce's Use of Bruno's Astrological Allegory," *New Alliances in Joyce Studies*, ed. Bonnie Kime Scott (Newark: University of Delaware Press, 1988), 210–16. The actual astronomy of this passage is discussed by Mark E. Littmann and Charles A. Schweighauser, "Astronomical Allusions, Their Meaning and Purpose, in *Ulysses*," *James Joyce Quarterly* 2 (1965): 238–46.

21 James Joyce, *A Portrait of the Artist as a Young Man: Text, Criticism, and Notes*, ed. Chester G. Anderson (N.Y.: Viking, 1968), 175. Subsequent references are cited parenthetically.

22 See Weldon Thornton's discussion of the idolatry of literary form in Oxen of the Sun, "Voices and Values in *Ulysses*," *Joyce's Ulysses: The Larger Perspective*, ed. Robert D. Newman and Weldon Thornton (Newark: University of Delaware Press, 1987), 244–70.

23 James Joyce, *Finnegans Wake* (N.Y.: Viking, 1939), 161.9–13.

24 I am indebted to Harry C. Staley for pointing out this *Finnegans Wake* reference to me. His discussion of it occurs in his unpublished manuscript, "No Word is Impossible."

25 Whereas the law of non-contradiction refers to any logical statement, the principle of identity is concerned specifically with substances. See *Metaphysics* 1041a7-32, *The Complete Works of Aristotle*, 2:1643–44.

26 Friedrich Nietzsche, *The Will to Power*, ed. Walter Kaufman and R. J. Hollingdale (N.Y.: Vintage, 1968), 280. See also Michel Foucault's "Theatrum Philosophicum," especially pages 184–87, *Language, Counter-Memory, Practice*, ed. Donald F. Bouchard (Ithaca: Cornell University Press, 1977), 165–96. Foucault states,

> The freeing of difference requires thought without contradiction, without dialectics, without negation; thought that accepts divergence; affirmative thought whose instrument is disjunction; thought of the multiple—of the nomadic and dispersed multiplicity that is not limited or confined by the constraints of similarity; thought that does not conform to a pedagogical model (the fakery of prepared answers), but that attacks insoluble problems—that is, a thought that addresses a multiplicity of exceptional points, which are displaced as we distinguish their conditions and which insist and subsist in the play of repetitions.

For Nietzsche's influence on Joyce see Joseph Valente, "Beyond Truth and Freedom: The New Faith of Joyce and Nietzsche," *James Joyce Quarterly* 25 (1987): 87–103.

27 Umberto Eco, *The Aesthetics of Chaosmos: The Middle Ages of James Joyce*, trans. Ellen Esrock (Tulsa: University of Tulsa Press, 1982), 3.

28 See Mikhail Bakhtin's attacks on Romantic and Formalist unification, particularly *Problems of Dostoevsky's Poetics*, ed. and trans. Caryl Emerson (Minneapolis: University of Minnesota Press, 1984); and *The Dialogic Imagination*, ed. Michael Holquist, trans. Caryl Emerson and Michael Holquist (Austin: University of Texas Press, 1981). Bakhtin's emphasis on the carnivalesque promotes the idea that literary works inherently resist the unification advanced by strict hierarchies. For a discussion of the distinctions among dialogics, dialectic, and rhetoric and of the applications of Bakhtin's dialogics to literary criticism see Don H. Bialostosky, "Dialogics as an Art of Discourse in Literary Criticism," *PMLA* 101 (1986): 788–97. For an application of Bakhtin's idea of the dialogic novel to *Ulysses*, see David Lodge, "Double Discourses: Joyce and Bakhtin," *James Joyce Broadsheet* 11 (June 1983): 1–2.

29 See, for example, Paracelsus, *Philosophia ad Athenienses* I, 10: "Nature . . . is a vast organism in which natural things harmonize and sympathize reciprocally. Such is the macrocosm . . . The macrocosm and the microcosm are one. They form one constellation, one influence, one breath, one harmony, one metal, one season, one fruit." For a lucid discussion of the distinctions between the symbolic and scientific perspectives see Gilbert Durand, "*Defiguration philosophique et figure traditionelle de l'homme en Occident*," *Eranos* 38 (1969): 45–93.

30 *Complete Works of Oscar Wilde*, ed. Vyvyan Holland (London: Collins, 1971), 1045.

31 In *Rabelais and His World* (Cambridge: MIT Press, 1968), 39–40, Bakhtin writes,

> The mask is connected with the joy of change and reincarnation, with gay relativity and with the merry negation of uniformity and similarity; it rejects conformity to oneself. The mask is related to transition, metamorphoses, the violation of natural boundaries, to mockery and familiar nicknames. It contains the playful element of life; it is based on a peculiar interrelation of reality and image, characteristic of the most ancient rituals and spectacles. Of course it would be impossible to exhaust the intricate multiform symbolism of the mask. Let us point out that such manifestations as parodies, caricatures, grimaces, eccentric postures, and comic gestures are per se derived from the mask. It reveals the essence of the grotesque.

Nietzsche aphoristically states, "Whatever is profound loves masks;" *Beyond Good and Evil*, trans. Walter Kaufman (N.Y.: Vintage, 1966), 40.

32 A. David Napier, *Masks, Transformation, Paradox* (Berkeley: University of California Press, 1986), 83.

33 See Cheryl Herr, *Joyce's Anatomy of Culture* (Champaign: University of Illinois Press, 1986) for a discussion of Joyce's appropriation of the Irish popular theater, particularly pantomime, music hall, and theatrical transvestism, in Circe.

34 The morris dance is a grotesque dance celebrating the summer and winter solstice. Ankle bells are usually worn by the dancer. A central character in the ritual is the Betty, a hermaphrodite, an appropriate allusion considering Bloom's transformation into the new womanly-man in Circe.

35 Jacques Derrida, "Plato's Pharmacy," *Dissemination*, trans. Barbara Johnson (Chicago: University of Chicago Press, 1981), 61–171.

36 René Girard, *Violence and the Sacred*, trans. Patrick Gregory (Baltimore: Johns Hopkins University Press, 1977), 202.

37 Sigmund Freud, *Totem and Taboo*, trans. James Strachey (N.Y.: Norton, 1950), 156.

38 In the *Poetics*, Aristotle cites a play entitled *Ulysses the False Messenger* as an example

of discovery arising from bad reasoning on the part of the audience: "An instance of it is in *Ulysses the False Messenger*: that he stretched the bow and no one else did was invented by the poet and part of the argument, and so too that he said he would recognize the bow which he had not seen; but to suppose from that that he would know it again was bad reasoning" (1455a12-16), *Complete Works of Aristotle*, 2: 2328. A footnote in the McKeon edition of Aristotle states "authorship unknown" in reference to this play, *Introduction to Aristotle*, ed. Richard McKeon (N.Y.: Modern Library, 1947), 646 note 31.

39 For an elaboration on the uncertainty principle in Joyce's works see Phillip F. Herring, *Joyce's Uncertainty Principle* (Princeton: Princeton University Press, 1987).

40 Jacques Derrida has demonstrated how the text works as a double-bind that anticipates the reader's responses, placing him within the text so that the reader becomes a meta-reader, reading *Ulysses* on *Ulysses*, "Ulysse gramophone: Hear say yes in Joyce," *James Joyce: The Augmented Ninth*, ed. Bernard Benstock (Syracuse: Syracuse University Press, 1988), 27–75.

41 E. D. Hirsch, *Validity in Interpretation* (New Haven: Yale University Press, 1967), 78–89. See also A. Walton Litz's attack on attempts to place *Ulysses* within the genre of the traditional English novel, "The Genre of *Ulysses*," *The Theory of the Novel*, ed. John Halperin (N.Y.: Oxford University Press, 1974), 109; and Brian G. Caraher's reading of *Ulysses* in terms of intrinsic genre, "A Question of Genre: Generic Experimentation, Self-Composition, and the Problem of Egoism in *Ulysses*," *ELH* 54 (1987): 183–214. Hugh Kenner states "*Ulysses* is the first of the great modern works that in effect create for themselves an ad hoc genre . . . and so entail an ad hoc critical tradition," *Ulysses*, revised (Baltimore: Johns Hopkins University Press, 1987), 3.

42 *Reauthorizing Joyce*, 135. Mahaffey calls *Ulysses* "an imaginative Odyssey, written in the double shadow of Shakespeare, whom Stephen calls a playwright of banishment, and his counterpart suggestively known as 'Homer.' "

43 In his deconstruction of Plato, "Plato's Pharmacy," Derrida discusses the chain of significations pertaining to the term "*pharmakon*," 95–117. For a reading of Murphy as psychopomp, see Gose, *The Transformation Process in Joyce's Ulysses*, 27–28.

44 Homer, *The Iliad*, trans. Richmond Lattimore (Chicago: University of Chicago Press, 1951), 302 (Book 14, line 320).

45 See Eugenio Donato, "The Ruins of Memory: Archaeological Fragments and Textual Artifacts," *MLN* 93 (1978): 575–96 for a discussion of the connections between the problematics of perception and representation and those of memory.

5 Milan Kundera's *The Unbearable Lightness of Being*

1 Janet Malcolm, "The Window-Washer," *The New Yorker* (Nov. 19, 1990): 56–106.

2 Milan Kundera, *The Unbearable Lightness of Being*, trans. Michael Henry Heim (N.Y.: Harper & Row, 1985), 245, 246. Subsequent references are noted parenthetically.

3 Terry Eagleton, "Estrangement and Irony," *Salmagundi* 73 (Winter 1987): 26.

4 In an interview with Jordan Elgrably, Kundera remarks, "Sabina is a woman endowed with a strong mind. I might even go so far as to suggest that her thinking is the most lucid in the novel, perhaps, as well, the coldest and the most cruel;" "Conversations with Milan Kundera," *Salmagundi* 73 (Winter 1987): 23.

5   Michel Foucault, *Discipline and Punish: The Birth of the Prison*, trans. Alan Sheridan (N.Y.: Vintage, 1979), 29–30. For an analysis of Foucault's view of the body see Greg Ostrander, "Foucault's Disappearing Body," *Body Invaders: panic sex in America*, ed. Arthur and Marilouise Kroker (N.Y.: St. Martin's Press, 1987), 169–82. For a related discussion of the political oppression of the body in contemporary American culture, the obsession over clean bodily fluids which the authors term "Body McCarthyism," see Arthur and Marilouise Kroker, "Panic Sex in America," *Body Invaders*, 10–19. Elaine Scarry's *The Body in Pain: The Making and Unmaking of the World* (N.Y.: Oxford University Press, 1985) presents an extended meditation and analysis regarding the connections between power and pain and the manner in which the creative mind attempts to express physical pain. Of course, Freud made the body (sex) the condition of the mind. Philip Rieff quotes him as saying that "the mental is based on the organic," *Freud: The Mind of the Moralist* (N.Y.: Doubleday, 1961), 4. See Freud, "Psychogenic Disturbance of Vision" (1910), *SE* 11:217 and *The Interpretation of Dreams* (1900), *SE* 4:41–42. For a feminist psychoanalytic and philosophical interpretation of the female body in relation to the problem of modernity, see Alice A. Jardine, particularly her readings of Lacan and Gilles Deleuze, *Gynesis: Configurations of Woman and Modernity* (Ithaca: Cornell University Press, 1985), 159–77, 208–23.

6   Lacan, "The mirror stage as formative of the function of the I" (1949). Laplanche and Pontalis link Freud's concept of primary narcissism ("Mourning and Melancholia" (1915), *SE* 14:249–51) to Lacan's mirror stage; *The Language of Psychoanalysis*, 251–52, 255–57. However, they also point out that Freud modified his views and came to conceive of primary narcissism as an objectless state in which ego and id were undifferentiated and relationship to the outside world was absent (*Group Psychology and the Analysis of the Ego* (1921), *SE* 18:130–31). His concept of secondary narcissism allows for ego formation through identification with another person and follows from the shift in his thinking to a conception of the id as distinct and from which the other agencies differentiate (*The Ego and the Id* (1923), *SE* 19:30, 46).

Laplanche and Pontalis also compare Freud's view of the autoeroticism that precedes primary narcissism to Lacan's discussion of the fantasy of the "body-in-pieces" (*le corps morcele*). However, they state, "Lacan sees the mirror phase as responsible, retroactively, for the emergence of the phantasy of the body-in-pieces. This type of dialectical relation may be observed in the course of psycho-analytic treatment, where anxiety about fragmentation can at times be seen to arise as a consequence of loss of narcissistic identification, and vice-versa," 251–52.

For a semiotic reading of mirrors that discusses Lacan, see Umberto Eco, *Semiotics and the Philosophy of Language* (Bloomington: Indiana University Press, 1984), 202–26. Eco argues that mirror images are not signs and signs are not mirror images.

7   Ellie Ragland-Sullivan, *Jacques Lacan and the Philosophy of Psychoanalysis* (Urbana: University of Illinois Press, 1986), 93.

8   Jane Gallop, *Reading Lacan* (Ithaca: Cornell University Press, 1985), 80–81.

9   Antonin J. Liehm, "Milan Kundera: Czech Writer," *Czech Literature Since 1956: A Symposium, Columbia Slavic Studies*, ed. W. E. Harkins and P. I. Trensky (N.Y.: Bohemica, 1980), 45. I am indebted to my student, Cathe Schultz, for pointing out this quote to me in a seminar paper on *The Unbearable Lightness of Being*.

10   In a note from 1797, Friedrich Schlegel defines irony as "*eine permanente Parekbase*,"

"Fragment 668," *Kritische Ausgabe*, Band 18, *Philosophische Lehrjahre*, *(1796–1806)*, ed. Ernst Behler (Paderborn: Ferdinand Schöningh, 1962), 85.

11 "The Rhetoric of Temporality," 219, 220, 222. See also William V. Spanos's rethinking of Heidegger's existential analytic in which he places de Man with other critics who perceive literature in terms of a spatialization of time. Spanos's essay is particularly relevant to a discussion of Kundera because he analogizes the conflict between spatial and temporal interpretation and the myth of eternal return; *boundary* 2 5 (1977): 421–48.

12 Elsewhere Kundera states, "the novelist is neither historian nor prophet: he is an explorer of existence," *The Art of the Novel*, trans. Linda Asher (N.Y.: Grove Press, 1986), 44.

13 I have in mind here Hayden White's theory of tropes in which he discusses the basic binary distinction between metaphor and metonymy. White considers metaphor to be essentially representational and metonymy essentially reductionist; *Metahistory*, 31–38.

14 Lacan presents this complex concept in *Four Fundamental Concepts of Psycho-Analysis*, 64–119. Ragland-Sullivan offers the following useful summary of the Gaze:

> It [the gaze] was introjected as a part-object in the pre-mirror stage before the eye acquired its function of seeing and representing the subject and, consequently, before there was any sense of alterity. In the mirror stage the gaze is the dialectical bridge to self-recognition; perceptually speaking, the prespecular objects of Desire become permanently enmeshed in a network of inner vision. In consciousness the intersubjective element involved in "seeing oneself seen" has to do with knowing that the other knows that one is being looked at. The intersubjective element appears mysteriously to consciousness when a person experiences "self" as an object of an-other's gaze—whether present or absent—and the gaze catalyzes a phenomenology of judgment in the form of shame, modesty, blushing, fear, prestige, rage, or so on. The other's look or words have connected with the repressed discourse linked to the Other's gaze. So essential is the gaze to Lacan's syntax of the unconscious that he has defined consciousness as the distinctive mark of the subject both oppressed by the inner gaze of the Other (A), and resentful of it. The Other's gaze triumphs over the eye, subjectivizing the relationship between gaze and eye, or seeing and knowing;

Jacques Lacan and the Philosophy of Psychoanalysis, 94–95. Arthur Rimbaud's statement, "*J'est autre*," seems prophetic considering Lacan's concept, and it is not surprising that this statement is frequently invoked in poststructuralist criticism.

15 *The Art of the Novel*, 134.

16 In the section of *The Gay Science* in which Nietzsche introduces the figure of Zarathrustra, he writes:

> *The greatest weight.*—What, if some day or night a demon were to steal after you into your loneliest loneliness and say to you: "This life as you now live it and have lived it, you will have to live once more and innumerable times more; and there will be nothing new in it, but every pain and every joy and every thought and sigh and everything unutterably small or great in your life will have to return to you, all in the same succession and sequence—even this spider and this moonlight between the trees, and even this moment and I myself. The eternal hourglass of existence is turned upside down again and again, and you with it, speck of dust!" Would you not throw yourself down and gnash your teeth and curse the demon who spoke thus? . . . Or how well disposed would you have to become to yourself and to life to *crave nothing more fervently* than this ultimate eternal confirmation and seal?;

The Gay Science, 341. In *Thus Spake Zarathustra*, he comes to celebrate the idea of eternal recurrence, and it is subsequently represented as one of Zarathustra's most significant teachings. In *The Will to Power*, Nietzsche refers to it as "the great *cultivating* idea;" 1053, 1056. He speaks of "the idea of recurrence as a *selective* principle," which functions "in the service of strength;" 1058, and asserts, "the law of the conservation of energy demands *eternal recurrence;*" 1063, trans. Walter Kaufmann and R. J. Hollingdale (N.Y.: Vintage, 1968).

17 Kierkegaard's most thorough discussion of the implications of identity in the context of change is *Repetition: A Venture in Experimenting Psychology, Kierkegaard's Writings*, trans. and ed. Howard V. and Edna H. Hong (Princeton: Princeton University Press, 1983), vol. 6. See also Louis Mackey's analysis in which he states, "irony is a necessary condition of repetition. Only the unsurprisable is absolutely surprised;" "Once More with Feeling: Kierkegaard's *Repetition*," *Kierkegaard and Literature: Irony, Repetition, and Criticism*, ed. Ronald Schleifer and Robert Markley (Norman: University of Oklahoma Press, 1984), 113.

18 *Soren Kierkegaard's Journals and Papers*, trans. and ed. Howard V. and Edna H. Hong (Bloomington: Indiana University Press, 1967), 1:94. Kierkegaard's fullest discussion of this subject is *The Concept of Anxiety: A Simple Psychologically Orienting Deliberation on the Dogmatic Issue of Hereditary Sin, Kierkegaard's Writings*, trans. and ed. Reidar Thomte and Albert B. Anderson (Princeton: Princeton University Press, 1980), vol. 8. Perhaps the most relevant contemporary critic concerned with the psychology and philosophy of revisionism in the reading and writing process is Harold Bloom. For a reading of how Kierkegaard's *The Concept of Anxiety*, the only major Kierkegaardian text never mentioned by Bloom, serves as the precursor text for Bloom's work, repressed through the anxiety of influence, see Stephen Yarbrough *Deliberate Criticism* (Athens: University of Georgia Press, 1992). Bloom mentions Kierkegaardian repetition in all of his major works, reading repetition as "the re-creation or revision of a paradigm," so that when "a strong poet revises a precursor, he re-enacts a scene that is at once a catastrophe, a romance, and a transference;" *The Breaking of the Vessels* (Chicago: University of Chicago Press, 1982), 45.

6 D. M. Thomas's *The White Hotel*

1 D. M. Thomas, *The White Hotel* (N.Y.: Viking, 1981), 90. Subsequent references are noted parenthetically.

2 In a 1908 letter to Karl Abraham, Freud asked Abraham to forgive Jung's spirituality. It is easier for Jews to accept psychoanalysis, Freud explained, "as we lack the mystical element;" Robert S. Steele, *Freud and Jung: Conflicts of Interpretation* (London: Routledge, 1982), 209.

3 Other critics, most impressively David Cowart, have noted some of the doubling of images and triangular relationships in *The White Hotel*; "Being and Seeming: *The White Hotel*," *Novel* 19 (1986): 216–31. However, none have seen them functioning as an integral facet of the narrative structure of the novel.

4 Marsha Kinder thoroughly treats the image patterns of trains, swans, and pines; "The Spirit of *The White Hotel*," *Humanities in Society* 4–5 (1981–82): 162–68.

5 In "Medusa's Head" (1922), Freud equates the terror engendered by the decapitated

head of Medusa with castration anxiety. Medusa's head represents the female genitals, the snake encircled head suggests the pubic hair, *SE* 18:273–74. See also Freud's "The Infantile Genital Organization of the Libido," *SE* 19:144 note 3. The conjunction with Venus and Ceres in *The White Hotel* is, of course, another instance of the joining of mirrored opposites. In a different but related context, Anna recalls observing jellyfish floating just beneath the surface of the lake at her childhood home and Freud's note tells us that she used the Russian term "medusa" for jellyfish (118). Since the jellyfish is womb-shaped, Lisa's recollection of a floating womb refers us back to the gliding womb at the white hotel and forward to the rape scene in the penultimate chapter. It also refers us to the etymology and primitive etiology of hysteria—the floating womb.

6 Kinder discusses the links between Freud's case study of the Wolf Man and *The White Hotel*, "The Spirit of *The White Hotel*," 155.

7 The critical material on *The White Hotel* has already noted the similarities between the case history of Anna G. and that of Freud's patient Dora in "Analysis of a Case of Hysteria." In a letter to me dated July 30, 1987, Thomas states that he was not consciously influenced by the Dora material. "The case I studied most intensively," he writes, "mainly for style and form, was that of Elizabeth in the Freud-Breuer series." One of Jung's patients, Miss Miller, also has several parallels with the case of Anna. Miss Miller writes poetry with an accompanying prose interpretation and experiences a pain in her breast, in this case, at the sight of the dying Christian de Neurillette in Cyrano de Bergerac. Jung writes of her "extraordinary capacity for identification and empathy," *The Collected Works of C. G. Jung*, 20 vols., trans. R. F. C. Hull, ed. Herbert Read, Michael Fordham, and Gerhard Adler (Princeton: Princeton University Press, 1957–74), 5:34. In one of her poems about creation, Miss Miller puts sound before light. She explains that the pre-Socratic philosopher, Anaxagoras, "Makes the cosmos rise out of chaos by means of a whirlwind—which does not normally occur without producing a noise;" *Complete Works* 5:45. With the transmutation of a few letters, "Anaxagoras" becomes "anagnorisis"—"Clarification! More light! More light! More light—and more love" (236). I am indebted to my student, Karen Riedel, for pointing out this connection to me.

8 Thomas has the fictional Freud write to Lisa, "my experience of psychoanalysis has convinced me that telepathy exists. If I had my life to go over again, I should devote it to the study of this factor" (196). The quote comes from a letter that the real Freud wrote from Bad Gastein to Hereward Carrington who was soliciting his support for parapsychological research; Ernest Jones, *Sigmund Freud: Life and Work*, 3 vols. (London: Hogarth Press, 1957), 3:419–20. Freud concluded this letter by stating "I am utterly incapable of considering the 'survival of the personality' after death even as a scientific possibility . . ." Cowart argues that Thomas conceived *The White Hotel* as a response to this final statement; "Being and Seeming: *The White Hotel*," 218. In addition to being a corresponding member of the Society for Psychical Research, Freud wrote several essays on the occult: "A Premonitory Dream Fulfilled" (1899), *SE* 5:623–25; "Determinism, Belief in Chance and Superstition—Some Points of View" (1901), *SE* 6:239–79; "Psychoanalysis and Telepathy" (1921), *SE* 18:175–93; "Dreams and Telepathy" (1922), *SE* 18:195–220; "The Occult Significance of Dreams" (1925), *SE* 19:135–38; and "Dreams and the Occult" (1933), *SE* 22:31–56.

9 The plagiarism controversy that emerged after the publication of *The White Hotel* is detailed by Lynn Felder, "D. M. Thomas: The Plagiarism Controversy," *Dictionary of*

Literary Biography Yearbook 1982, 79–82. The accusations focus primarily on Thomas's use of details from Kuznetsov's novel in "The Sleeping Carriage" chapter. Using the same premise, critics might have accused Thomas of plagiarism in the "Frau Anna G" chapter since it is largely modeled on Freud's analysis of Elizabeth; however, none have. What those who accuse Thomas of plagiarism fail to understand is how much the argument inherent in *The White Hotel* hinges on the revision of documents as aspects of the multiple narrative voices. For an as yet unnoted possible source, Richard Shelton's poem "The White Hotel," see my "Another White Hotel," *Notes on Contemporary Literature* (March 1991).

10   Several critics, particularly early reviewers of the novel, object to the inclusion of "The Camp" after the Babi Yar chapter. See, for example, Thomas Flanagan's review, "To Babi Yar and Beyond," *Nation* (May 2, 1981): 537–39. Mary F. Robertson states that "The Camp" is unconvincing because "its sense of renewal is aesthetic rather than ethical," "Hystery, Herstory, History: 'Imagining the Real' in Thomas' *The White Hotel*," *Contemporary Literature* 25 (1984): 472. My argument holds that the sense of renewal in the final chapter, although qualified by the lingering presence of Thanatos, is aesthetic and also ethical.

11   Cowart makes these identifications, "Being and Seeming," 225.

12   D. M. Thomas, Review of *A Secret Symmetry: Sabina Spielrein between Jung and Freud*, by Aldo Carotenuto, *New York Review of Books* (May 13, 1982): 3, 6.

13   *Agon*, 136.

14   *Freud and Philosophy*, 281.

15   Mary Robertson also objects to Thomas's portrayal of his female hero's knowledge in stereotypically mythic terms. In doing so, Robertson claims, Thomas fails to rectify history's horrors through his art, "Hystery, Herstory, History," 465.

16   I am grateful to my student, Diane Kirk, for noting these points in her seminar paper on *The White Hotel*.

17   *Agon*, 107.

18   The collision between two incongruous opposites, the one terrible and the other beautiful, is also the central concern of the grotesque. Certainly the frequent juxtaposition of human and animal as well as the conjunction of Venus and Medusa in *The White Hotel* contribute to a reading of the novel as a work of the grotesque.

19   *A Philosophical Enquiry into the Origin of our Ideas of the Sublime and the Beautiful*, 57.

20   *Agon*, 115. Bloom makes the link between Vico and Freud via Lionel Trilling's *Freud and Literature*, first published in 1940, and revised in *The Liberal Imagination* in 1950. Trilling writes,

> In the eighteenth century Vico spoke of the metaphorical, imagistic language of the early stages of culture; it was left to Freud to discover how, in a scientific age, we still feel and think in figurative formations, and to create, what psychoanalysis is, a science of tropes, of metaphor and its variants, synecdoche and metonymy;

Quoted in *Agon*, 93.

21   A connection with Arnold Schopenhauer's view of madness as revisionary memory might be suggested here. Schopenhauer characterizes the madman's memory as selective, the gaps of which he fills with fictions to create a comprehensible world, *The World as Will and Representation*, trans. E. F. J. Payne, 2 vols. (N.Y.: Dover, 1966), 1:193. Drawing in part on Bloom's theory of the anxiety of influence, Daniel O'Hara links Schopenhauer's

madman with revisionist theory. At the conclusion of his essay, O'Hara suggests that "revisionary madness could also be seen as an uncanny restoration to health . . . that the critic best embodies Freud's image from *Civilization and Its Discontents* of man as a prosthetic god," "Revisionary Madness: The Prospects of American Literary Theory at the Present Time," *Against Theory: Literary Studies and the New Pragmatism*, ed. W. J. T. Mitchell (Chicago: University of Chicago Press, 1985), 47. Bloom himself deems Schopenhauer's theory of the sublime to be the precursor of Freud's in that Freud's unconscious forgetting substitutes for Schopenhauer's conscious turning away, *Agon*, 124.

22 *Freud and Philosophy*, 402.

23 *SE* 19:227–32. In "Freud and the Scene of Writing," Jacques Derrida challenges Freud's premise that there exist finite origins to repression. Using Freud's statement from "Note Upon the 'Mystic Writing-Pad,' " "if we imagine one hand writing upon the surface of the Mystic Writing-Pad while another periodically raises its covering sheet from the wax slab, we shall have a concrete representation of the way in which I tried to picture the functioning of the perceptual apparatus of our mind," *SE* 19:232, Derrida agrees that "writing is unthinkable without repression," "Freud and the Scene of Writing," *Writing and Difference*, trans. Alan Bass (Chicago: University of Chicago Press, 1978), 226. However, he views that repression as ongoing rather than primal. David Hoy argues that Derrida sets up his examples after the fashion of Freud, locating "undecidability at the syntactical rather than the semantic level," "Jacques Derrida," *The Return of the Grand Theory in the Human Sciences*, ed. Quentin Skinner (London: Cambridge University Press, 1985), 55.

7 Exiling the feminine

1 Elaine Showalter, "Towards a Feminist Poetics," *Women Writing and Writing about Women*, ed. Mary Jacobus (London: Croom Helm, 1979), 25–40.

2 Jane Tompkins, *Sensational Designs: The Cultural Work of American Fiction 1790–1860* (N.Y.: Oxford, 1985); "Me and My Shadow," *Gender and Theory: Dialogues on Feminist Criticism*, ed. Linda Kauffman (N.Y.: Basil Blackwell, 1989), 121–39.

3 Hélène Cixous, *The Exile of James Joyce or the Art of Replacement*, trans. Sally Purcell (N.Y.: David Lewis, 1972).

4 Hélène Cixous, "The Laugh of the Medusa," trans. Keith Cohen and Paula Cohen, *New French Feminisms*, ed. Elaine Marks and Isabelle de Courtivron (Amherst: University of Massachusetts Press, 1980), 245–64; reprinted from *Signs* 1 (Summer 1976): 875–99.

5 "The Laugh of the Medusa," 259.

6 Hélène Cixous and Catherine Clément, *The Newly Born Woman*, trans. Betsy Wing (Minneapolis: University of Minnesota Press, 1986), 93.

7 Herbert Marcuse, "A Critique of Norman O. Brown," in *Negations: Essays in Critical Theory* (London: Allen Lane, 1968), 227–47. Quoted in Toril Moi, *Sexual/Textual Politics: Feminist Literary Theory* (London and N.Y.: Methuen, 1985), 122–23.

8 Thomas Laquer investigates the "one-sex story," in which woman is viewed as an imperfect version of man, and her anatomy and physiology are construed accordingly: the vagina as an interior penis, the womb as scrotum, the ovaries as testicles; *Making Sex: Body and Gender from the Greeks to Freud* (Cambridge: Harvard University Press, 1990).

9   Luce Irigaray, *Speculum of the Other Woman*, trans. Gillian C. Gill (Ithaca: Cornell University Press, 1985), 53.

10 Jacques Lacan, *Le Séminaire XX: Encore* (Paris: Editions du Seuill, 1975), 69. Irigaray uses the latter judgment as an epigraph for "Cosí Fan Tutti" in *This Sex Which Is Not One*, trans. Catherine Porter (Ithaca: Cornell University Press, 1985), 86.

11 Carolyn Burke, "Irigaray Through the Looking Glass," *Feminist Studies* 7. (Summer 1981): 292.

12 *Speculum of the Other Woman*, 88.

13 *Sexual/Textual Politics*, 140.

14 *This Sex Which Is Not One*, 106–18.

15 In her discussion of Irigaray, Carolyn Burke cites Nietzsche's consideration of whether "philosophy has not been merely an interpretation of the body and a *misunderstanding of the body*;" *The Gay Science*, trans. Walter Kaufmann (N.Y.: Vintage, 1974), 34–35. Cited in "Irigaray Through the Looking Glass," 303.

16 "Irigaray Through the Looking Glass," 301.

17 *This Sex Which Is Not One*, 24.

18 *This Sex Which Is Not One*, 213.

19 Monique Plaza, " 'Phallomorphic power' and the psychology of 'woman,' " *Ideology & Consciousness* 4 (1978): 8.

20 *Sexual/Textual Politics*, 147–49.

21 "Irigaray Through the Looking Glass," 302–3.

22 Julia Kristeva, *Powers of Horror: An Essay on Abjection*, trans. Leon S. Roudiez (N.Y.: Columbia University Press, 1982), 3–4.

23 *Powers of Horror*, 25.

24 Elizabeth Gross, "The Body of Signification," in *Abjection, Melancholia, and Love: The Work of Julia Kristeva*, ed. John Fletcher and Andrew Benjamin (London and N.Y.: Routledge, 1990), 86–87.

25 Fredric Jameson proclaims, "pornographic films are thus only the potentiation of films in general, which ask us to stare at the world as though it were a naked body," *Signatures of the Visible* (N.Y. and London: Routledge, 1990), 1.

26 Stephen Ziplow, *The Film Maker's Guide to Pornography* (N.Y.: Drake, 1977), 34.

27 Linda Williams, *Hard Core: Power, Pleasure, and the "Frenzy of the Visible"* (Berkeley: University of California Press, 1989), 107.

28 In his essay, "Fetishism" (1927), Freud writes,

> It is not true that, after the child has made his observation of the woman, he has preserved unaltered his belief that women have a phallus. He has retained that belief, but he has also given it up. In the conflict between the weight of the unwelcome perception and the force of his counter-wish, a compromise has been reached . . . in his mind the woman *has* got a penis in spite of everything; but this penis is no longer the same as it was before. Something else has taken its place, has been appointed its substitute, as it were, and now inherits the interest which was formerly directed to its predecessor. But this interest suffers an extraordinary increase as well, because the horror of castration has set up a memorial to itself in the creation of this substitute;

SE 21:154. Williams finds a basic fallacy in Freud's argument:

> . . . he seems to accept the visual truth of what the fetishist sees when he looks at the woman's body. Freud thus shares some of the fetishist's belief in the "horror of cas-

tration" embodied in the female genitalia, unable himself to see beyond appearances to recognize how social relations of power have constructed him to perceive women's genitals. Since Freud's scenario of vision asserts a self-evident perceptual "truth" of female lack, his very explanation originates in a fetishistic misrecognition of a sensuous, perceptual thing, followed by the creation of a compensatory substitute, the fetish;

Hard Core, 105.

29 Susan Sontag, "The Pornographic Imagination," *Styles of Radical Will* (N.Y.: Farrar, Straus, and Giroux, 1966), 54.

30 Benjamin, "The Work of Art in the Age of Mechanical Reproduction."

31 Georges Bataille, *Story of the Eye*, trans. Joachim Neugroschel (N.Y.: Urizen Books, 1977). Sontag refers to Bataille's book as an "erotics of agony," "The Pornographic Imagination," 61.

32 Jean de Berg, *The Image*, trans. Patsy Southgate (N.Y.: Grove Press, 1966), 9.

33 Pauline Réage, *Story of O*, trans. Sabine d'Estrée (N.Y.: Grove Press, 1965), 15–16.

34 Kaja Silverman, *"Histoire d'O*: The Construction of a Female Subject," *Pleasure and Danger: exploring female sexuality*, ed. Carole S. Vance (Boston and London: Routledge & Kegan Paul, 1984), 320. Silverman argues that the structuration of the female subject begins with the organization of the body.

35 *Jacoblellis v. Ohio*, 378 U.S. 184, 197 (1964).

36 D. H. Lawrence, "Pornography and Obscenity," *Phoenix: The Posthumous Papers of D. H. Lawrence*, ed. Edward D. McDonald (N.Y.: Penguin, 1978), 170–87.

37 Attorney General's Commission on Pornography, *Final Report*, 2 vols. (Washington, D.C., 1986), 1:98.

38 See Andrea Dworkin, *Pornography: Men Possessing Women* (N.Y.: Perigee Books, 1979) and *Intercourse* (N.Y.: Free Press, 1987).

39 Alan Soble, *Pornography: Marxism, Feminism, and the Future of Sexuality* (New Haven: Yale University Press, 1986).

40 Susan Griffin, *Pornography and Silence* (N.Y.: Harper and Row, 1981). See also Susan Gubar, "Representing Pornography: Feminism, Criticism, and Depictions of Female Violation," *Critical Inquiry* 13 (Summer 1987), 712–41.

41 Williams points to "couples films" and films produced by Femme Productions like *Femme, Urban Heat, Three Daughters, Christine's Secret*, and *Sensual Escape; Hard Core*, 229–64. The recent proliferation of erotica written by and for women in journals like *Yellow Silk* also testifies to this trend. For an examination of the burgeoning sexual content of mass market romance novels, see Carol Thurston, *The Romance Revolution: Erotic Novels for Women and the Quest for a New Sexual Identity* (Urbana: University of Illinois Press, 1987).

42 Laura Mulvey, "Visual Pleasure and Narrative Cinema," *Screen* 16.3 (Autumn 1975), 6–18; reprinted in *Visual and Other Pleasures* (Bloomington: Indiana University Press, 1989), 14–26.

43 Mary Ann Doane, "Film and the Masquerade: Theorising the Female Spectator," *Screen* 23.3–4 (1982): 74–87.

44 Williams, *Hard Core*, 214. Williams' insightful argument considers but diverges from Gilles Deleuze's investigation of masochism, which separates masochism from sadism; *Masochism: An Interpretation of Coldness and Cruelty*, trans. Jean McNeil (N.Y.:

Braziller, 1971). As Williams points out, Deleuze's study avoids the question of both female readers and female victims. Williams' concept of oscillation does draw on Parveen Adams' study of female masochism, "Per Os(cillation)," *Camera Obscura: A Journal of Feminism and Film Theory* 17 (1988): 7–29. Adams considers Freud's "A Child Is Being Beaten" and his case study of Dora while arguing against the fixed masculine or feminine identities Freud assigns.

Index

Robert D. Newman is Associate Professor of English at
Texas A&M University.

Library of Congress Cataloging-in-Publication Data
Newman, Robert D., 1951–
Transgressions of reading : narrative engagement as exile
and return / Robert D. Newman.
p. cm. — (Post-contemporary interventions)
Includes bibliographical references (p.) and index.
ISBN 0-8223-1280-8 (cl : acid-free paper). — ISBN
0-8223-1296-4 (acid-free paper)
1. Reader-response criticism.   2. Narration (Rhetoric)
3. Psychoanalysis in literature.   4. Tragedy.   5. Erotic
literature—History and criticism.   I. Title.   II. Series.
PN98.R38N48 1992
801'.95—dc20   92-13546 CIP